Seven Bamboo Tablets
of the
Cloudy Satchel

SEVEN BAMBOO TABLETS
OF THE CLOUDY SATCHEL

·

DENG MING-DAO

·

Portraits by
KWAN SAIHUNG

HARPER & ROW, PUBLISHERS,
San Francisco

Cambridge, Hagerstown,
New York, Philadelphia, Washington
London, Mexico City, São Paulo, Singapore, Sydney

Designer: Mark Ong

FIRST HARPER & ROW PAPERBACK EDITION 1988

Library of Congress Cataloging-in-Publication Data

Deng, Ming-Dao.
　Seven bamboo tablets of the cloudy satchel.

　Sequel to: The wandering Taoist.

1. Kwan, Saihung.　2. Taoists—China—Biography.
I. Kwan, Saihung.　II. Deng, Ming-Dao.　Wandering
Taoist.　III. Title.
BL1940.K93D45　　1987　　299'.514'0924　　[B]　　86-45819
ISBN 0-06-250227-1 (cloth)
ISBN 0-06-250229-8 (paperback)

88　89　90　91　92　MPC　10　9　8　7　6　5　4　3　2　1

In memory of
WOODROW W. ONG

Contents

Illustrations

Acknowledgments

Among the many who helped shape this book are Jade Snow Wong and Elizabeth Kalashnikoff. Their comments helped give me direction. Clayton Carlson, my editor, provided critical and supportive guidance.

Ms. Lien Fung of Singapore, Ms. Su Yung Li, and Mr. Li Hsi-Chih of Guangzhou provided invaluable personal recollections of Shanghai and Du Yueshen. Mr. John Service and Professor Frederick Wakeman generously augmented those memories with historical and scholarly views.

Ms. Yvonne Eastman typed and prepared many drafts with good cheer and efficiency.

Finally, it was Mr. Kwan Saihung who provided the true substance of this book, revealing the legacy of his Taoist teachers with clarity and drama. The spirit of this book belongs to those masters, but its faults and any inaccuracies are mine alone.

Introduction

When people meet Mr. Kwan today, they are usually struck by his appearance. With his husky frame, smooth and ruddy complexion, brilliant eyes, and lively movements, they often find it difficult to believe that he was born nearly seventy years ago. He dresses in contemporary clothing, converses easily, and appears to have assimilated well into American life. But in fact, his health is the outer sign of a lifetime of training, and the vast majority of his personality lies in prerevolutionary China and Taoist temple life.

Mr. Kwan was born to an aristocratic warrior family. His clan was an Imperial one. Though democracy had been declared by the time of his childhood, the family nevertheless remained loyal to the Qing dynasty. He was thus exposed to rare splendors, princely wealth, and high-bred standards. As someone who would continue the family name with a titled position, he was expected to become a scholar, government official, or general. He was allowed neither individuality nor mediocrity. His elders pushed, trained, and heavily educated him to uphold the honor and glory of their clan.

As was the custom, Saihung, his seven brothers, and three sisters became disciples of different spiritual masters. This system provided not only a religious and moral background but was also meant to give them the benefit of the masters' insight and mental rigor. Yet the elders never intended permanent initiation into a holy life for the children. Rather, the separated siblings, strengthened by monastic discipline were to return to the clan to compete for leadership. There was no familial affection: simply rivalry for power and honor.

Only Saihung renounced his family at the age of sixteen to enter monastic life. As was expected, he was branded a disgrace and he still recalls the times of doubt he had in his youth. But his craving for knowledge and spiritual perception led him to persevere.

The system that so deeply inspired him was Taoism, the only indiginous Chinese religion. He joined the Western school of Huashan and is a member of the *Chengyi* sect. Taoism's innumerable sects each stress varying approaches to the questions of immortality, longevity, alchemy, ritual, and the following of Tao. The Huashan school emphasizes physical purification, asceticism, celibacy, and lifelong meditation.

The pursuit of these goals meant daily practice under the strict supervision of senior priests. The system of self-cultivation had as its premise sequences of body postures and movements that would engender specific changes in the body and mind. These methods were the culmination of centuries-long observation and experimentation bound by a standard of sheer determination and repetition. Like a farmer tilling his field over and over or a student reciting from rote memorization, the acolyte was to practice until enlightenment came. Repetition was a horror of suffering until Saihung also realized that it was the scale by which he measured his progress. In the same way as a weightlifter suddenly able to complete a new lift, or a dancer able to make that higher leap, he saw that incremental progression could help him achieve in time what was once impossible.

Such effort requires unwavering faith. Mr. Kwan acknowledges that even a lifetime of practice does not guarantee success. He knew elderly priests who had not yet succeeded but who nevertheless continued with undiminished sincerity. They remained constant in their pursuit of knowledge, realization, and, if not the transcendence of death, at least its understanding. They lived life to its fullest, as defined by their broad and world-tested philosophy, and attempted to live in harmony with Tao, the Way.

The Way is the way of life, nature, and the cosmos. It is the current of existence, but has neither pattern, framework, nor fixed consciousness. It is more that the sequence of time, more than passages and shifting dimensions. It is the mystery that must be pierced, the unfathomable that must be plumbed, the irrational that must be encompassed. Ultimately, the only hope for understanding the Tao is through meditation and a commitment to following its mighty course. Descriptions are imperfect and worded in the paradoxical language of mystics. Only the Self is the proper instrument.

The masters told Saihung that every human being is a microcosm of the universe. As such the Way is within us and so too is the possibility of understanding. The body itself is the true temple. It is the dwelling of the divine, and it is in fact the self, immortal and pure, which is the true god. If an individual should wish to see heaven or merge with the Way, then he need only look within.

Since this suit of flesh is permeated with the radiant spirit, training proceeded from the physical through the mental and into the spiritual. Initial techniques focused on the breath—the gateway between the physical and mental—and exercise. The Taoists of Huashan particularly favored boxing and weaponry for such body development.

Martial arts goes far beyond a mere methodology of killing. It improves health, opens the energy pathways of the body, builds a resevoir of internal power, and fosters courage and discipline. Both meditators and warriors utilized the same internal forces—only their application differed. The spiritual people borrowed the martial methods. The warriors received a sense of justice and a way of life after retirement. In older age, many martial artists became holy men, since they had already cultivated the basic force, and this further consolidated the exchange between the martial and spiritual.

The priests themselves admitted that killing and holiness were incompatable, but China during that era was war-torn and lawless. There was an enormous threat of personal violence and the temples, as custodians of precious relics and large parcels of land, were favorite targets for outlaws and thieves. If a monk could not defend himself, then he would fail his duty and his years of self-cultivation would be negated by a premature death.

The warriors and ascetics had one over all priority in common: awareness. The ascetic needed the warrior's constant will to action, the fighter needed the meditator's perception. It was between warrior and meditator that the young Kwan Saihung sought to find his place. The man who today represents the unique product of the warrior-priests' awareness at one time struggled to find his equilibrium between these two standards. Within himself, he had to balance his own individual will with his spiritual quest. It is in the story of those struggles that we can bear witness to a unique and vital way of life, and find for ourselves inspiration to face our own challenges.

ONE

Master and Student

Saihung was the least likely candidate for holiness in the temples of Huashan. A young man of contradictions, restless and mischievous, he could alternate quickly from melancholy to euphoria, brashness to shyness, anger to reverence. His primary passion for boxing was not easily combined with his promise as an acolyte, yet his master continued to cultivate him in the hope of perfection. For him, divinity and evil existed within each person in continual struggle for the human soul; it was usually enough that divinity won most of the time. Anyone who knew Saihung would admit that neither side was assured easy victory. From minute to minute one never knew whether good or bad would emerge from Saihung; but for the moment, the good seemed to be on duty.

Before the dying night would be bleached by a lavender dawn, Saihung grasped a wooden bucket and held it over a well. The world would be awakening soon. The temples of Huashan in Shaanxi province, where he lived as an ascetic, would soon be stirring with priests and acolytes. China in early 1941, torn by civil war and soon to be drawn into global war, would awaken to another day of confusion and conflict. But there in the darkness it was quiet, and Saihung single-mindedly applied himself to his task.

He dropped the bucket down into the jet blackness of the well and heard a sharp, cracking sound. In the high mountains the nights were so cold that ice formed nightly over the pure well waters. He pulled up the bucket again and released it.

The next time he dropped the bucket, it filled with water. Saihung drew it up and for a second caught his own reflection as the disc of water angled into the weak yellow light of his paper lantern. The image was vague and imperfect, but he made out the wide jaw, smooth skin, large brilliant eyes, and long hair coiled into a top knot. He paused. He might have been anything: a duke, an official, a scholar, a general, even a bandit king. He could have claimed any of these lives as his birthright, since he was the son of a general, the grandson of an Imperial minister, the scion of a noble family that had been members of the aristocracy for dynasties. Instead, he was a Taoist adept and had been so since he was nine. Now in his mid-twenties he was still in the service of the Grand Master of Huashan. He quickly filled a large brown gourd with the clear cold water.

His hands were still numb from the water he had spilled on them as he tied the gourd to his body and picked up a basket that contained some firewood and fresh clothing for his master. He retrieved the lantern from where he had casually stuck it into the low eaves of the well's pavilion and made his way toward his master's temple. The light of the candle flickered in its paper sphere, a dancing spot at the end of a slender bamboo handle.

He followed the path around the crest of one of Huashan's many precipices. The surroundings were lost in black, and he could barely see the far mountain ranges through corpulent silhouettes of old pines. Individual pinnacles were smeared in the dye of night; the landscape was a simple division of rough, jagged land and a sky that still had stars and a crescent moon. He had been in these towering mountains for many years, yet he had neither explored them all nor known them fully. In a way, that incompleteness paralleled his experience in Taoism, a spiritual discipline more vast than the earth's myriad mountains. Taoism spoke of heaven and earth, the dimensions of time and space, and all that lay beyond. It spoke of simple human morality and it spoke of amoral Nature. It could degenerate into superstition, sorcery, and ritual, or it could soar into austere heights of asceticism and astral travel. It could engage in abstruse metaphysics or it could take equal delight in being a simple block of wood. Reach for it and it stretched away to infinity. Compress it and it shrank past atomic particles. Push it away and it could loom monsterously. Contemplate it and it changed relentlessly. Taoism was everywhere and everything. It was all that the universe was, all that it was not, and it could be both at once. It could not be escaped and yet it was the most elusive thing imaginable.

Saihung climbed quickly up the steep, rocky trail, his breath condensing into vapor before his face. He had to hurry. His master would soon be completing his night-long meditations. He ran up the stone steps to a tiny temple, and walked between two bronze cranes. The words "Hall of the Immortals" were carved above the gate. Its heavy doors were taller than a man by four or five feet. Their top halves were latticework, the lower sections inlaid with mosaic flower designs. He pushed them open with some effort and walked quietly down the tiled hallway to his master's chambers. He paused at the heavy wooden doors.

"Master! Master! Master!" he called out to announce his presence. As always, there was no response. He slowly pushed the door open.

Saihung stood at the threshold. His lantern barely lit the room. The brick walls and stone floor held the cold night air, the large bronze brazier had almost gone out, the morning mists had penetrated the walls of the simply furnished room. There was only a desk, a bookshelf, a bed, and a meditation platform facing a tabernacle. His white-haired master sat there, cushioned by a magnificent tiger's skin. He was erect and unmoving. In the uncertain light, with the swirling mist, his master could have been some ancient and mysterious votive object in a stone chamber. Saihung waited.

The dawning light slightly bleached the open skylight. The master's thin figure moved a little, and soon Saihung could hear breathing other than his own. His master was ready to begin his day. Saihung laid out clean clothing and quickly applied himself to his routine. He carefully opened lattice and paper windows, propping them open with wooden sticks. Then he heaped wood chips and coal into the brazier and fanned the pile to a small but intense flame. Walking quietly across the room he reverently drew the curtains on the intricately carved tabernacle. There were three beautifully fashioned figures inside. The central one was a Taoist saint and personal patron deity to the Grand Master. The flanking figures were the saint's acolytes. One carried a sword, the other a seal. All three were painstakingly painted and lit by an ever-burning oil lamp.

He checked to see that the flowers and fruit were fresh, the tea and wine cups full, and that no dust had accumulated on the altar. Then he tied the drapes back and lit the incense. The sweet fragrance of sandalwood filled the room, and smoke drifted up into the blue light like tiny gossamer dragons on the chase.

"Altars are for the weak," whispered the Grand Master behind him. He seldom spoke to Saihung directly in these early morning meetings. If he did, it was only to utter a few terse phrases. Sometimes it was an order to bring a certain tea, a specific book, or to prepare for a journey. At other times he would read aloud or simply make a few philosophical observations. Today he continued briefly on.

"Only those whose belief in themselves is inadequate must have some external image upon which to fix their

The Grand Master of Huashan.

attention. In actuality, heaven and hell are right here on earth—within each of us."

Saihung turned from the tabernacle, but his master's lips were motionless. The sepulchral silence returned as the Grand Master raised his right elbow and, with a smooth, languid motion, laid it upon a teak armrest. He nodded, a signal for Saihung, who stepped behind him to undo his hair.

The white strands, thick and full, fell down in a mass on the platform. Saihung combed it gently, tenderly. He remembered how the roles had been reversed during his initiation ceremony at the age of twelve. Then, as he had knelt before the altar, his master had combed his hair—symbolically purging attachment to worldliness–and had pinned the Taoist topknot for the first time. In the years since, Saihung had combed his master's hair many times, and each time it had strengthened a tie to the man who guided his life.

The Grand Master, it had been said, had been handsome and dashing in his youth. He had applied himself to the mastery of military arts and strategy, and had also excelled in scholarship. He had gone to the court of the Qing dynasty in Beijing, had entered into the Forbidden City itself to take the Imperial Examinations. Within the high red walls and airy halls of the palace, he had been tested over and over. He had completed essays, answered tests in history, mathematics, literature, astronomy, political theory, and dozens of other subjects. He had demonstrated his skills in poetry, calligraphy, horsemanship, archery, and physical combat. After days of trial in the grand capitol, he had been awarded the title "Civil and Martial Double Talent." It was one of the highest ranks, and he had been employed as an Imperial tutor.

He had thus walked the halls of royalty itself. He had absorbed the courtly etiquette and directed the mental progress of princes. Not long after his acceptance into the royal house he had married a beautiful woman of noble background, thereby completing his success.

But a tragedy struck him and he lost it all. Saihung's curiosity about this pivotal event had never been satisfied. No one could say what this event had been. Had it been court intrigue, the manipulation of vicious eunuchs? Could he have fallen into disgrace, advocating an unpopular viewpoint? Or had martial rivals murdered his family? Whatever the unknown circumstances had been, they had been traumatic enough for the Grand Master to have fled the world itself. He had sought solace in a life away from society. He had become a Taoist, by studying under two masters, and had entered into the priesthood. Two classes of religious life had then been opened to him: to become the resident priest of a temple, performing all public functions of ritual, divination, marriage, and funerals, or to become a renunciate following the tradition of monastic hermits. He had chosen the latter path.

He had gradually risen in the Taoist hierarchy until he had reached his present position. He was not simply the head of his particular sect, but the abbot who presided over all the temples of Huashan. His title therefore implied not only a supreme mastery of Taoist doctrine and ascetic practices, but a high temporal power as well. The acquisition of that power had taken decades, and the Grand Master was rumored to be over one hundred years old.

The worlds that formed the Grand Master's background were unique social structures with only vague parallels to world history. If one imagined a surreal combination of medieval Europe—when sword, sorcery, church, throne, and alchemy all coexisted; and classical Greece—when a pantheon of gods ruled the universe, philosophers headed up their own schools, and the Spartans were the standard of warriors—then perhaps one would have some inkling of the culture that had shaped the Grand Master's life. Nothing in the universe was ever really destroyed; people drew no distinction between ancient and modern. From the oldest methods of agriculture to the latest technological invention, everything had its place in the vastness.

The Grand Master embodied a sea of tradition, history, culture, and religion, and was a purist and strong theologian. He administered the temples with a firm and broadminded policy and tried to teach his disciples with the wisdom and strong sense of order and purpose that he had developed over his many years.

Tall, thin, but still possessed of a muscular vitality and deer-like grace, the Grand Master was an imposing figure. His beard was silky and as flowing as a mountain cascade. The eyes were large, luminous and clear. A scar that cut the right side of the upper lip was the only reminder that this man who looked like a fairy-tale character had also had a deep and real past traveling in the world.

Saihung often compared himself to his master. He too was lean, severe, and grave. But his muscles were inflated and hardened by weightlifting and martial arts, his black hair was thick and coarse, and his skin was darkened by years of exposure to the sun. He could see that he was markedly different. He was temperamental, impulsive, and without his master's deep serenity. He let out a soft sigh. In his eyes his master was a lofty figure. An inspiration, but perhaps a living ideal that he would never succeed in emulating.

Saihung wordlessly gathered his basket and his master's discarded clothes for washing. He noted with satisfaction that the room was warming and the mists had been dispelled. He placed the gourd of springwater at his master's side so that it would be available to quench his thirst after heat-building meditation. Saihung paused at the doorway to glance back. His master had crossed his legs, touched his fingers together, and closed his eyes. Within seconds he was again as motionless as a statue. As dawn finally rose on the mountain, Saihung saw the first ray of morning edge into the skylight and light his master's face.

Saihung left to wash, attend morning devotions, and eat a simple vegetarian meal with fellow monks. Afterwards, he went to fetch his master's breakfast. All along, he pondered his master's few whispered words. If heaven and hell were on earth, there might neither be reward nor retribution. If that were so, then there might neither be good nor evil. Furthermore, then, why should he worship and attend boring devotional services? As he walked toward the kitchen, he resolved that he would have to question his master more closely.

The kitchen was a hell of heat. Woks large enough to bathe a child in sat on roaring, wood-burning brick stoves. Young monks fed the insatiable fires, while others stirred the boiling rice. Some chopped vegetables or prepared them for pickling. They were all under the direction of a senior priest, who was known only as "the Old Cook."

A stubborn man whose spine and shoulders seemed fused, he was as thick and squat as the inscribed stone stele in the courtyard. His head was big and solid, the cheeks fat, and eyes round—dark, but registering a surprising awareness for someone of such a boar-like countenance. He was an impatient supervisor.

The abbots had long tried to calm his bursts of temper, as deeming them sacriligous and a poor example, but even Taoism could only do so much.

"You're late," grumbled the Old Cook with a bad-humored expression. "The vegetables are cold. Your master must be starving."

"This little one recognizes his sin," apologized Saihung.

He seized the covered wicker tray, the dishes clattering within, and rushed out the door to his master's chambers. None of the high-ranking priests ate in the dining halls. They were served by their students.

"Master! Master! Master!" he called at the door. Silence. He went in, and his master smiled at him. Saihung bowed and set the basket down. He took out the covered porcelain dishes and set them on the table. There was a tofu and gluten dish, freshly sauteed vegetables with mushrooms, peanuts and pickles, rice, and steamed bread. The fragrance—rich, clear, and fresh—burst like a cloud from each dish. Saihung could scarcely contain himself, and his mouth was watering as he poured tea and placed chopsticks delicately on their porcelain holder.

"How are your studies coming?" the Grand Master asked as he began to eat. Saihung adjusted quickly. Sometimes his master would say nothing for days. He had to seize the opportunity whenever his master was inclined to talk.

"It is hard to perfect oneself," replied Saihung modestly.

"There is a saying, 'The mind of a holy man is like a mirror. It neither grasps nor resists. It receives and returns. It is for this reason that the sage encompasses the world without hurt.' This is something which you must strive for. You must purify yourself. Do not occupy your mind with trivialities."

"Great Master, is there such a thing as good and evil, right and wrong?"

"Why do you ask?"

"You have said, 'Everything we do, we do ourselves,' and that 'Heaven and hell are right here on earth.' Does that mean that there is no external authority? And if not, who is to define right and wrong?"

"I will tell you a story to explain," said the Grand Master. "Once a beautiful and richly dressed woman appeared at a house. Naturally, the owner of the house welcomed her. He was dazzled by her ethereal loveliness.

"'May I ask who you are?' he said.

"'I am the Goddess of Fortune,' she replied. 'I bring luck to unhappy children, heal the diseased, grant children to the barren, bring untold riches, and fulfill every wish and supplication.'" The owner of the house immediately straightened his robes, bowed low before her, and personally gave her the honored seat in his home.

"Before long, another woman came. She was bent over and hobbled. Her face was dessicated, misshapen, wrinkled. Her hair was as tangled as dry rice grass. She stank. The owner was indignant and rudely demanded to know why she was trespassing.

"'I am called the Dark Lady. Wherever I go, the rich go bankrupt, high officials fall in disgrace, the weak die, the strong lose their might, women weep endlessly, and men mourn.'

"The owner immediately seized his staff to drive her away.

"But the Goddess of Fortune stopped him, saying, 'Those who would honor me must also honor her, for wherever I go, the Dark Lady inevitably follows. We are as inseparable as a shadow to a body. We cannot live apart.'

"The owner understood immediately and urged both goddesses to depart, now very much afraid that both might stay. The wise lead their lives in this way."

The Grand Master looked at Saihung to see if he had understood the parable. He saw only a quizzical student. The Grand Master picked up his chopsticks and ate quietly. After many minutes of thoughtfulness, he continued on.

"Good and evil do exist. There is bright Tao and dark Tao. There are demons and gods. There are good and bad people. But notice that there is no evil in nature, the constellations, nor in animals. These things are allied with Tao and have no volition of their own. They follow the Tao with no resistance. This is what is meant by the mirror that neither grasps nor resists, that perceives and returns simultaneously. But humanity and gods differ from plants, stars, and animals in one crucial respect: They have intelligence. They have rational, calculating minds. They have free will. It is because of their scheming that people have good and evil. They can make a choice, and there would be no choice without both good and evil.

"You know that *yin* and *yang* are the fundamental duality of the universe. Neither is mutually exclusive. For darkness to exist, there must be light. For day to come, night must precede it. If there is a right, then there must be wrong. This is the first meaning of the parable.

"The human race was created from *yin* and *yang*. We are both. If we had no tension and interplay between polar opposites there could be no movement within us or in the universe. There would be complete stagnation, a supreme stasis. Sterility would be the sole reality. Thus, we must accept relativity. We must accept good and evil, because they are part of the fundamental process of creation. If you can comprehend this then I must tell you one other thing: You must accept both good and evil within yourself."

"Great Master," broke in Saihung, "I am a Taoist. My endeavor is to live a decent life. I wish only to improve myself and to be a force for good."

The Grand Master laughed sarcastically. "How pious you are! There is nothing more disgusting than the pious."

"I don't understand. Isn't this what I've been taught since childhood? Is there anything objectionable to living a moral life? Why should I not yearn to live as a hero of justice?"

"Morality and ethics are for the stupid and unthinking.

Such people may lack discrimination, but nevertheless possess scheming minds. The sages invented morality solely to control such fools. Those who understand the Tao should not heed such things."

Saihung paused. He could not quite bring himself to accept the Grand Master's words. Surely he was not being told that morality and immorality were indistinguishable. "I am quite confused by your words. Please instruct me. You cannot be saying that to be evil is as valuable as to be good."

"I am only saying that morality is not for the discriminating," said the Grand Master in irritation. "The pious and moral person lives his life in fear of doing wrong. Whenever he commits a 'sin' he rushes to the temples to beg the gods for forgiveness and strength. He sees depictions of hell's retribution and trembles at the thought of falling so low. He reads scriptures, gives alms to the poor, and works himself into constant anxiety about doing 'good.' All this praying and mumbling is useless. He lives his life a babbling, idiotic slave of superstition. The gods are not in the least attracted by someone who bows and scrapes his way through life."

"Can I stop going to devotional service then?" asked Saihung mischievously.

"Rebellion!" exploded the Grand Master. Saihung shrank back. "You are a monk. You must do this as a type of etiquette, even a duty. But inwardly, you should understand the actual nature of what you are doing. For the public, you are performing an important service. For yourself, you must use this for self-control and self-discipline. In this way you reaffirm the good and do nothing to support evil. You are destined to be a holy aspirant.

"Those who have some wisdom accept that they embody contradictory elements. Thus, even while they cleave to the good, they know that they will inevitably do bad, but they understand themselves when they do. Committing evil should not be intentional. Do not say, 'Today I must do my quota of bad deeds in order to fulfill my destiny.' That is an utter mistake. Rather, you must always strive to understand a situation before you act. You must perceive what is required of you and then fulfill it. You must take this action whether or not it conforms to petty morality. This is the way of the sages. That is why the owner sent the two goddesses away. He understood relativity, and the inseparability of opposites. He chose the way of the wise: He chose neither good nor evil, but a transcendent path instead. A smartass hears the doctrine that he's both good and evil and thinks it a license for him to act as he pleases. He'll never understand that in doing so he will bounce eternally between the two poles.

"Take yourself, for example. You commit enough mischief for a hundred demons. I accept this as natural. But don't think you can use Taoism to justify it. Because you intentionally plunge into reckless behavior you have still not escaped duality. The sage seeks to transcend duality."

Saihung was scarlet with embarrassment. It was true. He was full of tricks. He tried to ask another question to divert the conversation away from himself.

"You have stated that good and evil exist within man," said Saihung, "and that even the gods may be subject to duality. But is there a metaphysical good and evil? If 'Everything we do, we do ourselves,' and if good and evil exist solely inside beings of volition, then good and evil can neither exist metaphysically nor can there be retribution. Then there can be no higher discriminating authority."

"You are a tricky one, I admit," said the Grand Master. "But such sophistry will get you nowhere. Let me explain. Good and evil are not as simple as heroes and villains in an opera. Good and evil exist metaphysically as destiny and fate."

"Destiny and fate?" responded a puzzled Saihung. "Aren't they the same?"

"No, they aren't. Destiny is that which you must fulfill in this lifetime. You are born with a task. During your life you must continually strive to identify it and complete it to its last detail. This is no simple errand, mind you. It is a terribly intricate and unique enigma for each person that must slowly be brought to fruition. The issue at stake is nothing less than transcending the consequences of past lives in order to be reborn in a higher state or, better yet, to escape all together. That is destiny.

"Fate is an active agent that exists solely to deter you from fulfilling your destiny. It struggles against you, impedes your progress. Fate functions through illusion. It is responsible for mirages which lead you astray. It is temptation. It tricks you, fills your mind with grand notions and proud thoughts. Fate would like nothing better than to deter you from your goal. Whenever you think of doing wrong or playing a trick, and you become aware of yourself, you have instantly found fate. Give and fate has won. Resist and it has lost. But it will be there, tirelessly waiting to distract you once more.

"This is what 'heaven and hell are right here on earth' means. Don't look outwardly for heavenly beings and hellish denizens. Look within you. Pursue your destiny and you are closer to heaven. Yield to fate and you slip toward hell. If you ultimately fulfill your destiny you transcend human existence. If you fall to fate you suffer in a quagmire of delusion and ignorance.

"Don't naively think that gods and devils administer you and the cosmos. Again, this is folk superstition. The gods *do* exist, but they don't look like the figures upon the altar. Furthermore, they have little interest in humanity. There is nothing we can do to gain a visit from the gods anyway; they cannot bear our human stench. No, don't rely on gods and don't be afraid of devils. They have their own problems, for even they must struggle with destiny and fate.

"This is what 'Everything we do, we do ourselves' means. If you understand good and evil as destiny and fate, you understand that your actions alone move you toward one or the other. Nothing else enters into your life equation. Solve a bit of your destiny and you triumph. Give in the slightest to delusion and your vision is all the more obscured. You used this saying to argue against a metaphysical authority, but the case is quite the opposite.

"There is no demon to punish you if you're bad. Hell doesn't exist after death unless you believe in it; the mind is strong enough to create exactly the place you envision and imprison your entire being in that dimension for an eternity. Retribution only exists within the mechanism of consequence. Consequence is not a being. It has no mind. It's not a thing. It is a force.

"All your actions have consequences. Put water over fire and it boils. Jump up and you will come back down. Action and reaction. In precisely the same way, your every action simultaneously has a commensurate reaction. In a person's life, the strands of consequence can become hopelessly tangled, imprisoning him in a matted and thick web. Such a person will be reborn a thousand times. But a net can also catch fish. The strands can be knotted into a net of good. This is the consequence of the devout person: The web of his past good actions continues to grow and generates more good, but he will still have to be reborn. The highest level is to transcend good and evil and erase one's consequences altogether. Then one leaves the wheel of life. So there is such a thing as divine retribution. It is neither the punishment decreed by the Jade Emperor nor by the King of Hell. Divine retribution is your simple interaction of destiny, fate and consequence. That is all."

Saihung tried his best to memorize and comprehend the words.

"Don't strain your mind," commented the Grand Master dryly. "You've not completed your life of mischief yet."

"I'll still try to understand," grinned Saihung.

"Good, good," laughed the Grand Master. "Keep trying."

As was his habit, the Grand Master ate only a very small bit of millet and a bird's sampling of the dishes. Saihung urged the Grand Master to eat more.

"I eat only to maintain my tie to this earthly plane," responded the Grand Master. "I could live on air and drink only the dew from trees, but I am not ready to relinquish my identity as a man. Sages who do not eat food already live half their lives in a divine state. As for me, I can only glimpse the divine and I accept that I have more to do in order to complete my task on earth. I do not want my body to deteriorate. The body must be maintained in an absolutely perfect equilibrium. It must be in peak health to function as one's spiritual vehicle. I eat only enough to satisfy my body. Please take these dishes away and complete your kitchen duties."

"As you wish, Great Master," said Saihung with a bow. He cleared the table and left the room.

Once around the corner, he glanced up and down the deserted hall. The white light that came through the lattice and paper window gave the wicker basket a warm glow. He set the basket down on the grey tile floor and opened it. He touched the lid of a dish. His hand felt the smooth blue and white porcelain. Saihung quietly set the lid aside and removed the dish. He brought it to his lips and the pickles and peanuts were gone instantly. One by one, he devoured every morsel of food in the basket before returning to the kitchen.

"Was the Grand Master pleased?" asked the Old Cook eagerly. Like any cook, he wanted his creations to be well received. Saihung wordlessly brought out the empty plates and displayed them triumphantly. The Old Cook's shiny face expanded in a joyous smile.

"He ate it all!" the cook marveled. "Tomorrow, we should send more. He's so thin! He musn't go hungry!"

"As you say, master," said Saihung humbly.

Saihung walked reverentially up the steep granite steps toward one of the most magnificent temples on Huashan, the Hall of the Three Pure Ones. The stone was so hard that countless processions had failed to soften the edges. He saw small puddles of water here and there, for the steps and portico had been thoroughly washed only an hour before.

The temple facade was set back from the mighty cinnabar-colored wooden pillars that supported the beamed ceiling. The hall was at least fifty feet high at the ridgepole, and its colors were brilliant in the sun. The lintels were painted in geometrical designs of red, green, gold, and blue surrounding small vignettes of holy scenes. Above the red-lacquered doors was a huge black plaque with the temple's name flowing in raised gold calligraphy. The doors of the temple were heavy and extended high enough for him to have walked straight in with another man standing on his shoulders. Avoiding the latticework, he placed his palms on the center, away from the inlaid floral design, and pushed the doors open with great effort. There was a rush of cool air.

The sheer verticality of the doors was matched by the soaring proportions of the hall's interior. Like most Chinese sacred halls, the ridgepole paralleled the front entrance; the hall was wider than it was deep. The lines of the roof sloping down in the rear, and the supporting pillars, which were naturally shorter towards the back, created an exaggerated perspective. Combined with the raised platform and larger-than-life-sized deities, the illusory perspective gave the hall a surreal sense of space.

The breathtaking architectural proportions were matched by the dazzling richness of color. All the supporting beams were carved and painted in a manner even more complicated than the exterior beams. The patterns of colors were too elaborate to take in at a glance, but they formed intricate screens and kaleidescopic backdrops.

Three altars were placed side by side, and each had a god framed by high gilded archways. On closer inspection, one could see that the gold filigree screens were formed of thousands of figures no larger than a finger's length.

The gods were painted to look as if they could be flesh and blood, giving a clear impression of substance beneath the robes, the contours of firm muscle or a swelling chest. The faces were painted a skin color, eyes and lips rendered in perfect detail. The hands of all three were exposed, but each was held in a different gesture. Lao Tzu, on the left, held a fan. The Original Being, in the center, held an orb that represented the universe. The Jade Emperor, on the right, held a scepter. All three had clothing so artfully carved that they draped like real cloth. The robes and prayer rugs were depictions of the wealthiest brocades. The lacings of gold leaf formed beautiful highlights that caught the worshiper's eye from any angle.

The thrones on which they sat crossed-legged were worthy of emperors. They too were carefully carved, as if every stroke of the sculptor's knife and every mark of the painter's brush was a gesture of devotion.

In any other context, the Three Pure Ones would have been considered sculptures of the highest quality. Any connoisseur of art would instantly have recognized not only the imagination, vitality, and craftsmanship, but also the epiphanatic element that is part of all great art. They had that mysterious ability to evoke reverence and awe, and to provoke thought and introspection. They had a sense of aliveness that transcended the physical reality of wood and paint. Art bridged the gap between humanity and heaven. Temples, sculptures, landscape paintings—all spoke of the human place in the scheme of things amidst the overpowering grandeur of nature and heaven. In creating art that transcended the human scale, artists tried to bridge the distance to heaven. They sculpted enormous figures too large to view at once. They painted scrolls too long to view at a glance. They built towers too high to scale in a few steps. All were attempts to take humanity out of its wretched reality and into the idealized proportions of art. This was the Hall of the Three Pure Ones: It was a masterful setting, achieved through the artistry and devotion of countless people, a place for the highest aspirations and acts of worship.

Saihung walked toward the high altar, which was already laden with huge vases of purple, yellow, and red flowers, unblemished fruit, food offerings, and fragrant sandalwood. Oil lamps were ready to be lit. The many ritual implements, such as bells, wooden knockers, gongs, and a jade scepter lay waiting. The red candles had been lit already, and hundreds more awaited lighting on the side. Saihung knew his master was purifying himself in preparation for the ritual before Taoism's supreme trinity. Soon the hall would be filled with solemn holy men, the fire of devotion within them burning as brightly as the hundreds of flames in the temple. Saihung didn't want to miss a single moment. He looked for a good vantage point in anticipation of the great event he had planned.

He would be able to see every corner of the hall from the beams some twenty-five feet above the floor. The only way to get up was to climb the gilded archways that framed the Three Pure Ones. He quickly put his fingers into the carvings. His toes found other openings, and he climbed up, stepping on the heads of the God of Longevity, the Goddess of Mercy, and a host of Immortals, Sea Dragons, and demons.

He swung himself in great glee onto the wide beam. He saw that it wasn't even painted on top, but there were decades of dust and incense soot in a grimy layer. Streaks of dark grey smeared over his clean blue ritual robes and dirtied his hands. Saihung didn't care. His excitement took him over completely.

He inched out to the very center of the beam and waited for the procession's approach. The mighty bronze echoes of the temple bells reverberated through the mountains. Every stone, each pine, even the flowing streams responded to the command of those mighty strikes. This was one of Huashan's holiest of days. There had been neither classes nor chores that morning, only ablutions and private devotions.

Saihung heard the procession approaching with the gentle sounds of gongs, clappers, and chanting. The temple doors were opened by young novitiates. The regular monks entered first, each one in blue gowns and pants, white leggings and straw sandals. Only the hats differed in shape, some round, others square, some with two peaks, to denote the rank of the wearer. The residents of Huashan filed in with solemnity and order. Their very steps were measured and their hands were clasped as a sign of discipline and preservation of holy energy.

The higher priests were dressed in more colorful clothes, embroidered with the same plethora of colors that decorated the temple interior. The Grand Master, as the leader, was dressed most colorfully of all. His black gauze hat had nine peaks, the symbol of the highest office of any Taoist monastic order. An oval piece of green jade was sewn to the front of the hat. His beard was full and dazzling white in the sunshine and it flowed like a river down his chest. The robe's predominant colors were purple, red, and gold, although many other colors had been employed to form embroidered symbols of cranes, bats, the word "longevity" in some of the "Ten Thousand Variations" and the trigrams of the *I Ching*. The satin surface of the robes was exquisite in its sheen, and brilliant in its color as only silk could be.

The Grand Master gracefully stepped over the eight-inch-high threshold of the temple doors. He hitched up his long, trailing sleeves and full hem with a subtle unobtrusive gesture, and walked closer to the Three Pure Ones. At no time did he glance down at the wooden threshold or the cracked tile floor. His mind and soul were fixed on the objects of his worship with complete concentration. Sai-hung could see the clear, nearly unblinking expression of the Grand Master's eyes, the half-smile of religious ecstasy, and the light, gliding walk of the enraptured holy man.

All the candles had been lit and the dark temple interior glowed with hundreds of pinpoints of golden flame. The incense from the central altar—a smoldering stick of pure sandalwood—wafted up in twisting clouds. The Grand Master lit three long sticks of incense and prostrated himself at each altar before offering the burning lengths on behalf of the entire mountain. Behind him, the other priests maintained their soft chanting. The long phrases of devout words formed currents of adoration that intertwined with the fragrant smoke. It was by that chain, raised ever heavenward, that the Taoists hoped to link heaven and earth.

The Grand Master returned to the central altar and opened the sacred scripture. Each Taoist deity had its own scriptures, and Taoists firmly believed that the figures of wood and paint could be awakened by the chanting of the appropriate texts. If the supplicants were sincere enough, the offerings sweet enough, and the place pure enough, the gods could be coaxed from the perfection of heaven.

The Grand Master's nasal voice rose like the sound of an oboe. It was reedy, yet full of deep and subtle resonances. It was an almost operatic ceremony; the gongs and wooden clappers maintained a steady pulse which punctuated appropriate climaxes in the reading. As the Grand Master's voice grew louder, and the incense had burned furiously to half its length, the sanctity of the ceremony was suddenly interrupted by a horrendous noise.

The priests broke their concentration. Although nothing was supposed to have the power of distracting them when they faced the gods, they turned involuntarily. One of the teak doors came crashing to the cold floor, sending up clouds of dust from the cracks that no sweeping had penetrated. It fell at an angle, and the impact sent a split like lightning down its length. Three men stood in the doorway.

The light from the south-facing doors was glaringly bright and many of the priests' eyes were dim from the darkness and smoke. The sentry priests rushed in while the others shrank back in panic towards the altar. The three men now charging to the temple center were clearly fighters.

Moving pugnaciously, their muscles bulging like melons in the sleeves of their corduroy clothes, the three glared viciously at the puny holy men. Their queues—which, like most martial artists, they still wore not as a symbol of allegiance to the long-dead Qing dynasty, but as a sign of their elite class—swung about them like live snakes. They planted themselves before the altar and simultaneously wrapped the braids around their necks. They had come to fight.

"Who is the Grand Master?" thundered the tallest.

"It is I," said the Grand Master gently. He came forward with a courteous bow. "Have we offended you worthy patrons in some way?"

"Damn you! Didn't you send us this?" One boxer pulled out a thin sheet of mulberry paper. Jet black calligraphy showed through the translucent fiber. "It says: 'You three dare to call yourselves Heaven, Earth, and Man. These arrogant titles are more than I can tolerate. In all my years of wandering in the red dust of the world I have never seen more pathetic caricatures of human beings. Your presumption to call yourselves martial artists on the basis of insignificant brawls with children is even more laughable. If you've any ounce of true courage, meet my challenge at the place and time I designate below. Only by eliminating you from the world can this life be cleansed of your foul presence.'"

"I assure you I never wrote that!" said the Grand Master hastily. "I am a humble and poor priest. I would not dare to compete with heroes such as yourselves. This is a great misunderstanding."

"Shut up! Isn't this your signature and seal?"

The Grand Master looked down as the letter was thrown to the floor. It was the only time in his life that Saihung had seen his master shocked. The old man's eyes were wide in disbelief and his mouth dropped open. The signature was his. The seal was genuine.

The tall man who represented Heaven took the Grand Master's surprise as an admission of guilt, and squared off for his attack. The Grand Master saw that talk was useless. His face became suddenly fierce, his body began moving warily. Even his robes seemed to bristle with electrical energy.

Heaven, dressed in dark-blue corduroy tunic and pants, moved with panther-like energy into the salutation of the

Golden Arhat system. He would not be fighting with fists and kicks, only with his palms. His dark face was lined and had a somewhat skewed appearance; his nose had been broken in his youth.

"Today is your funeral, old man," he snarled.

"Life and death are preordained by the gods," replied the Grand Master fiercely. "If I am to die, I am happy to do so before the gods. But you will not be the one to send me to King Yama."

"Raise your hands, old fool. I do not want gossip that I killed a defenseless man."

"Why cling to a nonexistant honor?" replied the Grand Master without raising his hands. "Attack when you please. If I use more then three moves to defeat you, I will consider myself dishonored."

"Die, then!"

Heaven lunged forward with a low growl. But the champion of hundreds of matches only managed a single strike that was blocked with the same hand that turned his head in a devastating slap. He fell unconscious.

Saihung could not contain himself, and began giggling. The Grand Master looked up and the face that was fierce for fighting became red with fury. But before he could speak, Earth attacked him.

Earth was a fat, pock-marked, and coarse man. His moves, derived from the Shaolin style, were not fancy. They were awkward and simplistic. But his sheer weight and strength had always been technique enough. Outweighing the average man by sixty pounds, he was a squat and ugly menace.

He closed in on the Grand Master with a reckless charge that the thin old man sidestepped. He came again. A look of regret flickered on the Grand Master's face. It would be like a pig before the butcher, but the martial code demanded fulfillment. He dodged and stepped forward. The sound of his fluttering sleeve was like a flag in a hurricane. He brought his palm slicing down on the kidneys and a kick then dislocated the knee.

Man was a thin, wiry creature with an ugly scar down the right side of his rectangular face. His salute showed him to be a Wudong stylist. Again, the Grand Master allowed his opponent to attack first. The attacker made a feint to the mid-section before a rapid jab to the eyes. The Grand Master's hand slid out of his full sleeves, grasped the wrist, and with a twist, threw Man to the floor. A flick of his toe knocked him unconscious.

The Grand Master stepped back and ordered people to carry the men out. Doctor-priests were sent to revive them and reset dislocated bones. The Grand Master had wanted only to incapacitate them momentarily. He knew they had been duped into the attack.

"Beast!" he shouted at Saihung. "Come down here!"

Saihung quietly slid down a pillar.

"Go to your quarters until you're called."

It was another three hours before the Grand Master's personal attendants, the two acolytes, escorted Saihung to his master's chambers. The Grand Master was still in his ceremonial costume. He walked slowly around his desk until he was face to face with Saihung. Saihung could sense a sudden acceleration in his master's body. His master slapped him sharply on the cheek.

"Kneel!" he commanded. "You evil child! This blasphemous act would have been unimaginable for any normal person. I knew you forged my name and framed me as soon as I heard you laugh. Only you, with your constant penchant for mischief, could have conceived such a scheme."

Saihung was quiet. He did not dare reply. But inside, he still reveled in the sheer excitement of it all.

"You made a serious error," the Grand Master continued. "You made a fool of yourself, dishonored me, and violated the sanctity of consecrated ground. Your sin is heavy indeed."

"But they deserved it," Saihung smirked. "What better way to humiliate them than to beat them before the Three Pure Ones? After all, the Trinity is even higher than Heaven, Earth, and Man."

"You are forgetting yourself by talking so freely!" interrupted the Grand Master. "You will be punished. But first, tell me how you arranged this shameful incident."

"I was begging for alms," recounted Saihung, "when I happened across their school. I went in to challenge them myself, but saw that I could not beat them. So I came back and sent the letter. Anyone so arrogant that they take such a high title deserves to be taken down a notch or two."

"You are wrong," scolded the Grand Master. "It is you who deserves humbling. Take him away."

The two acolytes took Saihung to a cave that ran far below the surface. The air was chilly and moist. Kindly, they had brought some padded clothing. All three were silent— the two acolytes because of solemnity, Saihung because he was still reliving his delight.

They came to a water-filled chamber. The place where a stalactite and stalagmite once met had broken centuries ago, leaving a jagged point over a round plateau about five feet in diameter. The rock platform was in the middle of a wide underground pool, and it was about ten feet above the surface. A heavy wooden plank stretched from the outcropping where they stood to the tiny island. The acolytes thrust the clothing and a gourd of water into Saihung's hands and ordered him across. Once he had seated himself, they withdrew the plank.

Saihung watched them turn and he saw the glow from

their torches fade in the darkness. His sentence was to sit in meditation for forty-nine days in order to contemplate his crime. During that time, he would have only rice gruel and water. Saihung closed his eyes, and the frigid air made him cough. The murmur of the water was a constant disturbance, and he heard uncomfortable shuffling noises from bats above. He knew he would suffer, but every time he recalled the day's events he would laugh. Repentance would not come easily when he found the delicious results from the crime so wonderful to savor.

A few jagged openings high above him threw tiny pale spots of dim light on the surface of the pool. He could see only a slight reflection of the drooping stone formations and grotesque irridescent cauliflower-like mineral deposits. The black liquid moved slowly and deeply.

He grew unhappy. There was no escape but memory. As he looked into the water he remembered the pools of sparkling aquamarine in the pine forests of his family estate. He recalled how, as a young boy, he had learned to swim. Third Uncle had tied two enormous gourds to him so the water would buoy him up rather than swallow him. The experience had been one of his happiest childhood memories.

Painful remembrances came as well. Sent at the age of seven to the village school to supplement his home tutorials, he had been beaten up daily. He had fought back, but could never overcome the apparently magical onslaughts of his tormentors. Ashamed to tell anyone, he had stoically borne his suffering until Third Uncle had noticed some bruises while they had been swimming.

"I fight, but they do strange things with their hands and legs and I always lose," Saihung had lamented.

"You silly boy," Third Uncle had scolded. "They're using martial arts."

"What's that?" he had asked. Only then had he begun to

learn not just techniques to defend himself, but a pivotal fact: His family was of a warrior class, descended from the Manchus of the Qing dynasty and of the God of War, Guan Gong. Until then, he had known nothing. All practice of technique and all weaponry were kept hidden even from the clan children.

As he began to learn martial arts he suddenly found himself in the deepest family conflict. His mother, an art and music tutor, had always intended that Saihung become a scholar ignorant of the ways of her battle-general husband. She had forbidden any martial activities. But that changed as Saihung learned of his heritage from Third Uncle. Now his father and grandfather took an interest in grooming him for the ways of the warrior.

As time passed, Saihung learned that warriors could be modern soldiers, like his father, who manipulated artillery and armies, or chivalrous knights, as his grandfather had been during the nineteenth century. He preferred the heroism of his grandfather's tradition to the violence of his father's. His grandfather was a gentleman, a poet, a calligrapher, and a musician, whereas his father was a shouting, drinking juggernaut. Saihung had spent more and more time with his grandfather as he had become estranged from his parents. His mother was unhappy because his warrior spirit had been aroused, his father was unhappy because he was not attracted to militarism, and both were unhappy because he was fond of playing pranks on servants and family members alike.

He liked tricks. He stole food from the kitchen and he hit people with bricks. For one of his most spectacular stunts he obtained a powder that would make a person break wind. He used this weapon in vengeance against an uncle who always lectured him on propriety. When a prince came to the mansion, Saihung put the powder in his uncle's tea. The poor man could not restrain himself and was severely punished. Saihung had watched his uncle's humiliation with no outer expression, but an inner glee. Playing tricks gave him some of his greatest pleasure. His relatives were his victims, and they punished him repeatedly and pressed him to reform. Even his grandfather, who never directly reproached him for his nearly daily misbehavior, spoke to him repeatedly about duty and the proper role of a young gentleman.

But the whole issue of roles became more complicated when Third Uncle had one day dressed him in long silk robes with a carp embroidered to the front, high platform shoes, a strange cap with a peacock feather, and a string of beads. He had not known then that he had been dressed in the clothing of aristocrats, nor did he understand why the servants had fallen down trembling when they had seen him. Old and young alike had knelt to touch his shoes.

"Why?" he had asked Third Uncle.

"Just let them do it," had been the reply.

Third Uncle had taken him to visit Emperor-in-Exile Puyi. The year had been 1927, the court had fallen in 1911, but the members of his family still presented their children to the Emperor. All the aristocracy clung to the old ways in the hopes of restoration. Third Uncle told Saihung that he had to learn the old ways.

He had become more aware of his clan's great legacy as he had felt their pressure to conform. Whether warrior, general, or nobleman, they wanted a disciplined, highly educated, and accomplished young man. There was no doubt that he was intelligent, but he was showing no signs of maturity. For his part, Saihung admitted to liking his grandfather and being partial to the old man's classical conduct, but he balked at the efforts of all other family members to control him. At the age of nine, his pranks had become so exasperating that his parents were ready to disown him. It had been his grandfather who had taken the decisive action.

His grandfather had taken him on a pilgrimage to Tai-shan, where Saihung had met the Grand Master for the first time. He remembered the meeting as something strange, the air mystically silent but nevertheless full of communication. Sensing some rapport between the two, his grandfather had arranged for Saihung to become the Grand Master's youngest student. It had been his way of rescuing his nine-year-old grandson from the pressures of the clan.

Saihung had grown up in the temples (though he still visited home), and had been raised by the Grand Master and his two acolytes, Mist Through a Grove and Sound of Clear Water. His master had become like a second father, the acolytes and his twelve classmates, all at least ten years his senior, had been like his brothers. It had only been on Huashan that he had known the security of a whole family, though he never gave up being the prankster.

Temple life could be dull, and when he was restless his old habits would resurface. Sometimes his tricks were merely for amusement, but often they were in response to some slight, real or imagined. He had put more farting powder into the food of monks who had claimed to be more accomplished than him, put a sage named the Bat Immortal to sleep with another herb and then shaved off his long hair and eyebrows, and had glued the Frog Immortal to a rock and beaten him with a stick. His master had punished him for each infraction. But Saihung accepted that as part of the game. Unlike his family, his master always forgave him afterwards and had continued to train Saihung unreservedly.

Gradually, he had blossomed, mastering not just martial arts but scholarly and spiritual arts as well. He had practiced extreme austerities while sealed in a cave for three years, and had even been an oracle for a year. During that time, he ate only herbs and had shrunken to a mere ninety pounds. His classmates had had to carry him around, all for the sake of making him a divine vehicle. When he performed his rituals, his own soul would leave his body and a spirit would enter to converse with the priests. It had always struck Saihung as ironic that opening himself up to the divine required his greatest physical weakness and that, despite the numerous times spirits had spoken through him, he had never heard the voices himself: While possessed, he had no consciousness of his own.

From physical weakness and communion with the divine he had plunged to the other extreme, when Japan had invaded China in 1937. Then he had left the mountain to fight and kill for patriotism. But after two years even that had lost any sense of purpose. Neither side ever won, he had seen atrocities that had made the tortures of hell seem like children's games, and he had seen the futility of politics. The Sino-Japanese War had also engulfed his clan, claiming the lives of some of its members, and laying waste to the once proud estate. In the few years since he had retreated back to the mountain community, he had tried to reconcile the disillusionment he had felt after all these events.

Meditation and the cool serenity of quiet and isolated incense-filled shrines had helped him to heal somewhat. Through his spiritual practice, he had been able to close the psychological scars more quickly than had other veterans. But war changes people forever, and he had been no exception. He never forgot the way fragile nationalism struggled with mighty nihilism on the battlefield, and he never quite lost the masculine pugnacity that had been his charm for staying alive. Stained as he had been by his clan's demands and the brutality of war, he had searched with more determination through the Taoist traditions for the key to understanding. Only by pursuing the deep and old ways of knowledge did he know a unique peace.

He felt there were answers in the past that the temples preserved. The wisdom of ancient times was not, for him, in the realm of archaeology. There was splendor, inspiration, and treasure. He felt a comfort in the antique, a hint of stability, an air of survival. In the worn buildings on high cliffs so close to heaven, he felt a resonance within his soul. He could reflect on the lapsed glories of old civilizations, muse on the passing of mortal things, and ponder the eternity of spiritual endeavor. Taoism spoke of immortality, and he had committed himself to its study not so much for the sake of longevity, but rather for the sake of finding the immortal poetics that would transcend his feelings of conflict, decay, and temporality.

But for the time being, he was condemned to the cave. He did see how his own faults had not only landed him there, but had interfered with his goals.

Saihung's initial attempts to make this a time of formal fasting and meditation gave out at some vague point halfway through his term. He quit the pretense. He was cold, hungry, and his thoughts were distorted. He spent much of his time sleeping—or perhaps simply lapsing from consciousness. He was oddly intriged to find that the hard rock had become an acceptable sleeping surface and that he barely cared anymore if his cheek was powdered with dust.

Forty-nine days later, his awareness trapped in a frigid stupor, he saw a wooden plank slide across the floor of his tiny world. It pushed a small heap of dust and dirt before it, and made an unpleasant scraping noise. He tried to look up, but it was difficult to make both his eyes focus on the same point. He saw flashes of flame, heard stepping noises, and felt a vise-like grip on his arms. The fingers squeezed him painfully. The muscles that he had once flexed so proudly now yielding flaccidly.

He coughed, but nothing came up through his dry throat. The smell of smoke made his cough worse. He found himself negotiating the flexing plank. The flowing ink below him was a molten night sky. The reflected torches were like dying suns, dissolving in rivers of spent gas and exhausted flame. He heard moans and whimpers from those expiring stars, but then he adjusted his consciousness and realized that it was the creaking wood. He was wobbly. His muscles disobeyed the orders to stabilize his movements. His adrenals had long ago run dry.

Saihung finally made out the faces of the two acolytes, and managed a half-smile.

They tenderly supported him as he stumbled through the tunnel to the outside. It was a cold dawn, but the breeze felt warmer to Saihung than the subterranean air. He opened his mouth to speak with what seemed like a gargantuan but ludicrous misaligning of his jaws. The acolytes only whispered to him to be quiet. They would take him to their own cell to nurse him back to health.

His dirty hair hung like withered roots, his face was grey with grime. Saihung's beard had grown into a chaotic jumble of black lines. He could have been a troll from the earth. He was a creature, a wretched, depleted, crumpled beast. Obstinate, rebellious, and proud, Saihung reflected that he was barely sorry for the prank that had led to this denigration.

He saw again the mountain beauty of Huashan, the towering vistas, the azure perfection of the sky. The legends, inspired by Huashan's gigantic tripod shape, had said the mountains were the very support to heaven's vault. As Saihung breathed in its clean air and tasted the bitter restorative given to him, he knew that the splendor of nature would hasten his return to normal life.

TWO

Two Butterflies

Huashan was a summit of beauty among all the poetic pinnacles of China, but it was a place where nothing could live unless it was strong. In its harsh climate only the hardiest plants and creatures could survive. The winds had twisted the pines into gnarled shapes; it had broken limbs and pruned needles, forcing the remaining branches to wave through the lighter flows of air, forming stark and idiosyncratic calligraphy. The rain had edged, marked, and deeply grooved the granite, polishing it to a near white and exposing its fine grain to the light. The sunlight was glaring on clear days, allowing some life to nurture itself on its rays, and pitilessly burning the weak. Yet the harshness gave the mountain a clean, pure austerity, perfect for the ascetics who lived so insignificantly in its crevices.

It was in the arduous mountain atmosphere that Taoist asceticism burst forth. It flourished on a paradox of barreness. No great human achievements, common wisdom would hold, could have come from such impoverished conditions. And yet Taoism came to full expression from precisely those circumstances.

Huashan—the name meant "Grand Mountains"—the West Peak of China's Five Sacred Mountains, was part of a high range situated between two ancient capitals, Luoyang and Xian. It was a circular grouping of five major granite peaks, accessible only by a single difficult trail. Rivers, lakes, waterfalls, forests, caves, and a predominance of sheer cliff faces made it an isolated paradise.

The Taoists had established schools, monasteries, and temples on each peak. All the buildings had been built by hand either from available wood, stone, and clay, or with materials arduously carried by men up the mountain's seven-thousand-foot ascent. With the exception of some buildings, like the Hall of the Three Pure Ones, most were plain, camouflaged from a distance by their earthy colors and hidden behind hillocks and pines, and shockingly poor. Their interiors had worn floors, thinly whitewashed walls, wooden window frames worn by rain and heat. Their furnishings were generally massive wood, heat was provided by coal burners, and beds were hard brick platforms with their own tiny fireplaces for heat. Such urban conveniences as electricity, telegraph, telephone, and steam power did not exist on Huashan. Food, generally short in quantity and variety in the north, was even less available on Huashan. The Taoists tried to grow their own vegetables in hothouses and small fields, and traded the rest from neighboring villages; but feeding the entire community of five hundred was a continual problem. Most of the priests were pathetically thin. Finances came from the uneven generosity of pilgrims and the meager earnings of priests as calligraphers, tutors, fortune-tellers, painters, and herbalists.

The temples were organized under the supervision of senior priests and abbots, and all the temples came under the jurisdiction of a council of elders headed by the Grand Master. Daily life was precisely regulated by the striking of planks or the sounding of sonorous bronze bells. An escalating cadence of five tones—three slow strikes ending with two rapid ones—aroused the adepts at 5:30 each morning. The young monks went about their assigned duties: fetching firewood and water, cleaning the halls, preparing breakfast, or attending to the masters as Saihung had done. The higher-ranking priests in the meantime washed and groomed themselves in preparation for the day ahead.

By 6:30, responding to the bell, most made their way to the shrine hall for morning devotions. There the prior would chant the scriptures in a high-pitched monotone, accompanied by strikes to a bell and a wooden fish. Saihung, now back to a regular routine, still found morning devotions utterly boring. When his master spoke he found the words alive and full of relevance. By contrast, he found all this mumbling quite dreadful. These words were hundreds of years old, formed by sages in the intricate patterns that would lead the aspirants to divine heights. But to Saihung, they were only a barrier to breakfast.

He could barely remain reverent as he entered the refectory with the sounding of another bell. Silence was absolute. Not only was talking prohibited, but even glancing at one another was punishable by a healthy stroke from the prefect's cane. The prior filled a bowl, while Saihung and his fellow monks stood in devotion, and offered it at the altar of a Taoist saint. Flanking the altar were two long trestle tables built from heavy timbers.

Saihung spooned up his bowl of rice porridge from the large wooden tub and sat down. There was a plate of pickled cabbage, turnips, and cucumbers for every two monks, and Saihung scrupulously ate only his half. He returned for a second bowl—the maximum amount allowed—and washed it all down with boiled water. "A pity it isn't a festival day," Saihung lamented to himself. Then at least he would have had a piece of fried wheat bread too.

After breakfast Saihung went to wash himself. The open-air washing pavilion had a series of enormous ceramic urns with holes at the bottom to drain the waste water. Two lengths of bamboo lined with copper tubing were fixed above the urns. The left-hand one carried water directly from an artesian well, while the right-hand carried hot water. Everything in the mountain was done by human labor. Two young monks heated the water in a large boiler over an open flame before diverting it into the pipe. Saihung undressed and stepped into the urn. The bottom was cold and the air was frigid. He splashed himself quickly and rubbed himself with sandalwood soap. He noted with satisfaction that his muscles were still hard and defined. Philosophy was fine, but physical prowess was tangible.

The hot water was too hot. He didn't know which was worse, cold water in the frigid morning air or the contrasting torture of the hot water. Saihung got out, dried off, dressed, and thanked the two boys. This morning he was scheduled not for lectures, but for class in the staff and sword with the Sick Crane Taoist. He started out in anticipation not simply of the class, but of seeing his friend as well.

The Grand Master had thirteen disciples, of whom Saihung was the youngest. The next oldest student was named Butterfly, and he was in his late twenties. The other classmates were much older than Saihung. They had all been ordained and had become accomplished men before Saihung had even been accepted as a student. Such men had had little interest in him as a child, but accepted him solely because he had become part of the Grand Master's inner group. Only Butterfly was within seven years of Saihung's age, and it was natural that the two formed a friendship through their growing years. If the Grand Master was like a father, Butterfly was like Saihung's elder brother.

He was the sibling Saihung could never have at home. Butterfly was warm, giving, and concerned. Saihung's own brothers were all intensely competitive, the result of his parent's high demands and ambitions. Each brother had been separated from one another and raised by different teachers in order to create extremely successful men. There had been no such thing as brotherly love to Saihung, only familial criticism and brutal comparison. He always felt short, ugly, and stupid when he went home. His brothers were great scholars, brilliant military men, rich merchants. Saihung was only a monk and would never bring prestige and fame to his parents and clan. It had thus been with the Grand Master and the thirteen disciples that he had finally known a family that accepted him as an individual. It had been with Butterfly that he had found a brother to look up to.

Apparently by coincidence, Saihung's given Taoist name was also Butterfly. The Grand Master had given Saihung the title for three reasons. First, Saihung was fascinated by beauty, due probably in large part to his family background. He was attracted to fine art objects, scenes of nature, and exotic flowers. Second, Saihung bored easily. He went from one subject to another, one infatuation to another, sometimes in moody swings. Finally, butterflies themselves seemed to like Saihung. They often hovered around him or even alighted on him. Saihung had thus been named the Butterfly Taoist. Like that insect fluttering from blossom to flower, he was drawn to beauty; but he never stayed for long in any single aspect of life. Huashan thus came to have two Butterflies: Saihung because he loved beauty, Butterfly because he was beautiful.

The elder Butterfly seemed to embody everything that a young man aspired to achieve. Intelligent, witty, and articulate, he was able to enter into a discussion with anyone from the most learned scholars to worldly state ministers. He could take part in contests where the participants spontaneously composed poetry—and this was only a hint of his command of literature, history, and philosophy. His skill as a musician was renowned, and even the grizzled old monks who supposedly did not care for earthly stimuli smiled when Butterfly played the lute.

He was handsome, with a physical perfection sculpted by years as a martial artist. His smooth-complexioned face glowed with athletic discipline, and his eyes were always vigilant. He usually had a charming smile for all who met him. People would turn to stare at him on the street in admiration, elders thought him good-natured and ready with sound advice. The youth of Huashan idolized him even more because he was not a monk: He had been an orphan adopted by the Grand Master and thus had the best that both the temple and worldly lives could offer.

When Saihung arrived at a small meadow, he saw that Butterfly was already there among the seven other students. Staff in hand, he tutored a few of his classmates. He learned quickly and wasn't selfish in helping friends.

"I'll never get this technique," sighed a slender youngster from Shaanxi province named Chrysanthemum.

"Nor will I," complained another with a heavy Shandong accent. "I had it and then Master changed some of the movements. Maybe he's forgotten."

"Yes, yes," agreed the first. "The Sick Crane Taoist is getting old. Maybe he's getting senile."

Butterfly laughed. "The Sick Crane Taoist is more vital than the three of us in the prime of our youth. He wins poetry contests and succeeded in the Imperial examinations."

"Yes, yes, we know all that," said Chrysanthemum. "But he still can't remember. We would have finished learning this set if he wouldn't keep meddling with it."

"Remember? Finish? You two have no classical background!" exclaimed Butterfly.

Butterfly, dressed in martial clothing.

"Classical? In this day and age?" retorted the Shandong student. "Wake up, elder brother, it's 1941!"

"Haven't you heard the old saying?" asked Butterfly patiently. " 'Sailing upon the ocean of knowledge, one cannot reach the shore.' He remembers many different versions. What he is actually doing is taking you through different stages of development. When you have absorbed one technique, he will refine it and make it more sophisticated. The set remains the same, but the movements acquire deeper subtlety. In this way your form is fresh and you will not lose interest. Since you never know exactly what will happen, your curiosity will be stimulated and you won't be bored.

"There must be variety in every kind of activity. Dance, drama, music, painting, and of course exercise must stick to the major themes yet still express the individuality and thought of the moment. The master changes things according to your understanding. He waits until you're ready to let go. He perceives when one version has become stale and is ready to give you a new little twist to move you forward."

"Hush!" broke in another classmate. "The master is coming!"

The students hurriedly fell into line. As they did so, Saihung looked at the two younger students and saw that Butterfly's talk had inspired them. But when he turned to look at the master, his heart dropped. He could see that the master was in a temperamental mood.

In his early sixties, the Sick Crane Taoist had thin dry hair streaked with white and tied into the traditional topknot. His skin was a deep copper. The darkness made his grey moustache startling in its contrast. The mouth was small, but still showed broken teeth.

A thin, aquiline nose divided two narrow eyes that seemed like two strokes of a Chinese brush. The corners came to sharp, narrow, downward turning points. Though he had no bags under his eyes, there were wrinkles from squinting, the result both of sunlight and hours of reading under an oil lamp at night.

The master's name was inspired by his looks. As slender as a stick, his back was slightly rounded, his chest hollow, almost caved in. His neck was noticeably longer than average. In fact, he seemed little more than a scarecrow. But Saihung had been invited to touch the master's body in order to feel a demonstration of particular muscle movements. The flesh had been tough and hard. One couldn't squeeze through to the bone.

The Sick Crane Taoist habitually held his hands behind his back. His grey robes had long sleeves that fell to his sides and he sometimes appeared altogether limbless, as a crane standing quietly appears to be little more than a head and body perched on spindly legs.

The master walked back and forth before the class, eyeing each student.

"Good morning, Teacher." said the class in unison.

"Humph! Don't call me your teacher! You have no discipline, talking and chattering like that. I could hear your noise all the way up the trail."

They said nothing. Talking was forbidden.

"Master," broke in Butterfly. "It was my fault."

The eyes like brushstrokes flared into onyx orbs. The hand came swiftly down. Tough as he was, Butterfly's cheek turned red.

"How dare you speak?" demanded the Sick Crane Taoist.

"I apologize, great teacher." said Butterfly with a bow. "This insignificant one is solely at fault."

"You are the eldest. You are responsible."

"Yes. I engaged them in conversation. I am the only one to blame. Please punish me."

The master relented.

Saihung watched him admiringly. "He takes the blame, but he knows the old man likes him too much to really punish him. He's crafty!"

"Alright," ordered the Sick Crane Taoist. "Ready . . . begin!"

The class instantly launched into a unison performance of the staff set.

When the class completed its performance, the Sick Crane Taoist nodded. He gave neither words of praise nor reproach. He had noted their level of accomplishment and his teaching would begin from that point.

"This is the proper execution of this technique," he said, picking up a staff. "The stick must not be held rigidly in the fists, but must be manipulated with the palms and fingers. When you bring the staff on a downward strike you emphasize the pressing movement of the forward palm."

He motioned to Saihung. "Little Butterfly, come forward. Show me this part of the set."

Saihung performed his movements with his utmost strength and skill. He was confident, for he had won boxing tournaments in the cities. The set itself was a routine of stances and fighting postures performed with lightning speed. Each was a distinctive collection of the style's hallmark techniques. Saihung proudly completed his movements.

"Barely acceptable," pronounced the master with a sigh. "Shouldn't it look more like this?"

The Sick Crane Taoist now jumped rigorously into the center of the meadow. Gone were his eccentric posture, the quirky walk, and the impression of pathetic thinness. His muscles snapped into lines, his limbs moved with tangible liveliness. The staff whistled angrily through the air and its ends flexed from the sheer force that propelled it.

When he stopped there was no panting for breath. The

Sick Crane Taoist returned to a casual posture that made it seem as if he had been no more than an old gentleman twirling an umbrella. The ferocious power that had been called up was withdrawn.

"Get into position." he said to Saihung. Saihung took a low stance and he felt the master come up close to him. It was an eerie feeling. He moved from posture to posture, but, with the Sick Crane Taoist touching him and gently directing his arms with nudges and pushes, Saihung felt that he was not moving of his own volition. Instead, the master's own life force had entered into him.

"There, isn't that better?" asked the master. Saihung had to admit that the subtle adjustments and the odd feeling of having something inside him had changed his performance and understanding.

Saihung became aware of a new attitude toward the staff. He felt its smooth surface against his palm and fingers, noted its rotation and changes in pressure as he directed it in different directions. It was hard, unyielding to his grip, yet flexible along its length. The staff vibrated almost imperceptibly to the force that he exerted through it, forming a response to his strength. This dialogue—made up in part by its obedience to his command, in part by the resistance of its weight—gave Saihung an added awareness of his own body. Moving the heavy staff, a thing outside himself, seemingly directed his attention inward. Saihung noted the stretching and contracting of his arm and shoulder muscles, the exertion of his chest, the contribution of his back. He noticed the rapid, bellows-like rhythm of his lungs and how they accelerated to meet the demands of the set. All this was somehow different, a change from his earlier knowledge. He wondered if it had been the Sick Crane Taoist's touch. It was said that there was such a thing as direct transmission of knowledge, and this might have been it. But such speculation was brief for Saihung as he returned his full attention to completing his set and immersing himself in his newly discovered awareness.

They practiced on for an hour, drilling over and over, reviewing, perfecting, and absorbing the movements. The Sick Crane Taoist watched them closely and gave corrections and instructions individually. When he noticed his students finally tiring, he said jovially, "Today, I want to teach some philosophy to you. Isn't that ironic? You, a bunch of aspiring holy men needing more philosophy."

It was a joke, but since laughter wasn't allowed in class, a daring few smiled.

"Let me tell you something further about the staff and sword," he continued.

"I want to give you an image to help you understand the staff's inner essence." The master paused. "The staff should be compared with the umbrella."

Saihung was puzzled. How could a stick be like an umbrella?

"Be a little imaginative," the master urged, delighted at having mystified them. Even Butterfly, with his greater experience, had never heard the comparison before. The Sick Crane Taoist revealed the secret.

"The proper execution of the staff requires that the stick be frequently angled away from the body. It is extended from the practitioner. It has reach. The body is like the shaft of the umbrella, while the stick itself represents the movement and extension of the ribs of the parasol. Sometimes a parasol is opened, sometimes it's closed; sometimes the stick is close to the body, and at other times it is thrust outward. But, just like an umbrella, the action is caused by the hand's leverage. The shaft and the ribs are distinctly separate parts. They always work at opposing angles to one another. This is the principle of the staff.

"Now we are about to shift to the sword. There is also an image for that. The sword may most properly be compared to a dragon. Its characteristics are virtually opposite to the staff. Where the staff is always a separate implement, the sword must have total unity with the practitioner. There is no distinction between man and weapon here. They are one. Together, they must twist, turn, coil, leap, and fly like a celestial dragon in the clouds. Take up your swords now and don't treat them like sticks. You and the sword are a single unit. Your limbs are part of that unit. All concentration comes brightly to bear on the very tip of the sword. Let the blade shine! Here is the dragon seeking his way! Begin!"

As the master had emphasized, the sword was seldom extended all the way, and it certainly lacked the reach of the staff. The movements were predominantly whirling ones, with the blade held close to the body. Inspired by combat, parries were executed at close range, the body and legs turning frequently to lead the edge in angled, slicing cuts. When the sword was thrust outward it returned by cutting its way along a different angle rather than simply being pulled back. The set had a liveliness that was indeed reminiscent of serpentine motion.

Few movements in this particular sword style were two-handed, and the free hand was never allowed simply to wave around. It, too, had precise movements to make, all the while maintaining a prescribed hand gesture of the index and middle fingers straight and the ring and little finger curled beneath the bent thumb. This gesture was not simply an imitation of the sword for the sake of symmetry; it was thought to be a talismanic protector. The early swordsmen believed that each time the blade passed near or above the head, the mystical power of the sword could injure the soul. The hand gesture protectecd the practitioner from harm.

The sword had been an integral part of life. Emperors and

officials always had beautiful swords inlaid with jewels. Noblemen fought with swords rather than coarser weapons like maces and axes. Even a poet like Li Po was expert in swordsmanship. Swords were believed to possess individual personalities, supernatural powers, and even their own destinies. A peach-wood sword was considered so magical that the Taoists used it in exorcism.

To Saihung, holding a sword was unlike holding any other thing. It was more than a training apparatus, for he was aware of its rich tradition. It was also more than a weapon, for he wasn't holding a real killing sword. A real sword seemed to have a life of its own. One could feel it immediately upon grasping it: it begged to be used. It had an "air of killing" as the traditional swordsmen put it. But what he held now, Saihung reflected, represented ritual, warfare, royalty, sorcery, and religion. He was touching part of swordsmanship and a fundamental part of life.

He sprang into the set. It felt good. He wasn't simply smashing his way through. The sword nature is refined and demanded grace and sensibility. He felt it draw upon different muscles, too: not the long ones, nor the large groups, as the staff required; the sword needed the dozens of little muscles deep in the arm and body. It needed fine motor coordination. Performing the staff was like painting a wall. Using the sword was like writing an essay in intricate and exquisite calligraphy.

He felt the sword take root in him and he felt his breathing extend to the tip of the blade. He gave himself up to the speed and momentum of the set. His feet moved automatically and he experienced one of those rare moments in any performing art or sport: The postures flowed on their own, effortlessly.

The Sick Crane Taoist noticed Saihung's performance,

but said nothing. Praise encouraged egotism. He only said, "Not bad," and instructed the class to review again and again.

These particular movements of the staff and sword were not meant for fighting, but for physical cultivation. Not so long ago—indeed, still within the memories of the elders—China had been a medieval society where recreational sports were almost nonexistent. A farmer who did his work without the benefit even of an ox to pull the plow, or a warrior who marched and fought man-to-man, would be little inclined to take up football. Exercise had been derived from everyday life in China, not conceived as a separate type of activity. When it had become necessary to train the young in physical culture, the elders had picked up two familiar things in Chinese life and adapted it to the needs of health.

A staff set differed in characteristics from a sword set. The staff taught the student how to coordinate both sides of the body. He had to move it and align its length to particular angles, turning it alternately from left to right, thrusting it outward to a predetermined distance. It also strengthened and sculpted the muscles by providing a heavy resistance during the full-speed movements of a routine that could last as long as fifteen minutes.

The sword taught grace, poise, posture, and positioning. Its execution could not be as physically powerful as the staff because it was a lighter and more fragile weapon by nature. Instead, its emphasis was on pinpoint concentration and precise cuts and parries. A real sword couldn't be used to block a weapon—it would break. This characteristic had influenced the movements of the exercise version and the practitioner twisted, turned, jumped, and crouched low in imitation of a dodging swordsman aiming for the smallest opening.

Both weapons were taught in a variety of weights. Initially, the weapons were light wood. As the student progressed, he was given heavier weapons in a system of graduated weight training. The heaviest ones weighed twenty-five pounds or more. After achieving a high standard, the student was given a very light weapon of perhaps a half-pound. Then he could perform the set with drama, expression, strength, and blinding speed.

After two hours the Sick Crane Taoist brought the class to a close and allowed his students to rest. But that was not the end. They all went for a walk through the mountains.

The Taoists had a thorough rationale for every activity, and hiking was no exception. It was of physical benefit because it increased stamina and resistance to disease. The stimulation to the circulatory and respiratory systems, as well as to the strength of the legs, was undeniable, but there were religious overtones as well. In the swift walking, one was allowed neither to trample plants nor insects. By walking in perfect silence, the students were expected to contemplate the beauty and meaning of the landscape they traveled through. Nature and the Tao were not wholly identical, but nature was a paradigm of the Tao. Thus, a student who could sharpen his perception and understand the subtle inner workings of nature, could also enhance his awareness of the Tao.

As they began walking Saihung was filled with impressions. He heard the crunch of his straw shoes on the dirt-and-gravel trail as he established his stride. He felt his leg muscles flex, the long bands of his thighs contracting and expanding, the movements of his hamstrings as he planted one foot firmly after another. The path began to lead uphill and he noted the corresponding shift in the interplay of his muscles as his quadriceps joined in the effort to carry him forward. He increased his pace, eager to walk and see.

A tangle of weeds grew beside the trail; grasses, vines, young tight-green shoots of yarrow thrust themselves above the competing thicket. Small red flies, and gnats that were like incandescent flecks in the sunshine, buzzed around in their own spiraling patterns. He filled his lungs deeply. Although it seldom got hot on Huashan, especially in springtime, this day was warm with a slight breeze. He welcomed the fresh pure air, and he smelled the grassy fragrance of the field. The grasses and weeds, the plethora of small plants, the small, low, blue-green leaves with tiny purple flowers, the yellow, many-petaled flowers that waved on tiny stalks, the spiky tops of a thistle, all these were as magnificent as trees, mountains, and streams. It only took someone to appreciate them.

As they climbed toward a ridge, shadows began to fall across his vision. Trees began to shade the sunlight. There were shadows like an indistinct lace, shadows of hazy grey, and shadows with intense spots of sunlight burned through them. He looked upward to see the beginnings of the spruce, fir, pines, and broad-leafed trees that forested the area. Some rose straight up in stately magnificence. Some had broken branches, limbs torn off by storms, pruned in ways that a gardener would have called ugly, but beautiful because it was natural. There were trees that arched over the trail at crazy angles, their bare white branches catching the light, making them a contrast to the forest canopy. He saw many whose girth would exceed his embrace, whose heavy trunks, like sinewy wooden muscles pushing from the earth, had stood for centuries.

The sound of water came to him. It was a brook that made its rocky tumble beside the trail. There was something about a stream's sound. It was hard to distinguish the separate voices of the stream, but it was nevertheless harmonious. Loudest, almost orchestral, were the falling and splashing noises as the water overcame fallen trees or piled rock.

The song of birds was loud in the air, a chorus above the water's sound, the percussion of branches moved by the wind, the sweeping rhythm of a thousand leaves. Above that background were occasional solos: the high delicate whine of insects, the buzzing of bees.

Saihung smelled the great moist earth where it had been cut by the stream. The air was colder under the trees. Blended with the smells of dirt and rock were scents of pine, spruce, and cypress. Smells excited him. They touched primeval urges. Of all the senses that humanity had made into elaborate methods of living or had stifled by repressive societal codes, smell was the last to be disciplined. Sight was appeased by painting, art, and cults of beauty. Hearing was entertained by music. Taste was obsequiously catered to with food. Touch was given a thousand sensual gratifications. All were correspondingly constricted by the ascetic and prudish. Sight was dulled by grey walls. Hearing was dulled by silence. Touch was muffled in heavy robes. Taste was tortured by plain foods. Only smell was unfettered. No one ever blocked the nose. That would have been suicidal. The nose had to be free, and as such it was free to exercise its sensitivity in any way it desired. It could convulse the whole body if it detected something putrid, or it could lead the body in search of pleasure upon noticing spice and musk. Even the saints had been helpless to sublimate the sense of smell in their urge for denial. They had had to give in to it, to placate it with pure mountain air and exquisite incense. Smell was a powerful sense that savored its own pleasures and catalogued its own memories.

The smell of the wet earth mixed with pine awakened thoughts of past walks. Saihung recalled the excitement of exploring the world, making new discoveries of different plants, the odd antics of insects, the wreckage of storms. He never tired of walking in the forests. Not once in his life had the mountain groves been unchanged. There was infinite variation, yet the forest always obeyed the seasonal cycles. That was the odd thing about nature. Everything was strictly obedient to a set order, yet everything was also individual and eccentric. Saihung glanced at one delicate set of branches that arched gracefully into the sunshine. The wood was homogeneous. The leaves were the same green with varigated edges. Yet there wasn't a single repetition to the twists of the branches, the pattern of the veins, or the angles of the toothed edges of the leaves. Nature was at once regular and wildly varied.

They climbed higher. Huge boulders, their undersides encrusted with moss and lichens, their upper surfaces bleached to bare grainy stone, began to dominate the land. The underbrush was beginning to be choked out. The richness was not possible amidst the rock and dry earth. Only the larger trees and plants could invade the rock crevices, thrust their roots deep into soil, and increase their height to survive in the more difficult environment. A few other plants took advantage—like the wood ears and parasitic ivies—but it was still the tall timber that was the major plant life. The trees stood higher than pagodas and their branches spread out mightily. But there wasn't the canopy that there had been in the lower valley. The sky shone through in large, beautifully abstract patches. The color was an intense cobalt blue—a hue so vivid that the sky, not the trees, seemed in the foreground.

They came to a section of the trail that led straight up a ridgeback. It was the belief of the Taoists that mountain pathways should follow the meridians of the earth. Just as the acupuncturists had established a science of meridians with points of energy, so had the Taoists established a study of the hidden lines of energy within the earth. One such type

of pathway was called the "Dragon's Meridian." This occurred on a mountain ridge whose profile resembled a
coiling dragon, and the main pulse naturally went up the
dragon's back. Switchback trails would thus have violated
the character of the mountain. Harmony was to follow the
natural flow of energy, but it meant a hard climb.

The rapid ascent nevertheless had its rewards in incom-
parable views of the far mountains. As the group climbed
higher onto bare rock mountain, the previously invisible
horizon came to stretch grandly across Saihung's field of
vision. Clouds, lower than his feet, galloped by like stam-
peding animals. Mountain range after mountain range
stretched to his left in a succession that finally merged with
the hazy blue. Before him he could see the thickly wooded
foothills punctuated by the white line of a waterfall. He saw
fields, the small patchwork evidence of humanity, and a few
villages thousands of feet to his right. The mountain dwarfed
him ridiculously as he climbed toward its summit; the scale
of nature made the evidence of civilization below seem
totally insignificant. There was something about being high
up, standing on a distant vantage point, that always aroused
in him an otherworldly feeling. He was totally divorced
from society, and yet on that towering platform he could still
see its traces. Even the brown, meandering course of the
Yellow River which snaked across the land was puny, and
the human world was already less than that mighty river.
Standing on that rock, seeing humanity many miles away,
Saihung did not care one bit for its pettiness.

They walked on for another mile before circling back to
their practice field. It was nearly noon and Saihung was hot
and thirsty. His hips and legs were sore, tired in a good way.
He walked to the shade of an old pine tree, picked a spot in
the midst of bark chips, pieces of pinecone, and soft grass,
and sat down. The Sick Crane Taoist began talking, the first

words anyone had spoken since the beginning of the walk. But Saihung, uninterested, began to examine a ladybug that had happened to crawl up his pants leg.

"Who noticed a special plant?" asked the Master.

"I did, Master," said the Shaanxi youth.

Good, thought Saihung. Just launch into your usual lecture and I'll rest. He sat back to enjoy the warm sunshine. There was always discussion at the end of the walk in which the Sick Crane Taoist asked questions or solicited their observations. He wanted assurances that his students were being observant. The Shaanxi monk was a poor physical performer but an ardent talker, and his classmates let him satisfy the master.

"Little Butterfly!" The intrusion was so abrupt that Saihung instantly realized how lost in his own thoughts he had become.

"Yes, Master," he replied quickly.

"A yellow-orange leaf fell as we passed. Tell me about it."

A falling leaf? In spring? Saihung thought desperately back. He could remember no leaf. His embarrassment was reply enough.

"You didn't notice it?" asked the Sick Crane Taoist with a shake of his head. "You who so pride yourself on being a fighter. What if it had been a dart thrown at you?"

The master paused to let him think it over. All Saihung could think over was that he hated being made to look so foolish. But, he reminded himself, he was there to learn both humility and awareness. He suppressed his pride and looked up at the master.

"One should notice these things," said the master softly and kindly. "Upon noticing such a thing, one should inquire why. Did it survive the winter? Was the tree diseased? Was it lacking for water? Had something knocked it down? Even to have noticed its exquisite color as it came down, a golden flicker against a mass of browns and greens, would have been acceptable. Not to notice it is insensitivity.

"We live on this mountain to be in nature. We shun the foul deeds of humanity, their pitiful lives, the mental pollution of what they vainly call civilization. We isolate ourselves from their loud noise, their stink, their obscene laughter, and their self-pitying laments. We withdraw to nature in order to purify ourselves and lead holy lives. Nature and her animals are innocent. We may think nature cruel and unmerciful when we find a deer's carcass or see a tree torn by a thunderstorm. This is nature's way and nature's logic. She lacks the wishful thinking and stupid sentimentality that humans possess. This purity and innocence is in tune with the gods, with the divine, with the Tao. Nature's way is the way of the Tao. If we want to attune ourselves with the Tao, we must place ourselves in an area that is in itself aligned with Tao.

"But it is of no use to live in a natural place if you fail to notice its gift. Nature is full of messages, though we often fail to see; and even if we do see we fail to comprehend. There are ten thousand sacred messages for you everywhere you glance, only you've not the eyes to see. That leaf could have been a sign to you, even a message from the gods. But you failed to notice it."

Class was over and Saihung began climbing the hillside for midday devotions and lunch. He was glad when Butterfly joined him.

"Little Brother, I'll be leaving again in a few days."

"So soon, Elder Brother? You've only been here this time for a month." Saihung felt a disconcerting emotion.

"Yes, but I'm growing restless. Besides, I have business to attend to in Beijing."

"And, of course, your lady friend."

"Yes, yes," smiled Butterfly. "Though there are many, she is more special than the rest."

"I envy you," said Saihung with a pout. "You roam the whole land in search of adventure. You see wealth and beauty. People adore and respect you. Your life is so full."

"Such a life is not for you, little one. Your destiny is to be a monk. It was meant to be. All can tell you were born for this role."

"But this is not life. I'm cold and hungry. Each day is completely regimented. Sutra recitation and meditation are boring, and physical practice is utter drudgery. Besides, all my efforts meet with constant disapproval. Nothing satisfies the teachers. They don't know how to praise.

"No one forced this on you."

"It's true," said Saihung with a sigh. "I was ordained at the age of sixteen. Though I made a choice, I still think about secular life, and wonder if I'm doing the right thing. Did you ever have doubts?"

"Yes, of course I did. Every man has his own doubts. That's why I travel so relentlessly in search of meaning. I learn as much as I can from the wise Taoists, and live life as fully as possible out in the world."

"You are lucky. You have the best of both worlds. When you want to rest, seek yourself, or recover from wounds, you come back to the temple. But when it suits you, you dress in the finest silks, wear precious jewelry, ride expensive horses, eat at lavish banquets, gamble all night long, and know the love of women."

"Ahh, I knew I never should have brought you to pleasure halls like the Red Peony Pavilion," said Butterfly with a smile. "If the Grand Master ever found out, he would punish us both."

"It was I who asked you to take me."

"Perhaps I should not have consented."

Saihung thought back to the few times when he had accompanied Butterfly in his travels. He remembered the glittering halls with gilded carvings, bright lanterns, splashing fountains, screens of fragrant camphor and sandalwood. He recalled the voluptuous girls draped in richly dyed silks. Harps and lutes again swayed his very soul, and smells of spicy dishes, musk perfumes, blooming orchids, and the faintly erotic odor of good opium returned to him. His fingers felt the domino chips again, those cool and rounded slabs of African ebony and Burmese rosewood that had become tactile fetishes. It had only been with great effort that he had remembered his vows of chastity.

"I'm glad to have seen such places," said Saihung, arousing himself from his recollections. "Nothing short of direct experience would have been adequate after all your exciting stories. But I found that that world wasn't for me. I don't like drinking, I don't like opium, I don't feel the need to break my vows of celibacy. Still, I wonder if this severe life of restraint and austerity is best."

"I know you are not interested in the outside world. But perhaps you should consider how it could affect you. The Japanese have enormous pieces of the country. Chiang Kai-Shek and the Nationalists are desperately trying to run a government from Chong Qing, fight the Japanese, and stab the Communists in the back at the same time. Beyond Asia, Germany has attacked Poland and the whole world is slipping into war. People are killing one another in numbers that have never been used to count corpses before."

"I fought in the Sino-Japanese War two years ago. I saw the horror. I fought to defend my people."

"The atrocities continue."

"What do you want me to do? Join Mao in Yenan? Align myself with warlords as you have done? I'm a renunciate. Politics never last."

"Can you deny that China has had war every day of your life? Now it isn't just China but the whole world that teeters on the edge of instability. All of Europe enters into the fighting. The fighting may spread to the United States and maybe even South America. While the whole world is destroyed, you sit on your meditation rug."

"Taoism is a philosophy of the heart," Saihung replied steadily. "It cannot be eradicated. The Tao is perpetual. Even the destruction of the planet cannot affect it. I can see our master. I can see our classmates. Observing the levels that they've achieved inspires me to reach for their level. I know that their achievements could not be touched by war or any other adversity, for they are triumphs within. I may have my own doubts, but politics is not the way to purge them."

"You are steadfast in your faith?"

"Yes, I am," said Saihung.

"The world may be coming to a final apocalypse and you do not consider changing."

"Through all my austerities, I feel that I am gaining results. I do not want to be like ordinary people. I want to be something more, something greater. Those people lead wretched lives, buffeted around by the whims of fate. That is not the life for me. I want to perfect myself."

"So do I."

"Yes, you are a perfectionist. Both of us had to sacrifice to gain our insights and abilities, only our goals differ. I believe in the Grand Master and in the Taoist path. While you . . ."

"I believe in perfection and discipline too. Otherwise, I could never have come this far. Don't be taken by the outer trappings of my life. Women and gambling is only a small part of it. I want to do something great, something heroic. The world will not come to an end. If you did not recognize that you would not be so calm. But it will take great men to bring order to this planet-wide degeneration. I want to be

one of those men. That will take as much discipline, courage, intelligence, a drive for perfection—and in a way, purity—as a monastic life."

"Are you saying that we're equal?" asked Saihung. He
was pleased with the comparison.

"I encourage you to study hard, Little Butterfly. The
monastic life and worldly life are two edges of the same
sword. They are inseparable. Neither could exist without
the other. Neither is better than the other. But it behooves
each of us to understand our destinies. Only by following
our innermost predilections can we find success. I urge you
to remain persevering in your asceticism. It's true that
physical and social needs are ruthlessly denied, but your
spirit will find satisfaction. Little Butterfly, you should not
allow discouragement to make you falter."

"Elder Brother," said Saihung, greatly moved. "You are so
eloquent. Why do you not become an initiate as well?"

"Perhaps I will," said Butterfly with a pensive look,
"when I finish my earthly wanderings. That's why I must
travel to complete my experiences. The masters say, 'Taste
the world before renouncing.' When I've had my fill of
worldly life, I will come back to stay for good."

"Then we could all be together—always."

"Yes, little one . . . always."

The mighty bronze temple bell reverberated throughout
the mountainside. It was time for devotions. They said
goodbye.

Saihung stood near one of the temple's antique bronze
incense burners and watched his elder brother leave the
courtyard. Saihung wondered if he would ever leave his
worldly life. He knew that Butterfly had lived in the world
for a long time, and his life had been scandalous. His mem-
bership in a secret society, his time as a warlord's bodyguard,
and his work as a protection escort for a drug smuggling

operation had brought frequent complaints to Huashan. The Grand Master did little, however, and Saihung puzzled over this.

While he himself had been punished many times for pranks, mischief, and laziness, he had never seen Butterfly punished. The Grand Master disapproved of Butterfly's life, but it was clearly a private part of their relationship. Whatever went on between the two men, whether it was discussion or reproach, was always behind closed doors. The Grand Master and the other priests continued to love him as a son, and Butterfly responded in the same way: He came back for the unwavering support of his adopted family, attributed his good achievements to his upbringing, and regularly supported Huashan with monetary donations. But Saihung wondered if that was enough to compensate for the many times provincial elders had climbed Huashan to report his misdeeds and demand his arrest.

Saihung walked through a series of gates before coming to the South Peak Shrine of the Jade Fertility Well. He entered, joining the ranks of blue-robed monks for the service. In the front of the group were the presiding priests in embroidered silk, reading aloud the divine words of sages. Musicians provided hymnal accompaniment.

Beyond the elaborate altar, Saihung saw the object of their devotion: the figure of a past Huashan ancestor who had become immortal through a lifetime of self-cultivation. Even from a distance he could see that the figure was covered with dust. But somehow, as the chanting and singing intensified, Saihung imagined that the god heard them, and that his eyes seemed almost to open in response. A feeling of sincerity arose in him. As this ascetic had attained salvation through cultivation, so Saihung hoped that he and Butterfly would succeed together in their destinies, and that somehow, his older brother would reform.

The Convocation

A great mountain-wide convocation was held once a month in a hall large enough to seat a thousand monks. During this time, those Taoists who had made important discoveries in their spiritual explorations. or who might have gained new insight into the esoteric passages of the canons, would be invited to share their understanding. Perhaps someone had completed experiments on a new herb, found a faster way to open the body meridians, or had seen new worlds in astral travel. Whoever had received such blessings was usually eager to discuss it unselfishly for the good of all.

There were many sects and subsects on Huashan, and within subsects were yet further divisions. Each master interpreted Taoism in a different way. A master might take a solitary sentence from one scripture out of ten thousand and spend literally a lifetime expounding upon it. Another master might adamantly refuse conceptualization and devote his entire effort to meditation. Yet another might advocate a preponderance of physical techniques, while his neighbor could feel as strongly about a dream remembered from decades past. Compounding such complexity was the perfectly acceptable practice of these masters' students emphasizing different facets of Taoism from their own teachers. But this was all agreeable to the elders of Huashan. They were willing to risk discord in order to affirm the diversity of Taoism and share that vitality.

Saihung went in early, a docile part of the crowd that filled the hall. He sat down on one of the hard wooden benches, almost uncomfortably squeezed between two other monks. As he waited for the opening ceremonies, he watched for others he recognized. Among them were the two acolytes, Sick Crane, Butterfly, Chrysanthemum, Red Eagle, and the two eldest among the Grand Master's thirteen disciples, Phoenix Eyes and Red Pine. Saihung immediately tensed upon seeing these two sit upon the benches reserved for the high priests. How stupid he had been to tell Butterfly the day before that he was inspired by his classmates! For the truth was that these two angered and embarrassed him.

Phoenix Eyes and Red Pine were challengers to the Grand Master's position. They advocated modernism and social action, in opposition to the Grand Master's advocation of classicism and orthodoxy. In previous convocations they had openly called for him to step down, to let young blood in. It was a terrible thing to do; the act of an elder disciple openly criticizing his master was tantamount to betrayal. But more disconcerting to Saihung was the fact that the pair had many supporters. They were masters in their own right, men with impeccable credentials.

Saihung let out a fatalistic sigh. Here was another enigma. Why had his master done so little to rebuff the attacks of Phoenix Eyes and Red Pine? Saihung looked up to the head of the hall, and proudly saw his master sitting among the elders of Huashan. Surely, Saihung reasoned, the Grand Master was a higher being than his students—even the men who flanked him were higher company than the two challengers could ever hope to keep. Those strange men with eccentric names to match their appearances—the Frog Immortal, the Bat Immortal, the Immortal Turtle—were universally respected for their wisdom; and by extension so too must his own master have been equally impeccable. But it did not seem true to Saihung. The thirteen disciples were no longer a family, no longer a comfort to Saihung, and they were a worry to the Grand Master. They were in disarray, and their polarization had now come to split the mountain. Politics had entered into religion, and the man who had floored three fighters, who whispered sage guidance to Saihung in the morning darkness, seemed oddly disinclined to respond to the crises.

The gentle reverberation of a gong and the muffled pounding on a huge drum aroused Saihung from his musings. He stood with the assembly as the elders made their obeisance to Wen Di, the God of Literature. Saihung gazed up obediently at the life-sized likeness that held a writing brush and a book inscribed with the words "Heaven Decides Literary Success." He saw the kind and unlined face, and the hair, which was real—long, thick, and black. Before the god was a well-laden altar table and an incense burner to carry their prayers towards his residence in the constellation *Kun* (Ursa Major). How easy it was to be a god, Saihung thought glumly.

As the last bell's clear, high note was still resounding, the Grand Master asked all to be seated. He then introduced the speaker for that day, the White Hare Recluse. According to the Grand Master's introduction, the Recluse had recently finished a painstaking, decades-long project. He had written a book on the theory and technique of power-words as a means to control the senses during meditation. The book would now become a part of Huashan's library and the White Hare Recluse would summarize its major points for the gathering.

The White Hare Recluse stood before the monks, prepared to address them without the aid of notes. He stood calmly, with his hands folded. They would not unclasp during his entire talk; a subtle sign of his concentration and meditative attainment. A short, portly man, he had a jovial round face with a big nose and pink cheeks. Clean shaven, his snowy hair carefully combed and coiled, with a smile always behind his thin lips, he presented a gentle and benevolent image.

"Elders, classmates, and initiates," he began. "I address you today in order to present the results of many years of research. We have reached these conclusions based on the teachings handed down by our predecessors and the experiences of my associates, students, and myself. I invite you to listen today and hope that you will favor me with your instruction.

"Meditation is the highest spiritual endeavor. Through its practice we can dispel the veil of ignorance and thus realize our essential nature. Our troubles stem from the fact that we are divorced from our inner selves and that we search far and wide for what is actually close at hand. While I know that so many of my worthy peers emphasize different goals—such as Thunder Magic, the Eight Trigrams manipulation, astral travel, or devotional chanting—I respectfully point out that all of us hold meditation to be important to our spiritual lives. Truly, it is said, 'All roads lead to the summit.' I do not quarrel with others' paths. But I do assert that the summit is unattainable without inner contemplation.

"My fear is that many along the way become distracted. It is easy to be pulled outward. All humanity is in trouble today precisely because they are turned outward. They are like an audience at the theater avidly viewing an opera. They are so engrossed that distinctions are blurred: They take the drama for reality. Having done this, they assume that all of life must take place in this narrow arena. They throw themselves headlong into outwardly directed action. They engage in business, travel, government, and warfare in the assumption that somehow their actions will make a difference. This is most lamentable. The more they direct their wills externally, the further they are drawn out, until all notion of the internal is lost.

"Humanity has thus taken a very different path than that of the meditator, and no one can deny the impressiveness of these efforts. Ordinary buildings in Shanghai are built higher and larger than a pagoda. There are now powerful locomotives and ships made of steel. Even here on the mountain we've sometimes seen machines that can carry a man into the air. But look what these accomplishments have been used for. Nations are now fighting other nations on an unprecedented scale. The Japanese, who once could scarcely travel from one island to another, now use aircraft, ships, and tanks to trample half of Asia. Another island nation, Great Britain, boasts that the sun never sets on its empire. All this outwardly directed energy, all this meddling in other people's business is a violation of the Tao.

"The meditator is different. His purpose is inner-directed. His goal is union with the Tao. Pain and ignorance, not warlords and nations, are his enemies. We are all familiar with the phrase, 'Without going out of the door, the sage knows heaven and earth.' That is a way of saying that the sage's contemplative powers are so great that nothing in the universe could be kept secret from his inner gaze.

"Many consider this ability of perception to be a great fruit of meditation. But I say even this is a trap. One must not become preoccupied with such knowledge. Although it is a result of inner-directed meditation, it is nevertheless detrimental. It will take some time before you younger initiates realize that meditative powers are a nuisance and that one must push more deeply into the inner world. No one can blame you when you first become thrilled with new-found psychic abilities. You will know of a person's approach long before his arrival. You will receive omens of the future. You will be able to read others' thoughts. Even in your sleep, you will find your now more powerful mind focusing on events of the previous day and perceiving underlying meanings. First you will go wild with these new feelings. You will think that this makes meditation worthwhile. Greedily and proudly you will hold yourself above mere mortals and think that you can indeed know heaven and earth without leaving your door.

"But in time, you will come to see that your mind is being wasted on trivialities. You become like a telescope, helplessly viewing things far and near, magnifying them out of proportion. So the meditator actually flees in panic from these things that others would call blessings. Their newfound abilities become a curse, an unwanted stimulus. Only now does he realize that he must plunge deeper. Only now does he realize that tranquility and freedom from the pull of the world lies in deeper meditation. Here the meditator must confront two significant obstacles: the mind itself and the sexual drive. In truth, the mind pulls the attention outward, while sexuality entangles the mind in emotion and desire. Unless each in turn is properly conquered, there can be no progress.

"The mind is an indispensable thing for us. It coordinates everything we do, great and small. It can accomplish great deeds, and it carries on the function of our body automatically. Through sensory faculties, it retains all the information necessary to ensure our survival. But the mind begins to grow domineering in its role. It begins to prefer one kind of experience over another. It differentiates between pleasure and pain and naturally prefers pleasure. Soon, the whole being is directed toward experiencing more and more pleasure. A little gratification means a greater drive for repetition. Disappointment engenders a seed of hatred and resolves not only to avoid unpleasantness, but to destroy its source. A vicious cycle ensues and the person becomes wholly entangled in desire. He becomes both a slave to his mind and senses and a bitter, vengeful creature opposed to anything that would thwart his pursuit of satisfaction. A pattern results that not only replicates itself but generates others as well. Every action, thought, and emotional obsession gives rise to ten others. Endless consequences occur and entangle one's life. In this way, we create our own bondage to this earthly plane.

"The person who endeavors to be spiritual is even more prone to abuse because of his greater knowledge and mental power. He will justify his pursuit of knowledge, his lust for spiritual attainment; but this is actually no different from the fellow who wastes his life away on opium and beautiful women. The mind can be used in the spiritual quest, but it can also become one's obstacle.

"Even the most mentally powerful person is vulnerable to sexuality. It is undeniably strong in everyone, for it is linked to the life force itself. Without it there could be no perpetuation of the human species. It cannot be suppressed. It will only come back more strongly. Nor does absenting oneself from women help. Although this is the case on Huashan, every monk here knows that this is not enough to completely cope with one's sexual urges. The mind conjures up lurid thoughts in the service of one's desire, and lust can actually drive one to do many shameful things in the need for release. Some have tried to cope with this through artificial means. But mortification of the flesh is not the answer. Such methods injure the body and ultimately fail to cultivate the mind. There is no understanding, only brutality and blind self-mutilation. The result is only bitterness, hatred, and ignorant piety, none of which will help one toward spiritual attainment. If one truly wishes to climb to the heights of the immortals, one must develop control of sexuality not by fighting it, but by giving the whole personality something to follow that will replace it.

"The pattern of the outwardly directed mind and the sexually driven organism must be broken. Desire must be eradicated. Delusion must be stopped. The senses must be tamed and turned inward in order to reverse the ever-expanding spiral of sensual involvement. There is a method. That method is a word.

"A *word* mollifies the senses. It becomes a substitute that occupies them and makes them not only too busy to engage in their normal activities, but also directs them inward. These *words* are not ordinary words of our language, but divine sounds that the sages have heard in deep meditation. They arise directly from the divine consciousness. They have no earthly origins and no earthly meanings. They can therefore not reattach one to worldly consequences.

"The *word* is not simply any sound. It is one, or a group, of sounds that can both satisfy the senses and turn the mind inward. The masters discovered these sounds and experimented upon themselves. They found that all sounds will affect us in some way or another, but discarded those that were insignificant or not conducive to their purposes. They kept only those that cleared away the undesirable tendencies of the mind and would turn it toward the good. One of the most important aspects was the unique ability of the *word* to guide a student to the same state in which the master had originally discovered the sound.

"The sages call this aspect of the *word* the 'Thread Through the Labryinth' technique. They compare it to a man who, exploring a deep and twisted cave, eventually finds a chamber with treasure. In order to find that place again, he returns to the opening, trailing a spool of thread behind him. Once he emerges, he can go back—or, more important, others can follow the thread to find the same treasure chamber. The thread, of course, is the *word* which can lead a student to a high state of consciousness.

"Other *words* can be beneficial to one's health. Every

sound has its own unique frequency of vibration. The sages discovered that particular sounds, when made with the voice, would resonate within a specific organ. The organ would be stimulated and tonified, and the health of the body would be protected.

"The ability of words to affect someone goes beyond the physical or meditative. It can also affect character. Simply speaking, we all may have excessive aspects to our character which can be compensated for through the mental or verbal repetition of words. If a man has a very fiery temperment, for example, the master may give a Water Word to balance his personality. In quite the opposite case, an unambitious and passive student should be given a Fire Word to build his will and character. The *word*, therefore, can be indispensable towards preparing the novitiate for greater endeavors.

"We have also experimented with *power words*. Our research would be incomplete if we did not clearly explore the wide range of effects possible within words. Through the repetition of words we have been able to conjure gold from thin air, dematerialize and rematerialize ourselves across vast distances, soar in the air above the clouds, enslave demons from the netherworld, and force people to do things out of character. We document these explorations for the future generations with the solemn injunction that they should never be used. We feel that their use is a reinvolvement in worldly things and a nearly irresistable temptation to abuse their power. We feel that the word should be used in the same way that talismans should be used: for healing, protection, and spiritual attainment. Any hint of profit seeking will mean the eternal damnation of the practitioner.

"We have not concentrated solely on contemporary Taoist words, but have sent representatives far and wide to visit, explore, and research in other temples and monasteries. My classmates have collected *words* from India, Tibet, China, and Southeast Asia. We have made every attempt to conduct exhaustive research. I leave it up to all of you to study further, but I mention these facts in order to point out that many words have no meaning in their original language. It is essential to note that these sounds did not arise from any linguistic thought, but from the one divine and universal consciousness.

"As we have come to the discussion of language, I would like to note that *words* are neither scripture nor prayer. Although divine sounds may manifest themselves in these forms, it does not follow that these forms are synonomous with *words*. They may be important for devotion, but they do not necessarily bring predictable results. Personal prayers are just that: a psychological act to focus the mind and comfort the weak-willed.

"In summation, we advocate the verbal or mental use of *words* for the purpose of turning the mind inward and leading the meditator toward self-realization. We feel that this is the only true use of words. We do not care one whit for powers, possession, invocation, prayer, or spells if they do not bring us closer to the divine. *Words* must be handed down through a verbal tradition. Thus, while we have written a book, we recognize that the true transmittal of the spiritual tradition is the unbroken chain of master to disciple. Should any of you wish to explore these techniques further, we invite you to join us in this holy endeavor. I invite the elders to examine our research and to put aside false courtesy in criticizing our faults. My fellow Taoists: I humbly present our findings."

The audience applauded as the White Hare Recluse's acolyte, a young boy of fourteen, brought forth the five volumes of research. The Recluse took the books in both hands, and with a bow presented them to the Grand Master. All the elders stood, in a magnanimous gesture of courtesy.

"I accept on behalf of all Huashan," said the Grand Master. "Thank you for your most worthy efforts."

The Grand Master urged the elders to be seated. He then opened the floor to discussion. This phase of the convocation was a forum in which anyone could discuss ideas for the better progress of Huashan and Taoism. After several minutes of announcements regarding meetings with other mountains, Saihung became bored. Although he had been most excited by the White Hare Recluse's talk, he hated administrative matters.

He saw Phoenix Eyes stand up. The older priest was an imposing figure, and the other monks looked up quietly and expectantly. Phoenix Eyes was clear voiced, speaking in the flamboyant, almost theatrical Beijing dialect.

"I ask permission to speak."

"Permission granted," responded the Grand Master.

"Gentlemen: It is well known that the nation is undergoing one of the worst periods of warfare and social instability in its five-thousand-year history. At no time has our country been so weak and humiliated before the armies of inferior nations. Is this not because its spiritual vigor has ebbed away?"

There was a murmur of agreement from the assembly.

Phoenix Eyes continued. "Where has Taoism been in the face of this decay? The only indigenous Chinese religious tradition is in itself weakening before the times. Our chief rivals are the Buddhists, and they influence a greater number of people with their magnificent temples and promises of paradise. In addition, Islam has always been strong in the North, and now the missionaires from the West are directly seducing our people."

In spite of rumors that the Christian missionaries engaged in barbarous rituals and ate roasted babies, people were increasingly converting to Christianity. Many monks

Phoenix Eyes.

still regarded the cathedrals and churches recently built in Beijing and Shanghai as yet another capitulation to the Europeans.

"My brothers! Where have we been? Haven't we all vowed to bring the spiritual light to humanity? Instead, we stay isolated on our mountain and seek our own success, while ignoring the suffering of the populace!"

The hall erupted into chaotic discussion. The monastic discipline faded with Phoenix Eyes's emotional address. The Grand Master asked for silence.

But before they could quiet down completely, Red Pine shouted, "But our policy is noninterference with society!" Others agreed. They were renunciates, pledged to a life away from society.

Phoenix Eyes gazed confidently at his audience. It was the cue he needed. He pulled himself straight and stroked his smooth and shiny beard.

"This has been our policy. But is it correct? Or is it just the muddle-headed direction of old-fashioned traditionalists? It is precisely because of their conservatism that we have failed to bring glory to Taoism."

Saihung looked around and saw many arguments taking place. Some shouted at Phoenix Eyes to sit down. Others supported him.

Saihung looked to his master to refute Phoenix Eyes. But the Grand Master only looked placidly upon the assembly. "Why doesn't he fight back?" Saihung asked himself. It was utter defiance for an eldest student to attack his master publicly, as forbidden as patricide; but no retribution seemed forthcoming.

"I support my classmate!" cried Red Pine as he stood up. His sad features became animated, but he looked ridiculous waving his long sleeves excitedly. "The intrinsic principle of Tao is change. We must change and adapt. We have made

Red Pine.

great accomplishments and we've gathered a formidable body of knowledge. Now is the time to use it to save humanity! The world is slipping into a war that may destroy the planet. It is the time for action, not monasticism!"

"Yes, my brothers," said Phoenix Eyes shrewdly. "How will there be Taoism if the country is bombed to oblivion? We must act to stabilize the situation. If our elders cannot be flexible enough to accept reality, then they should step aside for the younger generation."

"Your position has no merit!" thundered the Immortal Turtle, abbot emeritus. Saihung was surprised to see the small man jump up so hotly, but he was relieved. Finally, the elders were responding. The wrinkled face pulled taut and the eyes blazed fiercely. "Why don't you shut up? It is clear you have no true understanding of Taoism. What you propose is contrary to the rule of asceticism!"

The Immortal Turtle was the former Grand Master of Huashan. He had voluntarily stepped aside in favor of the present Grand Master. As a past abbot, he still held considerable prestige. The assembly quieted somewhat.

A single priest stood up. Saihung recognized him as someone from the East Peak, but he did not know him. The man was tall, slender, and had a handsome, clear-complexioned face. His clothes were neat and impeccable, and he was well groomed.

"Asceticism is not the only way," said the priest. "Many of us are trained in other disciplines. But of what use is it to argue? Such conflict is contrary to our calling. Let us merely say that it is our duty to be compassionate. Withholding our help in these dire times is as cruel as a swimmer failing to rescue a drowning comrade."

"This discussion is a perversion of order," said the Immortal Turtle. "You youngsters have no faith. The Tao will continue whether or not we continue to exist."

The Immortal Turtle.

"You are admirable in your doctrine," said the priest from the East Peak. "But I cannot agree and you know this is my prerogative. Just as you stepped down, I believe it is now time for the present Grand Master to step down. Times have changed."

"It is not up to you to dictate the policy of this mountain," retorted the Immortal Turtle sharply.

"Let us put it to a vote," Red Pine challenged.

"Nonsense!" shouted the Immortal Turtle. "The rules must be followed. The elders will discuss this issue, I promise. We will have our decision in time for the next convocation. For now, I will accept no more discussion. I order you, as your superior, to sit down."

The three had no choice but to acquiesce to his command. They could not afford to alienate the assembly with open defiance. The Immortal Turtle signaled for the closing ceremonies to begin.

Saihung could barely bring himself to mutter the scriptures. His emotions burned deep in his gut. He felt betrayed. The Grand Master was like a father to him, and Phoenix Eyes's challenge was repulsive to Saihung. Above all else, he valued loyalty as one of the highest virtues.

The service ended and Saihung saw many young monks crowd excitedly around Phoenix Eyes. Saihung angrily watched him walk down the center aisle with his new-found supporters. Saihung grew hot. A bitter taste suddenly welled up in his throat.

"You son-of-a-whore!" Saihung cried as he pushed a young monk over and jumped before Phoenix Eyes. "If you want to start trouble, let it be here and with me!"

Phoenix Eyes was utterly calm. His stately dignity remained unchanged and his prayer gesture showed not the slightest tremble.

"It is sin to utter such blasphemy, Little Butterfly," he intoned softly.

"You horse's ass," screamed Saihung. "I'll do more than curse! I'll smash you down to King Yama's realm!"

"You're hotheaded," said Phoenix Eyes smoothly. "Hotheads need cooling off."

"I'll knock yours off!"

"Come on, if you dare," said Phoenix Eyes proudly.

Saihung charged, but the two acolytes quickly restrained him. He threw one off, but then Butterfly also ran up. It took three of them to hold him down.

Phoenix Eyes walked quietly up to him. Saihung could feel his breath as he spoke. "Such a bad-tempered bull! How appropriate that you're restrained. After all, a pen is the only place for a stupid ox."

"I'll kill you, you bastard!" screamed Saihung wildly. But Phoenix Eyes only walked away.

"Stop struggling, Little Butterfly," said Sound of Clear Water, one of the acolytes. "You've committed a grave sin today."

"I can't stand that monster attacking the Grand Master!"

"Neither can we," said Mist Through a Grove, the other acolyte. "But it is not for us to act. The convocation is the forum for anyone to speak their minds openly and without retaliation."

"Let go of me!"

"Calm down, first," said Sound of Clear Water.

"I will not! I'll strangle him right now!"

Butterfly pressed Saihung back firmly.

"You're crazy. Stop and think, fool. You know that his martial ability is ten times greater than yours. He would have squashed you."

"Just leave me alone!" grumbled Saihung.

"They will not!" It was the Grand Master. "Take him to my chambers for punishment."

They forced Saihung out of the temple hall and up the steep slope towards the South Peak Shrine. The Grand Master permitted no talking as they made their way. Saihung was still angry. It was Phoenix Eyes who had sinned. Why should he be punished?

It was only when they had reached the Grand Master's study that they released him. The Grand Master sat down at his desk, the only furniture in the bare brick room besides the rows of bookcases. The light burned its intricate lattice pattern onto the Grand Master's back. His white hair blazed like flame as he wearily removed his hat and set it down.

"Kneel!" he commanded.

"Master, I've done nothing wrong!"

"You uttered profanities before your elders and the God of Literature. Is this not sin enough?"

"I was protecting you."

"I do not need this type of protection."

"Master, why didn't you fight back? He was challenging you. Why didn't you defend yourself?"

"Why should I be affected by such an insignificant matter? I've practiced a lifetime with faithfulness and sincerity. My accomplishments and thoughts need no approval from others. As long as I can live with myself and honestly face the gods with nothing hidden in my heart, I have nothing to fear."

"Don't you see that your own students are plotting against you? How can you allow this?"

"They are priests as well. Everyone's viewpoint has merit. They are only trying to express themselves sincerely."

"No, Master, they are trying to overthrow you."

"Do I need this position to feel complete? How absurd! If they feel they can do a better job, that's fine. But they cannot.

It is only because they know I oppose them that they try to publicly attack me. They are all motivated by temporal power. This is incorrect. As long as they try to use Taoism for profit, as long as they want to become this era's Chong Toling, they know that I am their biggest obstacle. I stand against them, but I need not fight them."

"Master, I don't understand you."

The Grand Master laughed. "Someday you may understand what 'noncontention' means. That is Taoism, too. For now I order you to stay away from Phoenix Eyes and Red Pine. Take no action on your own. Do you understand?"

"Yes, Master."

"Good. You may go."

Butterfly followed Saihung out of the temple. "I'll walk you back to the dormitories, little brother," he said soothingly.

"Who is that East Peak priest?" asked Saihung. He was not interested in comfort.

"His name is Intercepting Imprint and I know him," said Butterfly casually. "In fact, I learned some of my techniques from him."

"What kind of techniques?"

"Things you would not like . . . techniques of dual cultivation in which a man and woman unite to seek realization."

"Oh, he practices sexual techniques," said Saihung scornfully. "I should have known that Phoenix Eyes and Red Pine would have recruited such a perverse ally."

"Don't forget, dual cultivation is also a part of recognized Taoism. It has its own scriptures, rituals, and discipline. As one who practices its techniques, I can attest to its efficacy."

"You are not a priest," said Saihung dryly, "why should you live like one?"

"But he is also a priest."

"His whole school is a shelter for perverted old men so oversexed that they had to lock themselves away to keep from humping themselves to death."

"Spoken like a cranky celibate. You are exaggerating."

"Damn! You know Master teaches that such methods are evil and contrary to the teachings!"

"They are contrary only to his sect."

"Well, that's good enough for me."

"You've never tried it."

"Stop your absurdity. I've sworn to be a lifelong celibate."

"Let's hope your path gets you to heaven, because you surely won't experience it on earth."

"Just shut up! I'm tired of talking."

Butterfly fell silent. Saihung walked back to the dormitories and sat down on the sleeping platform. One of the temple cats sauntered up and arched his back to rub against Saihung's legging. Saihung was quiet. A renunciate had no family. The literal translation for renunciate was "one-who-has-left-one's-family." But he had never been a wholly solitary man. The Grand Master and the twelve classmates had always been his family. Now that family structure was decaying, and he realized that that was what hurt most of all.

It was natural, he supposed, for such things to happen. He reviewed the lessons he'd learned about the various phases of change. Everything had a zenith, but every zenith inexorably led toward a nadir. For every rise there was decline. Huashan and his class had been the perfect world for him, but now that world was as uncertain as China's future itself. Decline had to be accepted, his teachings told him, but he hated it. He cursed. All philosophy did for him when he felt bad was make him feel worse.

He brooded until the evening bell. Saihung stood up to go to his evening lessons. There was nothing to be done. His master seemed unconcerned. He realized his duty was to return to his lessons. Sometimes duty was a comfort; it gave a role when times were uncertain. Perhaps it was just because of life 's odd uncertainties that Chinese society so emphasized duty: It would hide his anger, frustration and confusion.

FOUR

Begging for Alms

A week after the convocation, Saihung and the two acolytes accompanied the Grand Master on a rare excursion away from Huashan. Saihung had received his instructions in an early morning whisper from his master. But he personally found the timing very odd. Surely the master was not abandoning the mountain to Phoenix Eyes? Perhaps it was a way of doing penance or getting back in touch with the humble meaning of the priesthood. Or, Saihung concluded gravely, maybe his master was going to organize other temples for a countermovement. There was no way to know. As Saihung steadied his backpack on the rocking train to Xian, he settled back upon the official reason: They were going begging for alms.

Begging for alms was the general name for journeys undertaken by every monk up to four times a year. The journeys were usually made by a large group, forming a procession that would travel to nearby towns. Occasionally, a small group or even a single monk would wander for great distances to visit other temples and solicit donations from patrons. Socially, begging was not an altogether acceptable occupation. The hardworking, pragmatic, and conscientious people looked upon beggars as men who would not support themselves. They felt no compulsion to give money to people they felt were lazy vagrants. Seeing a beggar dressed as a monk did nothing to modify the judgment. Some disapproved so greatly that they had signs at their gate saying, "No gifts to Buddhist and Taoist monks."

The priests of Huashan did not beg for their daily meal as spiritual people in other parts of Asia sometimes did. The begging bowl they received upon ordination was a symbol rather than an implement. Begging for alms had evolved into ways of soliciting donations of cash, grain, oil, or other gifts. Sometimes, the scale was much larger than a mere bowlful. The priests visited wealthy patrons, through past connections or letters of introduction, seeking funding for the building of a temple, renovation of buildings, or some other large-scale project. Huashan depended significantly on the proceeds from these begging expeditions.

As the son of a noble family, Saihung had an almost inbred distaste for begging. He hated going from door to door and putting himself in the position of meek supplication to common folk. But his begging trips had developed into great adventures, for he enjoyed traveling and visiting friends. Whenever he came to a town, he would stroll along asking for donations to the temple. He would then talk to anyone who came up to him and would perform any priestly function requested of him. Divination, geomancy consultations, exorcisms, herbal prescriptions, osteopathy, calligraphy, weddings, funerals, and miscellaneous blessings were all services he exchanged for donations to Huashan and, hopefully, a banquet for himself.

He loved the freedom of traveling, and this somewhat mitigated his aversion to begging. There were no restrictions on where he could travel when he was a mendicant monk, and Saihung had traveled to all the frontiers of China accompanied only by a little mule to carry the gleanings of his efforts. As a wandering Taoist he did not have to follow the stringent monastic codes, and he therefore used these journeys to sample the rich cuisine of China and engage in his own research of martial arts. In each town he would fulfill his mission, but at the same time he exercised his rich tastes in the villas of patrons, lavish teahouses, and homes of his boxing comrades. On the mountain, he was a wretched student; but in the cities, he was often honored. It was unusual to see a monk of his rank. Seeing the Grand Master was even more rare.

Even on the train many people noticed them as Taoists having "descended the mountain." The words were resonant in meaning and carried the connotation of an extraordinary person descending from a half-way-to-heaven hermitage. Folklore was full of legends and mythology about supernatural beings who cultivated themselves through mystical methods, and the appearance of such a being usually evoked much superstitious awe and respect. Many people saw the four of them not simply as holy men, but mysterious creatures capable of sensational powers. The appearance of the Grand Master of Huashan was considered a doubly unusual event. There were many whispers that a living saint had descended the mountain.

But people were curious and pragmatic, even in their awe. The train station in Xian, a broken-down and dirty terminus for the railroad from Loyang, was packed with people. Many crowded around the quartet, staring unabashedly at these fairy-tale creatures incarnate. They pressed closer, and some even dared to finger the acolytes' clothes. Even though they were homespun, they were a finer cloth than most of them would ever feel touching their own skin. As the four tried to leave the station, many people begged for blessings or asked about their fortune.

The two acolytes positioned themselves on each side of the Grand Master and held their arms out. It was tradition that a venerable master supported himself while walking by resting his forearms on those of his acolytes.

"Master, allow us," said Mist Through a Grove.

The Grand Master felt insulted. "You know I dislike this convention," he whispered.

"It is tradition. The people expect it," said Sound of Clear Water.

"Are you saying I'm old?" demanded the Grand Master.

"Master, Master," said Mist Through a Grove soothingly, "just until we leave the station."

"Now you're humoring me!" grumbled the Grand Master. "But I suppose we musn't disappoint them." He took their hands and looked forward. He saw an enormous and dense crowd of faces. The Grand Master sighed.

"If we are ever to get to the temple before they lock the gates, we must get through this crowd," he said. "I guess we'll have to unleash the Little Butterfly."

"Yes, Master?" said Saihung eagerly.

The Grand Master waved his hand in consent. Saihung enthusiastically jumped in front of the Grand Master and faced the crowd. He pushed his Taoist hat down at a rakish slant.

"I'm sorry, but we must go. Come see us in town tommorrow." With that announcement, he began pushing and shoving his way through the crowd. His master and the two acolytes followed close behind him. There was no other method for them to penetrate the crush of curious onlookers.

Xian, "Western Tranquility," formerly named Chang An, "Eternal Tranquility," was a beautiful old city that was spilling out beyond its quaint medieval walls and surrounding moat. As if the city could barely contain its history and culture, it had slowly expanded to become one of the proudest centers of northwestern China. One of China's Eight Ancient Capitals, having served intermittently as the center of eleven dynasties including the Zhou, Qin, Han, Sui, and Tang, it had flowered as the culmination of rich commerce, imperial power, fertile land, and diverse peoples.

Unlike other capitals, however, Xian, in the rich Yellow River valley, had its origins in the earliest beginning of civilization. The earliest primitive tribal societies had been born from the rich silt of the flood plains, nourished themselves from the mighty river, and had begun the settlements that would lead to one of the world's greatest cities. Xian was at its mightiest when it had become the terminus for the famous Silk Road, the route that led through the northern deserts into India and Persia. The population of the city thus evolved as a reflection of both the geographical fertility and cultural diversity, as Moslems, Indians, and Persians settled in the area. Bringing with them their own artistic treasures, religions, and ways of life, they contributed to the deep and resonant character of Xian.

Three great religions coexisted in Xian. Aside from Taoism, there was a significant Moslem population. Their adherents were clearly known by the white cloth wrapped around their heads. The Moslems had an ancient mosque, which looked like a traditional temple save for the Arabaic writing juxtaposed beside Chinese writing. The Buddhists also had many temples, but their most famous landmark was the Big Wild Goose Pagoda, built to house the scriptures brought back to China from India by Hsuan-tsang, a devout Buddhist priest.

Old temples and pagodas, dusty with the yellow soil and centuries old, were only a part of the architectural and physical character of the city. There were also the predominantly single-storied mud or brick edifices, built in a style unchanged for hundreds of years, which formed the maze of crowded lanes. Short, squat, and walled, they formed narrow corridors for a kaleidescopic variety of people. Among old and young, among every shape, height, and facial type, Saihung was fascinated by bearded Persians, rectangular countrywomen, angular Manchurians, willowy urban ladies, misshapen beggars, big white-capped Moslems, and rosy-cheeked children. The streets were so crowded that they were lost in the human river.

They arrived at the Supreme Purity Taoist Temple, a small compound situated in the midst of a crowded and poor neighborhood. The sun was just meeting the horizon, and its blazing golden light lit the front gate of the temple. The still warm breeze was made hotter by the evening meals, cooked over coal and wood fires. The smell of food and burning wood gave way to the drift of incense.

At the announcement of their presence, the abbot and his attendant came out to greet them. He was a serious-looking priest with a long, wispy beard. He and the others bowed low in deference to the Grand Master's status. The thin but erect man, monolithic in his long-sleeved blue floor-length robes, cordially invited them in for a drink of tea. Saihung was impressed. Although the abbot lived in the city and exercised the primary duties of caring for the religious needs of his congregation, he was nevertheless as severe and upright as anyone from the monastic system. His type was familiar to Saihung: the absolutely orthodox priest who would never compromise his religion.

Saihung knew that his master would engage in all-night philosophical discussions; so, after politely sipping tea, he made the excuse of going to rent a donkey before the stables closed entirely. The Grand Master knew better than to hold back a restless youth, and gave his permission.

Saihung rushed joyfully out the gate. He noticed the food stalls nearby, with their great steaming baskets and vats of boiling oil. He could not resist, and bought some delicious steamed buns filled with sweet bean paste. He savored their aroma and delightedly felt the sandy texture of the filling as he bit in. He pulled out a few more coins, bought three more, and turned away quickly. In his excitement he nearly collided with two men who instantly sobered him. They were of the class that had been dubbed the "useless flotsam." They had their shirts unbuttoned flamboyantly to reveal their muscular chests, and their sleeves were rolled up immodestly. One had a crooked face, a long broken nose, and a scar under his pointed chin that was a red line connecting both his ears. The other was more handsome, with perfect white teeth and arched eyebrows, and lashes so dark that he could have been wearing mascara.

"Why don't you watch where you're going, you damn monk," said the handsome one. Saihung felt his temper rise. "Why not beat these two for fun?" he thought.

"Stop, stop," said the one with the scar. His voice was hoarse. "It's unlucky to hit a monk."

"You superstitious bastard," said the first. "You believe that crap?"

"No, not really," smirked the scarred one. "But forget it. I'm hungry."

"All right." He turned to Saihung. "Get out of here."

Saihung knew that starting a fight would reflect badly on the temple that was only a few yards behind him, and he swallowed his pride.

"That kid must be a damn deaf-mute."

Saihung walked off. He was unhappy. The frustration of not fighting would be with him all night.

He stopped at several more stalls. Maybe he could eat his irritation away. He was certainly determined to make up for the months of austerity he had suffered through. Small cakes, deep-fried doughnuts, even nuts and dried fruit were some of the quick snacks he snatched on his way to the stables. He reckoned that he was only half-full. If he was careful, he could fill the other half on the way back and still arrive in time for the temple meal.

"Young Yao," he said greeting the groom at the mule

stables. Saihung always came here to rent mules. They knew him and gave a discount to priests. "Is your father in?"

"Yes, yes he is, Master," replied the tall youth. "Father! Father! That monk from Huashan is here."

The father came out, a broad man with skin the color of a roast goose, and teeth more chipped than the broken city ramparts.

"Ah! Ah! Kind sir! It's been so long since you last honored me with a visit."

"I'm afraid I had to ascend the mountain," said Saihung formally.

"A true monk," cried the old mule-keeper. "You'll soon be an immortal!"

"Uncle is too kind," said Saihung humbly. "But this time even my master has descended the mountain."

"By the gods!" exclaimed the mule-keeper. "The stars must be in concordance for such a rare event! I suspect you want a nice mule for your master."

"It's only proper, uncle. I'd be grateful for your help."

"The mules have been rather thin of late. Feed is harder to get nowadays. But I do have one fat one I've been saving. I won't rent her as a cart-puller. Why don't you take her?"

He turned to his son and barked an order. Before long, a brown mule was brought in from the smelly and noisy darkness of the shabby stables. Saihung saw that the mule was satisfactory and, even rarer, did not have big patches of mange. He had the mule fitted with a saddle and put the few required coins into the old man's hands.

"I'll bring her back in a few weeks."

"As you please," replied the man. "Only don't be too hard on her. You know Taoists—they can even outwalk a mule."

"Uncle, you exaggerate!"

The old man smiled. "Off you go, little monk."

"May the gods bless you."

"And good fortune to you."

Saihung followed his plan meticulously, eating his way home, pulling the mule behind him. Upon his return to the temple he went to a side gate to bring in the mule. As he came to the doors and knocked, he was surprised to see the useless flotsam pair leaning against the temple wall. Both were smoking cigarettes and looking away from him. Saihung quietly slipped into the temple and questioned the gatekeeper.

"Young brother," he asked, "have you ever seen these two?"

"No, elder brother, I have not," the young novice replied. "But they came when you did."

Saihung gave the novitiate the mule's reins and crept to the wall.

"Have you heard about those spectacular robberies in Beijing?" It was the hoarse voice.

"Yes, no one knows who the man is, but his martial skill is extraordinary."

"Haven't the papers dubbed him the 'Heaven Soaring Spider'?"

"Yes. He can leap from one rooftop to another. The police have trapped him twice, but he killed them all. They had guns, too."

"Rumor in the underworld has it that he's one of Du's men," continued the hoarse voice. "That gangster is strong, even in the North."

There was some street commotion. "Come on," said the hoarse one. "We've got to get ready."

Saihung was chagrined. He had hoped to hear more than some gossip.

Saihung, the Grand Master, and the two acolytes set out very early the next morning, when the sky was just turning from black to blue. The air was, gratefuly, cool, for the spring days were often unbearably hot in Xian. Saihung saw a crescent slice of the moon and the skittering flight of small silhouettes that were bats rushing home before dawn.

Sleepy people wandered through the dim streets, a few with lanterns in their hands to help them find their way. Shopkeepers were unboarding their store fronts, and the ubiquitous food stalls were stoking up their stoves. Dogs paused to sniff and bark. They traversed the city square, where men and women performed their early morning calisthenics and *taijiquan*. One fat man was determinedly jumping around with a staff, but his movements were so stylized and languid that he could have been poling a boat.

Through all these early morning street scenes, the Grand Master remained quiet. At his stage of spiritual attainment he could lapse in and out of outside awareness. The divine always shined its light on him, even in the ambiguous dawn atmosphere; he cared not for the world. But he was purposefully exposing himself to the people. This was his responsibility.

When people came to their procession, the Taoists responded with whatever service was needed and collected whatever donation the pious would give. But this sort of alms never would be enough. In spite of their devotion, poverty and frugality always kept them from giving any significant sum. The larger donations lay with the established and wealthy patrons who requested their presence.

Saihung led the mule upon which his master rode, and the two acolytes flanked the Grand Master. They slowly walked past the Small Wild Goose Pagoda; and by the time they passed the Big Wild Goose Pagoda, the sunlight was pink and full on the eroded but still elegant seven-storied pinnacle.

They arrived at a wealthy villa in the southern suburbs. A high brick wall surrounded the estate and private guards stood sentry at the steel gates. They admitted the four travelers instantly, and ushered them through vast and lovely gardens alive with lush greenery, flowing streams, and massive rockeries. They came to a brick hall with unchipped roof tiles of green glazed ceramic, pillars elaborately carved with dragon and phoenix motifs, and a proud sign above the entrance proclaiming the House of Li.

Patriarch Li, a fat man with a grey goatee and a pockmarked face, greeted them enthusiastically. He was dressed in an expensive high-collared, blue brocade gown. An ostentatiously large rectangular jade ring glittered on his left index finger.

"Forgive me for not greeting you myself," said the Patriarch.

"Not at all, please don't be so formal," replied the Grand Master with an elegant wave of his yak-tail whisk.

"Please, sit down."

They seated themselves on carved rosewood chairs that formed a corridor down the center of the room from the door. The patriarch's chair was in the center, facing the doors. Serving girls brought out covered tea bowls for the guests to refresh themselves.

"You honor me with your visit, Great Teacher," said Patriarch Li, picking up his tea bowl. "Please, try the tea."

The Grand Master gracefully lifted the bowl by its saucer and wrapped his fingers around the rim. He grasped the lid with the other hand and gently scraped the tea leaves still on the surface away from him. He took a sip, using his long trailing sleeve to cover his mouth. Patriarch Li watched him shrewdly.

"The Grand Master is a man of manners and cultivation. Few today know proper etiquette."

"You flatter a worthless hermit," responded the Grand Master. "You serve him in Sung dynasty porcelain, you lavish this expensive picked-before-the-dew-has-dried Dragon Well Tea on a withered priest and his insignificant students. We are most unworthy."

"What a connoisseur!" exclaimed the Patriarch. "You are a man of refined taste who is entirely too modest about his status in the world."

"Not at all. Not at all."

"Please. Everyone drink."

After a few minutes, the Patriarch put his tea bowl down and sighed.

"The Head of the House of Li should have no reason to express sorrow," said the Grand Master.

"Revered Master, you cannot know the responsibilities facing me."

"May I be of service?"

The Patriarch looked up with an expression of pure delight. It was a theatrical look of enlightenment, as if he had met someone by chance who could help him. Everyone knew that he had a reason for inviting them. They were merely playing out the customary formalities.

"It is my son," said the Patriarch. "Although he is now of mature age and though he was educated in Europe, he is still unmarried. I've tried to arrange some matches, but he resists, saying such things are no longer fashionable. But how is he to get a mate? My son, you see, is somewhat homely in appearance. Reverend Master, can you use your power or give me a talisman or chant in order to make my boy handsome and less prone to odd ideas?"

"Patriach Li," replied the Grand Master, "this is not something to ask for. There is no proper way to make a homely boy handsome, nor is it right to bewitch him even at a parent's request. But I will offer a bit of advice. Think what is now possible for your son if he is free from the distractions of handsome men. Beauty may be a curse, ugliness a blessing. The gods have given us all a measure of good fortune to balance out the sorrow we inevitably experience in life. It is up to us to ascertain our gifts."

"What you say is correct, though it makes my heart

heavy," said the Patriarch sadly. "I should reconcile myself to it. But it is hard to deal with him. He has so many ideas about what is modern."

The Grand Master stood up. "Let us stroll in the gardens. You must restore your tranquility before we discuss this further."

They went out into the gardens and the patriarch did indeed cheer up as he boastfully showed them his bountiful estate. He insisted on showing them all the principal buildings, including the family living quarters, the ancestral shrine, and pavilions made especially for viewing features of the gardens. As they walked beneath covered walkways and over zigzag bridges, they could see lotus leaves floating on the water, rock imported from Lake Taihu, and old willow trees doubled by their reflections. The Patriarch ushered them through a garden wall with a moon gate to another family compound. It was the home of his son, second only to the patriarch in the family business.

The Grand Master paused. "Patriarch Li, what is this in the front courtyard?"

"My son's European education has been a great boon to me," said the patriarch. "But he has some odd interests he picked up there too. When he came back, he wanted to tear out the gardens planted five generations ago and put in a Western-style one. I absolutely refused. In rebellion, he had these potted trees and shrubbery moved in to imitate a Western garden. He wanted to remember the tree-shaded places in France, I suppose. It's ghastly the way those foreigners cut trees, but I'm told it is fashionable."

"This is against the laws of geomancy," murmured the Grand Master.

"Reverend Master, surely to ape the foreigners cannot be completely inauspicious."

"I will explain," said the Grand Master. "Whether you

believe it or not is your choice. Your son's home faces south. Formerly, it overlooked the flowing stream and pond. There was a large and spacious courtyard in between. Now he has filled the courtyard with tall trees that not only block the sunlight, but inhibit prosperity from finding the entrance to your son's home. The junipers that once were in the small beds close to the gate have been torn out, and the view to the pond obscured. In my opinion, this is the source of your trouble."

"Reverend Master," said the Patriarch respectfully, "you know that I cleave completely to the old Chinese customs. But today's youth. . . ."

"It doesn't matter if you believe me or not."

"I believe! I believe!" said the Patriarch hastily. "Only East and West are difficult to resolve."

"Thus you have trouble in your family," observed the Grand Master. "Let me explain. Not all Chinese and Westerners have set minds. East and West are two world views, but they are not immutable. Nowadays I am quite aware that some Chinese have learned to think like Westerners. Some, like your son, have the skill to make significant achievements. Similarly, the time will one day come when Westerners will accept what harmonizing with nature means. Some will understand how to observe and combine the subtle duality of *yin* and *yang*, they will learn to cooperate with nature instead of combating it. This style of a garden symbolizes the West's attitude towards nature. They want to dominate it, contain it, strip it of its secrets and force it into a geometrical pattern of their own invention. But one day it will be possible for them to see a different way."

"It is this cursed foreign garden that is ruining me," said the patriarch ruefully.

"Just a minute. I am no xenophobic dogmatist. It is the

position of these trees that blocks your prosperity. Were they Chinese or wildly grown, they would still ruin your geomantic potential."

"The Reverend Master is giving me a lesson, but I am failing to understand."

"I know you have conflicts with your son. On one hand, he introduces some convention from the West and because it does not compromise you and is profitable, you embrace it. But you are a traditionalist and when he goes too far you oppose him. You despair at his appearance but fail to recognize his inner character. Your family's difficulty is not only a case of bad geomancy, but one where father and son fail to fulfill their obligations to one another.

"I cannot accept the authority of ignorant foreigners over my beautiful native culture," declared the patriarch. "We Chinese had vast civilizations and refined lives when they were nailing their god to a cross. He should get married the Chinese way. The House of Li must have heirs!"

"It is true that East and West differ," said the Grand Master. "Here is a tree. The Westerner is like a pine tree in the mountains, driving its roots into solid rock, splitting and penetrating it to survive: The West is constantly fighting and striving for the unattainable. The Chinese is like a banyan whose roots encase rock, run like rivulets over it. It gives way to the rock, penetrating the spaces in between, and in its grip it becomes one with the stone. The East accepts life as it is and seeks to harmonize with it. But there are nevertheless crass Chinese as willing to exploit and subdue the land as foreigners, and there will one day be a movement of Westerners who will seek the quiet of holy mountain temples."

"Reverend Master, are you saying that East and West will meet?"

"The West will be in turmoil for seven years more. Its conflict is still in ascension. Other countries will enter the Great War and humanity will see a new and terrible weapon that will be like a sun falling to earth. The East will be plunged into deeper trouble that will last another thirty years. It will be three hundred years before humanity finds peace."

Patriarch Li clasped his hands and bowed. "Your wisdom is incomprehensible to me. Truly abstruse is the Tao."

The Grand Master smiled. He could see that the old man could not understand his discourse. "Forgive a deluded hermit's mutterings. We were talking about your son and I went off on a tangent. My advice is simple. Clear the courtyard. Do not block prosperity from your gate. But at the same time, try to understand your son. You need not compromise your own traditions, but do look deeply into your dilemma. The solution lies not in changing your son's appearance, but in understanding his nature."

They stayed the rest of the afternoon, meeting the various members of the Li family and accepting their hospitality. Saihung was especially happy with the banquet in his master's honor. There were rich dishes of cold sliced jellyfish, sea cucumber, crispy duck, roast goose, braised yellow fish, spicy freshwater crayfish, venison, pheasant, and fresh vegetables. The wine was so fragrant and heady that Saihung could smell its aroma even from its place on the table. The Grand Master ate only the vegetarian dishes cooked for him, but he leniently allowed his disciples to eat whatever they pleased.

Everyone was happy and content when they returned to their temple in Xian. They had helped the family, had been well fed, and had received a pledge for donations. The late evening air was still warm. The two acolytes went to do their chores. Mist Through a Grove went to draw water from the well, Sound of Clear Water propped open the wood-and-paper windows for a cross-draft. Saihung uncoiled his master's hair, gently pulling the sandalwood comb through the thick white strands.

"It is not enough," said the Grand Master to Saihung, "merely to talk about geomancy and talismans. As priests we must be sensitive to the true problems of our constituents. In the case of Patriarch Li, I had to approach his difficulty on two levels. On the one hand, I had to correct the geomancy of the house. This will have a real effect on the family. On the other hand, I saw that much of the problem lay in the conflict between father and son. Using the guise of geomancy, I pointed out the true reason his family is in conflict and attempted to resolve the anxieties involved. But a priest must not overly interfere with destiny. He speaks poetically to ensure that a person will respond only if he himself is ready. If he does not understand, it is his destiny."

Mist Through a Grove returned with the water and said, "Little Butterfly, the mule seems ill."

"What? He was fine this evening."

"Perhaps he got overheated," said Sound of Clear Water.

"Master, my expertise with mules is not great. May we all go investigate?" asked Mist Through a Grove.

"Yes," consented the Grand Master. Go resolve the problem."

Once they were outside, Saihung confronted his elder brother. "It cannot be that bad. Why drag us out?"

"Quiet," whispered Mist Through a Grove. "This has nothing to do with the mule. A man in black with his face masked attacked me at the well. We exchanged several blows before he fled."

"Was he a good fighter?" asked Sound of Clear Water.

"Not bad," replied Mist Through a Grove. "He clearly wanted to kill me, but was unable to. I think I injured him.

"What is his motivation?" asked Saihung. "Could it be robbery?"

"No. I don't think so," said Mist Through a Grove. "If he had wanted to rob the temple, he would have gone toward the main hall and scripture hall where the treasures are. Why come to this little compound only for guests?"

"That leaves only one conclusion," said Saihung. "They want to kill our master."

"It's possible," said Mist Through a Grove. He turned to Sound of Clear Water. "What do you think?"

"I fear that this is a likely reason, though I do not know why anyone would attack the Grand Master stealthily. At any rate, the only way to find out is to set a trap."

"Agreed," said Mist Through a Grove. "But they are watching our every move. We must be careful."

The Grand Master began meditating at 11 P.M. and it was then that his students took action. Saihung, following the plan laid down by Mist Through a Grove, walked plainly across the courtyard with a lantern. He went to the opposite side and through the gate to the latrines. He waited quietly inside and tied his sleeves. The smell of the air was unpleasant. Fortunately, his only weapon, a folding fan, would help him survive the wait. It was not long.

As Mist Through a Grove had clearly predicted, an assassin came for Saihung. If the target was the Grand Master, the attackers would know that his students were all martial artists. They would try to pick off the Grand Master's defenders in a simple divide and conquer plan.

At the sound of footsteps, Saihung leaped out of the latrine. A dart came whistling through the darkness but a quick flick opened the fan, forming a shield in front of his face. Sidestepping quickly and twisting the fan, he deflected the short blade. Saihung peered through the ribs of the fan. He could be watchful, but hide his intentions.

A black-clad masked man jumped down from the temple wall holding two long daggers. Small arcs, like freshly sliced pieces of moonlight, flashed as the twin points sought Saihung's flesh. Saihung snapped the fan closed. He parried expertly until his opening came. At the moment of a thrust he struck the back of his opponent's left hand with the edge of his bamboo fan. The small and delicate bones, held taut by the tension of gripping the dagger, shattered from the impact.

That still left the other dagger, however, and the assassin renewed his efforts. He used a lightning flurry of kicks as a harrassing distraction before bringing the blade into play. He stabbed at Saihung's most vulnerable points—the wrist, the throat, the eyes—with smooth expertise. Saihung sensed that he had to gamble to win.

He retreated two paces to bait his attacker. As the man advanced a step, Saihung threw the fan whirling into the air like a spinning boomerang. The assassin looked up for a split second and Saihung threw himself rolling on the ground, siezed the dropped dagger and brought it up in a two-handed slice that ripped through several layers of cloth and stained the polished steel red. A line of blood ran down the blade's groove. Saihung stepped once, turned away in a feint, and thrust back into the same cut, with an upward stab beneath the sternum and into the heart. The muscles resisted, the membrane of the diaphragm was tough, but he slammed the hilt home. It happened so quickly that he was able to leap up and catch his fan before it hit the ground.

Saihung quickly searched the man. As he unmasked him he recognized the eyes bulging from a smooth skinned face. The lashes were so thick that they could have been painted with mascara.

He undid the clothing. Aside from a jade talisman around the man's neck, he found only a promissory note for the payment of a thousand ounces of silver drawn from the Red Peony Casino.

The temple bell, much smaller and less sonorous than the ones in Huashan, signaled midnight. Saihung knew that the two acolytes, who had stayed close to their master, would be executing their part. He went to the courtyard gate and he could see Sound of Clear Water escorting a tall cloaked figure, who was wearing his master's veiled hat and holding the yak-tail whisk. Sound of Clear Water had a staff and his full bundle of clothes. They walked in panic-stricken steps, giving every indication of hasty flight. They did not even close the gate.

Saihung waited in readiness until his instinct told him to act. He dashed across the courtyard, using the silent shuffling run known as the "rat step," just as two more assassins jumped from a neighboring rooftop. They charged straight at the master's chambers. Saihung's job was to divert them.

He attacked fiercely to prevent the pair from drawing their weapons. In the first exchange of blows, he could see that they were both skilled fighters. One was taller, but weaker, and Saihung concentrated on him. He siezed the man's arm and threw him into the other man with a wrestling move. It was time for another gamble.

Saihung moved between his opponents and the gate. It was a risk, since the way to the building was now clear. But he took a flamboyant pose with one hand upraised, the other in a fist. It was a taunting, insulting posture to the martial artists, because it mocked their inability to attack. To be sure, Saihung called them every obscene name he could think of.

In Saihung's experience, weaker fighters were always impetuous. His gamble paid off when the tall assassin drew a curved broadsword and rushed him in anger. A slap to the midsection, an arm around the neck, a quick throw, and the man was through the gate. Sound of Clear Water's staff came down crushingly, but the man dodged. It was now a whirling broadsword against the staff.

The trap was now clear. Mist Through a Grove's strategy had not been simply to draw them with a decoy Grand Master. He had intentionally wanted the assassins to believe it a clumsy ploy. The assassins, thinking Saihung would be dead and seeing the two acolytes' attempt to lure them, would then think the master was unprotected. They would charge to kill him. Saihung would then drive them out the gate where they could be killed without the Grand Master knowing.

The final assassin now realized the sophisticated strategem that had ensnared him. His only objective now was to flee. He drew a long, straight sword from its scabbard and charged Saihung. He made several quick slashes and two thrusts before he ran away from the gate and along the wall. Running quickly to pick up speed, he jumped up, grabbed the top of the wall and swung himself over. Saihung ran through the gate.

Sound of Clear Water was still engaged with his opponent. He brought his staff down, shattering the shoulder blade and snapping the clavicle. The jagged end of the broken bone tore out of the flesh. The assassin dropped his broadsword. In two thrusts—one to the stomach, another to the throat—the acolyte brought the man down.

The other assassin had escaped, only to find his way blocked by Mist Through a Grove. The acolyte had his own sword, but it was an unusual one. It was a wider straight sword, wielded with two hands. The steel had been treated with chemicals and heat to a purple color. Instead of a blood groove, there was an open channel down the center of the sword. It was a cruel weapon: When thrust into a body, the flesh would close by suction around the blade and into the opening. Pulling the sword out would tear large pieces of flesh with it.

Since his straight sword was too delicate to withstand a direct clash with the acolyte's sword, the assassin used spinning movements to dodge the purple blade. His sharp point aimed at strategic spots. The wrist, the navel, the throat. The acolyte, having a heavier sword, swung back with less delicacy but more accuracy. The assassin gathered his courage and attacked ferociously. Mist Through a Grove pointed the purple sword down and slapped him insultingly. The enraged man charged, the acolyte retreated and knelt down. His blade rose abruptly and the man could not check himself, impaling himself on the blade. Mist Through a Grove jumped up and thrust the blade clean through the body and raised the blade into the stomach. He wanted the man's throat to well with blood so that his death would be silent.

The three disciples searched the bodies. As Saihung expected, the swordsman was the man with a scar. But all three were astonished to see a Buddhist monk. It was impossible to tell if he was a real monk or if it had merely been a disguise. They opened his clothes and found a letter that warned of a new religious conflict between Buddhists and Taoists, and that Huashan would be coming to eliminate the monk. The letter was signed and sealed with a name they did not know. Someone had manipulated the monk into attacking.

Saihung took out the promissory note. The Red Peony Casino was the same one he had visited with Butterfly. How could it be connected with an attempt on his master's life?

The acolytes immediately made the connection.

"The Casino," said Sound of Clear Water, "is said to be owned by the chief disciple of Phoenix Eyes."

"It is our classmate who is behind this," said Mist Through a Grove.

"But that's outrageous!" burst Saihung hotly. "Has he become that desparate for control? Has he so forgotten loyalty?"

"When you've lived longer, you'll learn not to be surprised at the treachery of others," commented Sound of Clear Water. "But this does fit in with rumors. Phoenix Eyes is the advisor to several warlords. That's why he wants control of Haushan: to swing the weight of an entire holy mountain behind a drive for control of the nation. Naturally, he needs money and influence. The casino and others like it provide considerable revenue, as well as a link to the wealthy underworld."

"It is a sound strategy," said Mist Through a Grove. "After all, everyone knows it is the Shanghai underworld and their millions from the opium trade that keeps Chiang in power."

"But to kill our master!" cried Saihung. "It's despicable. I'll kill the bastard myself."

"It is not so simple," said Mist Through a Grove in a calm tone. "Phoenix Eyes is a Taoist, a supreme strategist. What can we prove? There is no tangible connection with the casino. It belongs to his student. He can deny everything. He doesn't actually care if the assassins fail. He *wanted* us to find the note. That's enough of a hint. We must be wary. Phoenix Eyes is hemming us in."

"But what do we do?" asked Saihung. "The Grand Master does nothing."

"He has his reasons, and these are not for us to question, he is wise. He will tell us what to do. Right now, we must dispose of these three and return to him. We must protect him."

Saihung and the two acolytes dragged the bodies away from the temple. In those days of war and poverty, people died on the streets every day. It would be another three bodies and a mystery for the police. They went to clean themselves and change their clothing. It was nearly one o'clock in the morning by the time they were done. They had to go into their master's room to change the incense and bring water.

They went solemnly into the room and found their master sitting cross-legged on the clay sleeping platform. He opened his eyes.

"Did you take care of it?"

Saihung and the two acolytes looked at each other with concern.

"Yes, Master," said Saihung. "The day's work is done."

"Good," murmured the Grand Master. But as he closed his eyes, his students looked at his furrowed brow and knew that he had not been referring to the mule.

FIVE

Nocturnal Lessons

The four pilgrims returned to their mountain retreat with no additional attempts on their lives. No one talked about what had happened, and Saihung was left with the promissory note and letter, two pieces of mute evidence. He silently delivered the grain, jewelry, cloth, and pledges to monks at the North Peak gate and prepared to return to monastic life.

The trip had been a tonic for him. With renewed determination, he readied himself for the meager meals, the four periods of scriptural recitation per day, the variety of classes, the hard work, and the intensive meditation. He renewed his commitment to master the challenge of temple life and gain for himself unbreakable will and spiritual perception—qualities he knew could come only from cloistered cultivation. Having returned from the outside world, something in him was temporarily satiated, and he was ready to accept isolation again.

His master had always told him, "Live life to its fullest, and then renounce." He wanted his student to taste the best of what life offered and then gradually, with the perspective of his philosophy, renounce those things that were not conducive to spiritual growth. In this way, Saihung would progress through the stages of his life with no regrets about what he was leaving behind.

The Grand Master was an able, conscientious teacher, and he guided his students carefully.

One of the most important forums for him to transmit his knowledge was an evening class with a few students.

Saihung, the two acolytes, and one other student met in the Grand Master's chamber a few nights after their return. They sat on floor cushions while the Grand Master sat upon his meditation platform.

He delicately pulled back his sleeve and rested his right arm on the meditation crutch.

"Tonight," began the Grand Master, "I want to begin a little differently. You students always ask me questions. This time, I will ask *you* a question:

"What is Taoism?

"Little Butterfly. You have been here with me since the age of nine. Surely you can give me an adequate answer. Please respond."

Saihung flushed. He felt nervous being put on the spot, and struggled desperately to put together a coherent reply.

"There is something that pervades all things," Saihung said. "It is a movement, a force, a progression to the vast universe that is so mighty even the gods are subordinate to it. This power is so great that humanity can only perceive its minor manifestations. The constellations, the seasons, the changes of nature, the history of civilization—all are manifestations of the Tao, yet none of them can be siezed upon as the Tao itself. The metaphysical components of the universe—the ten thousand things, the five elements, *yin* and *yang*—are parts of Tao, yet they are not the whole. A human being cannot know the Tao in its entirety, but one can learn its principles and live in harmony with it. In this way, they can follow the stream of life and attain immortality.

"Taoism is a system that was handed down by the gods, sages, and realized beings. Humanity, in its ignorance of the Tao, engages in vain striving. The sages gave us the doctrines of the Tao in order to show us the way to liberation. Taoism has developed internal and external alchemies, scriptures, and meditations in order to sustain the devotee in his quest. This is a brief summary of my understanding of Taoism."

The Grand Master sat with his eyes closed and listened intently to Saihung's discourse. He was silent for a few moments, and then he opened his eye and fixed his gaze on his young disciple.

"Is that all?" he asked.

"This is all I can muster at this time," said Saihung hesitantly.

"What you say is acceptable, but perhaps not quite deep enough. I agree with you that our discussion should begin with the Tao itself. But let us be sure that this Tao is indeed that which underlies the whole universe. We can begin by observation. We see an order to the world of phenomenon. In the regular cycles of the stars, planets, and seasons we discern a cosmology. No serious thinker would think that this is all there is. We must inquire further: What animates these things? Where did they come from? Some might answer that the gods created and govern the universe. But this is not a satisfactory answer, for then we must ask, 'Where did the gods come from?' In addition, we know from scripture and even mere folk tales that the gods are themselves subject to causality. There must thus be something beyond the gods in our search for the underlying force of the universe, some force that is in itself related to the cause of things.

"Notice that I said *force*. The universe cannot be reduced to matter. Rock, no matter how finely ground, cannot account for life, movement, time, and the dimensions. No, neither nature, the gods, nor matter are the ultimate fabric of the universe.

"The scriptures say, 'Being was produced by Non-Being.' Examine this. The only possible, totally irreducible origin of the universe can be non-being. Only it is irreducible.

"In the beginning was nothingness. Out of nothingness came a random thought. A thought caused a movement within the stillness that generated infinite ripples. Movement gave rise to *qi*, vital breath. Breath congealed into the five elements—metal, water, wood earth, fire, symbolic of matter. Then this chaos became organized by *yin* and *yang*. Breathing knew inhalation and exhalation, the universe was ordered according to duality; for only in the interaction and tension between polar opposites could movement and evolution arise. The interaction of all these things finally brought forth the gods, humanity, and all the myriad phenomena. That first thought was like a stone dropping into a pristinely still pond. All that came after that may be called the Tao.

"The Tao is therefore not that which is totally irreducible, for only nothingness qualifies for that definition. But the Tao is only one shade away from nothingness and one could say it has a very intimate interaction with nothingness. In Tao's changes and hidden permutations—the ripples on the pond—heaven and earth and the ten thousand things issued forth and are all still inseparable from the Tao.

"Words do not serve a mystic well. I can only indicate, point the way. You must perceive this yourselves. Do not accept my words or even those sayings of enlightened creatures as a satisfactory substitute for experience. When I say these things, I am describing those phenomena I have seen in meditation. This is why the holy ones say, 'Without going out of the door, the sage knows heaven and earth.' If you would have such wisdom, you must meditate.

"Now, what does Taoism mean?

"Taoism is the method of studying and bringing ourselves into harmony with the Tao—or, still further, it is the procedure for uniting with the Tao itself. The sages say, 'Tao is forever and he that possesses it, though his body ceases, is not destroyed.' However, there is no one simple method. People are different and the Tao is never static. Different ways of life must be tailored according to the needs and destinies of individuals. This is why the *Seven Bamboo Tablets* catalogue 360 ways of self-cultivation.

"Taoism is a spiritual system of many levels. Where other religions strive to totally define their beliefs to the exclusion of all others, the vast, sprawling range of Taoism embraces the whole universe. One of its most fundamental points of philosophical origin is to accept humanity and the world as they are.

"Starting with humanity itself, the Taoists appreciated its intrinsic characteristics of sin and aspiration, wretchedness and nobility, savagery and artfulness, emotion and intelligence, perversity and purity, sadism and compassion, violence and pacifism, egotism and transcendence. Unlike other sages, the Taoists chose not to reject humanity's evil impulses. The duality had to be accepted and worked with.

"Once both sides of dualism were accepted, the Taoists clearly saw that individuals combined good and evil in varying proportions. Taoism therefore evolved into a system large enough to satisfy the needs of all the different people. Taoists gave morality and piety to the common man; faith and loyalty to the hero; martial arts and sorcery to the power-hungry man; knowledge to the intellectual; and, for the rare few looking for even more, they gave meditation and the secret of transcendence. Then they turned everything inside out and said, 'Not only are these segments of the world's people, but by the principle of microcosm and macrocosm, they are also inner realities of every individual.'

"The Taoist is always a pragmatist, not an idealist. His interest is always to deal with what is there before him, rather than to impose his will upon reality. Perhaps it is for this reason that Taoism is sometimes accused of being too slippery and elusive to define. Some might even say it is an opportunist's doctrine. But actually, all Taoism cares about is dealing with the situation before it, the one that always changes, the Tao.

"Historically, there are five major antecedents to Taoism. Shamanism, philosophy, hygiene, alchemy, and the school of Peng-Lai, were the components of what would develop into a massive spiritual movement.

"Shamanism was Taoism's earliest beginning. The primitive peoples believed in a world of gods, demons, ancestral spirits, and an all-powerful Nature that was mysterious and even unresponsive to humanity. They turned to their leaders, shaman priests who used magic to cure the sick, divine the hidden, and control events. The priests intervened through their personal power between their constituents and a hostile world.

"Cults of divine beings sprang up to further make life understandable. Chief among these cults were the worship of ancestors—for the joint work of agriculture made the family unit essential—and the worship of nature gods of the earth, mountain, lake, trees, harvest, and so on. Indeed, every conceivable feature of the landscape and agricultural life was believed to have its divinity. The Yellow River, for example, was called the Count of the River, and he was believed to ride a chariot drawn by tortoises. The people sought to placate his cruel and temperamental flooding by human sacrifices equally as terrible. It was only through the intervention of enlightened sages that the people gradually progressed in their consciousness. Emperor Huang-Ti was known for his discourse on medicine. Emperor Fu Hsi taught divination and formulated the Eight Trigrams. Emperor Shen Nung experimented with herbs upon his own body. Emperor Yu tamed the floods. These emperors of prehistory shaped shamanism and originated elements of

Taoism that still persist today. Many of our traditions of nature worship, divination, geomancy, talismanic art, exorcism, and spirit oracles harken back to the centuries that preceeded recorded history.

"The philosophical school of Taoism, the pure Conversation School, can be held to have originated during the Zhou dynasty. Lao Tzu was such a Taoist. When he left Luoyang to renounce the world he came for a time to Huashan. But because of his discourses in the court with Confucius, his philosophy took a twin course: It became part of Taoism, and it gradually became a somewhat secular philosophy for the literati. In the third century A.D. schools of thought, centered around such thinkers as Chuang Tzu and Lieh Tzu, advocated a Taoism that propounded noncontention, theories of government by virtue, relativity of opposites, and the search for the Tao through meditation. The schools that arose from this period may therefore be considered to have advocated an intellectual class of Taoism that paid little attention to divinities, shamanism, or physical practice.

"Physical practice arose with the hygiene school, and our sect in large part is descended from this tradition. The essential premises of this lineage are that both the physical body and the mind must be disciplined and cultivated as a means to spiritual attainment. What is called physical is considered but one side to a continuum that extends to the pure spiritualism. The hygiene school had its roots sometime around the fourth century B.C., but did not come into full prominence for another five hundred years. From the first to fourth centuries A.D, the school's teachings were codified first in the *Jade Classic of the Yellow Chamber* and then the *True Classic of the Great Mystery*. It was in these early centuries that doctrines arose of the three *dan tian* vital centers: breath circulation, diet, meditation, martial arts. All this was united in a principle postulating the existence of 36,000 gods within the human body. Given the assumption of the person as divine receptacle, it is easy to see how they believed that the body should be kept pure and strong—for it was believed that the gods would abandon an unfit body. There was a strong leaning towards asceticism. Wine, drugs, and all external means were rejected, since they could potentially offend one's resident gods.

"The goal of the hygiene school was initially physical immortality. But they gradually became aware of the doctrine of reincarnation, and their priorities shifted to the creation of an immortal soul within the earthly shell that could transcend death.

"The alchemists, by contrast, continued to believe in physical immortality. Their origins were in the Five Element school of Tsou Yen, who came into prominence about 325 B.C. It was from this lineage that the *fang shih* originated. The *fang shih*—Formula Masters—were so called because they experimented constantly to find the formula for immortality. They engaged in endless combining of herbs, minerals, and chemicals, and all sorts of smelting processes. Unfortunately for their health, most of their early efforts concentrated on such minerals as mercury, sulfur, and lead. Eventually, they adjusted their research—if only in the interests of self-preservation—towards the use of herbs, ritual, sexual alchemy, meditation, and magic. It is this division of Taoism that inherited the early shamanistic concerns of demon enslavement and sorcery. We can best contrast it to the hygiene school by noting that the alchemist embraces external methods, whereas the hygienist clings to the internal.

"We come finally to the cult of Peng-Lai, the school that is most unabashedly concerned with simple physical immortality. Some time around the fourth century B.C., a legend arose about magic islands somewhere in the Pacific where the Mushroom of Immortality grew. Expedition after expedition was launched to find the islands. By the time of Emperor Qin Shi, who united China in 221 B.C. and ruled a mere sixty miles from Huashan, the cult of Peng-Lai combined with the alchemist-magicians. Along with their arts of spirit possession and witchcraft, they advocated the cult of Peng-Lai. Emperor Qin Shi wanted to live forever, and the man who ordered the Great Wall built became a fanatic about Peng-Lai and alchemy. The emperor sent ten thousand girls and boys to search for Peng-Lai, with orders to succeed or be punished with execution. The ten thousand found the islands of Japan, but no Mushrooms of Immortality, and opted to stay rather than be executed. The emperor's efforts at alchemical preservation of his own imperial person were no more successful. In fact, it is rumored that the illness that killed him was brought on by ingesting some poisonous formula.

"From the fourth century A.D. to the present there has been enormously complex cross-pollination of these five basic aspects. Sixteen centuries of the Taoist movement have generated endless combinations and recombinations. All the thousands of later sects and forms of Taoism can be distinguished as either left- or right-handed Taoism. On the left is sorcery, alchemy, sexual practice, and demon enslavement. Roughly, it is a path that believes in external methods. The right-handed path advocates asceticism, celibacy, and meditation. Roughly, it is an internal path. Somewhat common to both are studies in scriptures, worship, meditation, divination, chanting, pursuit of immortality, geomancy, talismanic art, vision quests, and so on. All ostensibly seek union with the Tao, they only differ in their methodology and interpretation of Taoist principles. All are considered valid and orthodox methods. All yield results, and high masters of any sect can demonstrate supernatural power and manifest great spiritual insight.

"But I am rigorously opposed to the left-handed path. There is too much temptation. Admittedly, one can practice asceticism sincerely and honestly and gain only content-ment, tranquility, and piety. One is not necessarily freed from tribulation. The left-hand path grants great power with a simple incantation or ingestion of pills. But the results are not honestly gained and the adept, not having undergone the struggle to gain his position with a sound set of values, finds it too tempting to abuse his power. Levitation, transforma-tion, seeing into the future, and controlling demons, are all instantly available on the left-hand path. But nothing is free in life. Consorting with the dark side requires payment, and one's only form of barter is the human soul. Each time the force of dark Tao is tapped it feeds upon a small bit of the human essence. The whole person is eventually trans-formed into an agent for the dark Tao. Immortality and power are yours for eternity, but you have sacrificed your soul for it.

"In conclusion, I say that the Tao is awesome and tran-scends human conception. Taoism, with its centuries of great minds seeking to know the Tao, has expanded into a labyrinthine sprawl of different doctrines asnd schools. There are Taoists for every facet of the Tao—even if it is Tao's evil side. But I say to you that in spite of this staggering amount of human effort, the Tao remains an enigma and mystery that nevertheless inexorably surrounds our lives and destinies." The Grand Master paused.

"Are there any questions?"

"Master, how does one properly follow the Tao?" asked Saihung. "There are so many methods that it is quite mind-boggling."

"It's true," replied the Grand Master. "In fact, Little Butterfly, you must fully master and surpass the *Seven Bamboo Tablets* before you can consider yourself firmly on the way."

"But I have neither seen the books nor had their contents explained to me. How can I master them?"

"Not the books, not the words," said the Grand Master. "The teachings."

"Why can't I see them?"

"You're not ready yet."

"But surely the books set down a course of study to follow," said Sound of Clear Water. "Wouldn't it be more efficient if we knew what to do?"

"Course? Do?" laughed the Grand Master. "There is no set course to the Tao! You must use your own initiative to set your own course. How you end up is how you end up. Act on impulse. Whatever you feel is right. You might want to be a recluse. That's Tao. You might want to live in a big city. That's Tao. If you have joy in the world, that's Tao. If you get angry, that's Tao. You are looking deeply into life."

"Then one may act freely?" asked Mist Through a Grove.

"Why not? The Tao has no fixed pattern. The Tao is free! Flexible! Constantly changing! Followers of the Way should do no less." The Grand Master giggled at his confused students.

"Imposing any rigid pattern, even if it's derived from the Taoist canons, is wrong," he continued. "Wearing priestly robes, a topknot, saying sutras, praying every day is all worthless. You can burn incense day after day and the gods may not listen. It's only you yourself who makes things happen."

"So why shouldn't I just indulge myself?" asked Saihung bluntly.

"Self-indulgence is Tao too," replied the Grand Master

immediately. "But it has no purpose. No motivation. Thus it's dead when compared to the Tao."

"Oh," thought Saihung. "I knew it was another trap." But the Grand Master had found a foil for his act and went on to complete his talk.

"One should have purpose, conviction, and goals. Self-indulgence is Tao, too; but is it freedom? In your self-indulgence you could destroy yourself wrecklessly. In the pursuit of your self-indulgence you might have an impulse to do something, but you would not be able to achieve it because you lacked ability. Therefore, you would have no freedom and I would judge freedom better than mere self-indulgence."

"So there's no getting out of temple life?" asked Saihung.

"Not if you want to achieve any goals. If you do not want to live a life solely devoted to gratifying your baser instincts, then you should try to achieve something great. If you have a goal, then you will gladly sacrifice lower things for the sake of gaining something higher."

"It does seem that the Taoist life is one of sacrifice. It's paradoxical," commented Mist Through a Grove.

"Not just sacrifice," reminded the Grand Master. "I am not advocating blind self-denial. Pure asceticism can be mentally and physically dangerous if it is unbalanced. Vegetarianism without the tonic herbs to balance it is wrong. Celibacy without technique is insane. This is the test of your mastery: How do you attain balance? You must always ask yourself this.

"Asceticism is only to fulfill your potential. Strictness develops you quickly into special individuals. Then you will fulfill your destinies and be in a position to help others. That is also the Tao."

The Grand Master looked at them and smiled. "Too much talk is boring, even for monks. Action, not words, is what is important. Transformation, not speculation, is the goal. An important part of your progress lies in securing your physical and emotional well-being. Tonight, I wish to teach you the Six Words *Qigong.*

"This is a method that was developed to preserve the organs. Several weeks ago you heard the White Hare Recluse's discourse on the effects of sound as *words.* Today I will give you a simple and concrete example of the use of words to stimulate and maintain the organs.

"The method is this: You are to perform the indicated motions while simultaneously making the prescribed sound and mentally tracing the meridian associated with that sound. Six words are used: *Shu, Ke, Hu, Sss, Chui,* and *Xi.* The organs they affect are, respectively, the liver, spleen, heart, lungs, kidneys, and triple warmers."

The Grand Master stood up and his disciples followed. The movements were performed slowly and with the muscles relaxed, as if they were ballet dancers underwater. The liver exercise consisted of raising the arms to the side before folding them in and lowering them with a pushing down motion. The raising of the arms coincided with inhalation, and the lowering with exhalation. Exhalation was the long expelling of breath while making the sound "Shuu-uuuuuuu," drawing the word out at the end of the breath and movement. The Grand Master taught them each sound and movement and instructed them to do each posture seven times.

When they had learned the movements, the Grand Master taught them the meridians to imagine. At the beginning of their exhalation and sound, they were to begin mentally tracing the meridian from one end to the other. By the time they reached the terminus, a duration of about ten seconds, they were to have completed the sound and breath. The entire line was imagined as a thread of brilliant light.

Taoism and the internal martial arts stress that mere physical technique divorced from its psychic content is ineffective. Every technique, besides having its outward movements, had its mental procedures to direct the flow of energy. The *qi* took on certain patterns in accordance with the body posture, but it also required the mind to fully exercise the technique.

Many Westerners believe that a true "scientific" technique should work regardless of an athlete's state of mind. Health and physical prowess are to be developed by clear-cut exercises free of any mystical overlay. However, this viewpoint ignores what the Taoists believed to be humanity's true nature—that people are mind and spirit as well as body, and that mind has control over the matter of the body. For them, the body itself was merely a coarse manifestation of the universal mind.

"This method allows you to control the organs," said the Grand Master as he unrolled a scroll with anatomical diagrams. "The sound enters the meridian like an electrical impulse. The energy will push through blocked points and restore health and balance. It is the same effect as an acupuncture needle, only the practitioner uses sound and mental concentration instead. Only an unblocked meridian properly transmits energy into its respective organ. Through the proper posture and sound, the organ is actually gently vibrated and massaged. This is the Taoist way to promote good health.

"The organs are believed to be the residence of emotions. The *Yellow Emperor's Canon on Internal Medicine,* which dates from the twenty-seventh century B.C., but was expanded to twenty-four volumes in A.D. 762 by Wang Ping, states these concordances between organs and emotions: the liver with anger, the spleen with sympathy, the heart with joy, the lungs with grief, and the kidneys with fear. The triple warmer, being actually a system of organizing the functions of the five organs and six viscera, is a compensating organ and can be used to bolster any of the others. Since the emotions have a mutually dependent relationship with the organs, they not only affect the health of the organ but, inversely, the emotions can be controlled through the organs. The Taoists believe that the physical can therefore be used to subdue the emotions.

"The Six Words is thus a useful method to preserve the health and stability of the practitioner. Physical maintenance must be firmly wedded to spiritual achievement. If one studies, reads, or even meditates excessively, the organs and body can weaken. The Six Words will preserve you if you practice faithfully every day."

The Grand Master heard the low reverberation of the temple bell. He ended the class with a prayer and his students went home.

The night air was cool and slightly damp. Smells of moss and pine mingled with the respiration of the trees. Saihung walked quietly along the covered temple walkway. The spaces between pillars divided the gardens into perfect views of balance and poetry. He went to a lone meditation cell and lit a candle.

Night came as a blue-blackness flooded over the faded wooden temple eaves, and sight and sound ebbed. All the day's endeavors were past and any cares that still existed could be put off until the next day. The quietness that gradually grew in the holy interiors was a neutral ground, a passive space. Saihung's mind projected brief flashes to fill that stillness. There were worries, but worrying achieved nothing. There was loneliness and longing, but he pushed that aside. There were plans and just mental talking, but he put no stock into those words. It was quiet. Perhaps the teachers were right to insist on silence. It was inevitable, they said, that man would utter something impure and blasphemous and thus drive the gods away. Only in soundlessness might there be sufficient tranquility to attract the divine. He turned away from his emotional vexations, his internal dialogue, even that which he considered duty and responsibility. He turned away from memories that floated up through his consciousness in an apparently random sequence: walking in his grandfather's garden, a restaurant he'd been to in Beijing, the night's lessons, a smile from one of his master's friends, the fight with the assassin. He turned away from the traces and shadows of his life and instead looked within.

He wondered if any man could sense his own destiny, or whether any man could defeat an impulse from a higher source. Saihung sat down and crossed his legs. His spine automatically straightened to assume the position he'd known for years. The neutral darkness of the room changed to a feeling of positive serenity. Self-dialogue had given way to introspection. Introspection gave way to contemplation. His attachment to the day faded. Contemplation focused on the gentle rhythm, the high and low tide of his breathing. He noticed his pulse and it seemed he could even hear his blood flowing, his nerves firing without any direction on his part. But he soon plunged deeper within himself and his awareness reached beyond his own body functions. It was true that spirituality was rooted in the body. The body could even be said to be indivisible from the spirit. In the soft viscera, pungent body fluids, viscous blood, tangled veins, grainy bones, and foul excrement, spirituality rose up.

Saihung had learned that the source of human spirituality was at the base of the spine. It wasn't in the head, or some other romantic spot. It was there in the morass of nerve endings, in the loins, smothered close to the genitals and anus. That was the bottom of the well, black, dark, mysterious, hiding all. It was from that depth that he had to draw out a shaft of light, a slender thread that needed to be pulled as smoothly, as steadily as reeling silk from a cocoon. Then he could lead the energy up the channel of his spine, out of the basest elements of his body towards the crown. That point was metaphorically called the Thousand-Petaled Lotus. Deep in his meditation he sought to urge the expanding energy upward, now like a glowing, slender stalk. He had an urge to move it higher, to make the lotus reach its height and blossom. That was his purpose: to draw the pure lotus of his own divinity out of the muck and tangle of his earthly life and his own imperfect biology. He had to plunge deep into the darkness of his personality, transcend his boundless unconscious mind, reach down into the well to draw up that precious essence.

From deep in his subconscious arose something his master had told him long ago.

"The heart of the perfect man is pure. Even in a swamp he remains unsullied. Though thunderbolts destroy mountains, and winds churn the four oceans, he is unafraid. He flies through the clouds, sails above the sun and moon, and transcends the world. Life and death cannot sever his unity with the world. His heart is with all things, but he is not one of them."

This last shimmer of conscious memory dissolved in light.

A Quest

One day the Grand Master summoned his disciples before him. He surveyed them sternly.

"I have a quest. Who is willing?"

"I am, Master!" said Saihung quickly.

"It is true that I need a man captured. But I'm not sure if you're the one."

"A martial quest is even better!" said Saihung enthusiastically. "Who is the man?"

"It is someone I have forgiven nine times. I can forgive him no longer. Really, my hand has been forced. The provincial governor himself came to me and threatened to level every temple on Huashan unless I did something."

The Grand Master paused and looked directly at Saihung.

"This man has been dubbed the Heaven Soaring Spider." Saihung suddenly recalled the hoodlums' conversation that he had overheard on his journey. "He recently robbed a government gold convoy, killing many guards. His acrobatic skill, which can carry him from rooftop to rooftop or over walls, is almost supernatural. He fights with two daggers and is an Eagle Claw boxer."

Saihung mentally tabulated this data. He wanted to fully understand his quarry.

"He is a notorious playboy," continued the Grand Master. "A pimp, a drug smuggler, and a member of the Green Circle Gang. In fact, the governor is after him precisely because this libertine seduced his wife. He is now in Beijing, making a spectacular exhibition of himself in the papers. Every week there is news of his criminal behavior."

"Master," asked Saihung respectfully, "why are you interested in such a man?"

The Grand Master sighed for a moment. A look of resolve set his face firmly.

"I raised this man from childhood. He is your elder classmate, Butterfly."

Saihung was solemn.

"Are you sure your personal feelings won't interfere?" asked the Grand Master. "Even Guan Gong let personal feeling interfere with duty."

"No, Master," said Saihung. "He has gone too far and has betrayed you and our sect. I will not let him go."

"You speak like a young man."

"I will not fail, Master."

"Then you must go. You leave tomorrow with Wuyung and Wuquan, two sentry monks. You will pursue Butterfly and bring him back quickly."

"But Master, what about Phoenix Eyes?" asked Saihung.

"This is my concern. Bringing your elder brother back is yours. Go quickly and ask no more questions."

Within a week Saihung, Wuyung, and Wuquan were on a westbound train. Saihung was dressed in the flamboyant manner of a rich martial artist: a green silk brocade, high-collared gown, a sash of heavy black silk embroidered on the ends, and black cloth boots; discs of precious jade hanging from his belt symbolized his aristocratic class. His long hair was tied in a queue, illegal in Republican China, and hidden beneath his gown like some of the weapons he carried.

Saihung always returned to his ancestral home in northern Shaanxi, whenever he left the mountain. Although he had formally renounced his family ties, they nevertheless accepted him back each time. His own rooms and a personal library were maintained in the mansion and his custom-made weapons, forbidden in the temple, were stored in the

Saihung, as he appeared during his pursuit of Butterfly. The sash and jade pendants were all symbols of his rank and class.

arsenal hall. He could thus change his identity from poor begging monk to that of wealthy nobleman and knight-errant. His family's descent from the God of War himself gave Saihung a vast store of resources to draw upon. Now he was dressed in silk, embellished with jade, financed with gold, armed with steel, and motivated by a romantic purpose. The Little Butterfly had become a steel lion.

Saihung looked at the brothers Wuyung and Wuquan seated across from him. Both in their forties, who had come to Huashan to renounce the world and become novitiates. They were sullen, large, and mean, and Saihung suspected that the two had had a rough past. Somewhere along the way they had been given sad names that had stuck with them even in the temple. Wuyung meant "useless," and Wuquan meant "powerless."

Wuyung, the elder brother, had a head shaped like an old melon. His skin was rough from some childhood illness, and his brows were often tensed in his most typical demeanor of pensive melancholy. He was hard muscled, with shoulders like a bull, and his heavy body swelled his black and purple gown.

Wuquan had more angular features. His dark brown face was like a bronze mask, the slits for eyes were narrow, uneven, and shadowed. Belligerence had been worked into every fiber of his face and body, and there was barely a trace of mercy to alloy it. His brown and grey gown was vainly tailored to show his titan frame.

The brothers were close in a rough and unsentimental way. Theirs was the silent alliance of blood and of men who had faced life and death together. The years of battle had made the sad-eyed Wuyung superstitious, while Wuquan was slyly cynical, especially regarding his older brother's outlook. They rarely exchanged words. They were two journeyman warriors. Saihung realized that his master was not a gambling man. He was sending two hulking killers after a nimble-footed one.

They stayed on the train day and night, enduring the unyielding benches, the constant swaying, iron cacaphony of wheel to rail, and the even louder human noise of fellow travelers. The smelling, chattering crush of people packed on at each stop, stuffing their squealing bodies and make-shift luggage into the narrow confines of the train. They pushed, jostled, hung out the windows, screamed in peasant voices down the cramped, shaking car. But they shrank away in fear from the three warriors. They saw the clothes, noticed Saihung's aristocratic insignia, and spied the wrapped swords. Although it had been almost two decades since the collapse of the Qing dynasty, the fear and awe for the elite noble and warrior class was deeply ingrained into their simple outlook. Everyone knew the old saying: "A swordsman only carries a sword to kill. A sword can never be resheathed until it has tasted blood."

They transferred to a train on the Beijing-Shanghai line at a filthy and crowded station where the tracks were littered with debris. Saihung was glad to board the steam-engined train. It only unnerved him a little bit to watch a man stroll nonchalantly down the tracks and begin to bang away at the wheels with a hammer. This seemingly random pounding on the train made the whole contraption seem more ridicu-lous. Wuquan explained that the tie rods were being tapped back into place.

Their train headed northward, and in a few hours it passed into Japanese-occupied territory. Butterfly's gang connec-tion and his presence in the war zone would make the task of capturing him more difficult. They would have to try not to alert his confederates or meet any Japanese patrols.

As Saihung's train lurched on its twin rails he passed mud-brick houses, farms, orchards, and towns. But he also saw old bomb craters, devastated villages never completely repaired, and sleek dogs fattened from scavenging the dead. The war had settled into ineffective and bumbling skirmishes between the Chinese and Japanese, and the territory was a confusion of Japanese military administration, remnants of Chinese bureaucracy, soldiers, guerillas, and gangsters. The fighting had evolved into a grim ennui where the Japanese occupational forces traded freely with Chinese gangsters and opportunists. Opium and heroin were the chief commodities, and thousands of pounds enriched both sides. China, from the Yellow River to the coast, was a surreal mix of death, cruelty, narcotics trade, and fumbling militarism. Heroism had long ago vanished as the rare and volatile quality it was. This was now a place of scoundrels.

They arrived at the train station for Qufu in Shandong province in the afternoon. The skies were a dense grey-purple pall that dissolved into a heavy downpour upon their arrival. The air was hot. It let up after a while, but the roads were already a quagmire of brown sludge. They still had nine-and-a-half miles into Qufu. Since the town was both the birthplace and burial site of Confucius, geomancy and respect for the Great Sage would not permit the line to go directly there. The three of them hitched a ride on a farmer's cart.

They passed under a stone archway, the old drum tower, and found their way through the broken-down streets and lanes to an address the Grand Master had given to them. It was an herb store with a dark interior rich with a pungent aroma.

The proprietor was a stocky man in his fifties. Balding and bespectacled, he was nevertheless energetic and forceful. He greeted them from behind a counter.

"What would you like to buy?" he said.

Seeing that they were strangers, he waved his hand to direct their attention to his wares. Hundreds of tiny drawers lay behind him in cabinetry that went from floor to ceiling. There were no labels. He knew where each herb was.

On the opposite side a display case showed such esoterica as ginseng, tiger bone, rhinocerous skin, *lingzhi* mushroom, deer antler, dried lizard, goat forelegs, and various dried organs of bears, deer, and sea lions. A pair of middle-aged men sat in chairs nearby. This in itself was not suspicious— an herbalist's cronies often came to chat the day away. But these two looked like murderers.

"I come with an introduction," said Saihung.

"Is that so?" responded the herbalist noncommitally.

Saihung pushed the letter forward.

"Come back tomorrow," said the herbalist after he read the letter. "Your master's prestige is great. I won't refuse you."

When Saihung returned the next day he was told that he could meet the people he wanted. The herbalist had discussed the request and there was an agreement. In two days there was to be a council meeting. The three of them would then have an audience with the Elders of the Martial World.

There were two great underworlds in China: the criminal underworld, and *Wulin*, the world of martial artists. Whether good or bad, they considered themselves bound by chivalry, honor, and principle. They obeyed a King of *Wulin*, councils of elders, and policed themselves by their own law. The outlaw martial artists were particularly interesting. They viewed themselves as champions of justice. Rewarding the loyal, punishing the traitorous, and generously helping those who caught their fancy were hallmarks of their style. Though they were still criminals, they were part of *Wulin*.

Of course some of these people also fell into the second

underworld. That underworld was controlled by secret societies like the Green Circle Gang, the Red League, the Trident Society, the White Lotus Clan, and the Iron Shin Society. Many of those gangsters did not belong to any tradition of masters, schools, discipline, or honor. They were hoodlums, pure and simple; greedy syncophants, brutal sadists, and strongarm masterminds obsessed with bullying and riches. It was true that many of the secret societies, such as the Red League, had begun as patriotic anti-Manchu organizations dedicated to the overthrow of the Qing dynasty. But over the years the underworld societies concerned themselves more with opium, heroin, prostitution, gambling, graft, extortion, assassination, and political manipulation.

Both underworlds formed a criss-crossing net of contacts throughout China, and to almost all parts of the world where there were overseas Chinese. Both would be essential to the successful completion of Saihung's task. For now, Saihung had to begin with the martial world. Only they could guarantee that Huashan would be spared until he could catch Butterfly.

The martial world was administered in territories by a head patriarch and a group of elders, and all martial artists were obliged to follow the council's dictates. The elders settled disputes, sanctioned duels, directed collective actions, and ordered the execution of those who violated the code of chivalry. It was to such a council that the three monks went to present their petition.

The meeting was held on a hot and humid afternoon in a private mansion of courtyards, gardens, flowing streams, and magnificent pavilions. In one dark hall chairs were set up in rows like a theater, and the various members of the martial world sat in audience. At the head of the pillared hall was a round table where the ten elders sat. They each wore long Chinese gowns except for two men. One, with greying hair, wore the olive drab uniform of the Nationalist army. The other was a man in his fifties dressed in Buddhist robes. Together, the ten represented religion, government, and business, as well as martial arts. If it concerned power, the martial world had a hand in it. The Buddhist monk was the Patriarch of the Martial World. His name was Qingyi, which means "Pure Mind." He had a smooth-shaven skull, although his face had begun to sag and wrinkle and his eyes were slightly puffy. His goatee had forgotten how to grow long or thick, but his shoulders hinted at a past broadness. His robes were a khaki color and a shawl of deep brown with a golden pattern like mortar between bricks angled over his chest and a shoulder. He wore a rosary of 108 beads around his neck, punctuated every thirty-six beads by one of brilliant imperial jade. He also fingered a smaller rosary.

Qingyi called the meeting to order.

"I call the three monks from Huashan. Step forward."

They stood up and approached the table. Some of the elders did not even bother to look at them, but remained smoking cigarettes disinterestedly.

"Speak."

"I am the Butterfly Taoist of Huashan, student of the Grand Master," said Saihung. "I come to petition the elders to stay the hand of the Shaanxi governor. He wants my classmate who seduced his wife. Unless we turn him over immediately, he will order the army to destroy all Huashan."

Qingyi glanced at the Nationalist Officer. He smiled derisively and looked at the tip of his burning cigarette. Why trifle over a mere woman?

"In my Master's opinion," continued Saihung, "it is an internal matter for Huashan to settle. We will resolve the issue within the context of *Wulin*. We ask the Elders to intercede on our behalf."

Qingyi looked around the table. No one spoke. There was

only nodding and hand gestures. Saihung saw one man shake his head no. The rest agreed. Qingyi looked up.

"We will give you one hundred days only. After that, we cannot protect you."

"We thank the Elders," said Saihung with a bow.

They left the meeting and hurried back to their inn to prepare for their trip. Saihung was satisfied. He knew that the Elders would use their considerable leverage to enforce their rule. The army officer would send formal governmental orders, the businessmen could withhold money and supplies. Saihung had no doubt that Huashan would be safe from troops for one hundred days. He hoped his master could hold out against Phoenix Eyes as well.

Their train drew nearer to Beijing. The sun was a flaming sphere, parching the barren land. The fields were scratched pitifully from the dusty soil. Laboring peasants, tied emotionally to the land in spite of warfare and natural calamity, worked for hours to pull crops of corn, wheat, millet, and potatoes from the chunks of clay. Bent over, hobbled, they stained the hot earth with whatever moisture they could divert to their fields, and endured the sandblasting brawn of the wild desert winds.

Dynasty after dynasty, generation after generation, year after year, Beijing stood at its chosen location. It was supposed to be an ideal geomantic site, the center of the world itself, yet it was no paradise. The clouds of hot yellow dust blew over the city like cavalry, the sun made the air dry and hard to breathe. Grit accumulated quickly between the lips and the corners of the eyes. Trees, crops, pack animals, and people alike withered in the climate of Beijing. The magic that the founders of the "Capital of Swallows" had used to establish the very pivot of Chinese civilization had diminished. As the train rushed toward its terminus, Saihung thought of the many armies that had, over the centuries, charged across the plains to sack the city and usurp its emperor. The tramp of marching armies, the pounding of hooves, and the crushing of tank tread had been heard throughout history as attackers from the north, peasant rebels from the south, European armies from across the globe, and Japanese invaders from the ocean sought to breach the vermillion walls of the Forbidden City.

The train terminal was outside the old city walls and the three began walking toward the center of the city. For once they were glad of the hordes of people, since they could use the crowds to camouflage their presence from the occupying Japanese and the ever-watchful underworld spies. They made their way through narrow, crowded streets, between mud-and-brick houses that seemed as if they would sink into the earth with a good rain or heavy earthquake. It was like being in a labyrinth. Because of an old decree that no building be higher than the Forbidden City, and because the old-fashioned population refused to distance themselves from the earth, the city had become a sprawl of low buildings, grey walls, and dusty lanes.

Walls were the major surface presented to the eyes in Beijing. Most homes and compounds had a wall around them. Some were weathered and broken, with yellow grit and coal dust caking the crevices where mortar once cemented the brick. Others had irregular patches of eroded whitewash and stucco, showing the brown rammed-earth blocks beneath. Windows were seldom seen on buildings close to the street, and those that were visible were usually translucent paper or a glass so dirty that they might have been clay anyway. Bright sunlight failed to enliven the utter dinginess of the walls, even though its rays occasionally caught tatters of old New Year's couplets or progressively faded cheap woodcuts of door gods.

Dogs, their coats a patchwork of mange and pink flesh, prowled the corridors and nosed into the garbage piles. Urine, both animal and human, stained the walls. Black tiles—cracked, broken, host to weeds and grass that had grown in accumulated dirt—topped the walls. Most doors were closed tightly; occasionally a half-open door would reveal a crowded and cramped room colored in charcoal tones. Walls were everywhere, and it was anybody's guess what went on behind those walls. They might have hidden anything. More than likely they kept starving families— struggling, clawing, desperate victims of poor urban life— penned neatly into compartmentalized squalor.

If these tiny little walls, these innumerable thick subdivisions, were the basic geometry of the city, then it made sense that the whole city should be walled. (Is it any wonder that the first emperor of Qin tried to wall the whole nation?) The old ramparts of the city still stood in the forties. They were high, angled brick walls with gap-toothed crowns. Although they were in disrepair, with tumbled sections of missing or disintegrated brick, it was a testimony to their original scale that they still stood as fairly forbidding parapets. History and time had carved intaglio records of their passing, and the gaping holes left by cannon fire from the Allied attack in 1900 were unrepaired.

All travelers entering Beijing's walls were required to register with the city magistrate. They went immediately to a brick building with red pillars and tiled roofs and found an empty reception hall with a stage and heavy rosewood desk and chair. A doorway on each side and a mural of two cranes above a frothing ocean made the room completely symmetrical. Except for the absence of chairs, it could have been a tiny theater.

A red drum on a high stand was adjacent to the open doors. At the center of the taut yellow drumhead was a large red dot. Saihung grabbed a stick and struck the drum loudly. This was an unrefusable demand to see the magistrate.

Soldiers in olive drab Western-style uniforms and rifles filed out of each doorway at the end of the room. They walked silently and expressionlessly down the steps and turned to face each other. The attendant, a dessicated, coat rack of a man, came out in an ill-fitting blue gown. He had tiny glasses and a moustache and goatee that looked like they had been scribbled on.

"The Magistrate of Beijing!" he announced pompously. Saihung and his companions dropped to their knees. The stone floor was hard and cold.

The Magistrate made his entrance with all the drama of an opera star. A squat, tough, no-nonsense bureaucrat dressed in black brocade, burgundy vest, and black skullcap, he sat down formally and with such an upright posture that a carpenter might have measured a plumb angle with his spine. His red face was like a boar's. His beard bristled like a scrub brush. His eyes were round but heavily lidded, conveying an uncaring, cynical outlook.

Saihung, Wuyung, and Wuquan kowtowed three times, each time touching their foreheads to the floor.

"The supplicants will state their request," ordered the assistant.

"We request permission to enter the city in search of a man," replied Saihung. He looked at the floor as he spoke—it was considered discourteous to look at the Magistrate.

"Your papers!" demanded the attendant imperiously.

Saihung offered his identification with both hands held above his head. He was still looking down. The attendant walked down the steps and took them to the Magistrate. Two soldiers took the others.

The Magistrate unfolded Saihung's passport, a long accordion-pleated piece of paper bound between two hard covers.

On one side was an oval photograph of Saihung along with his address and signature. There was a text signed by the Grand Master of Huashan telling the purpose of Saihung's business. The enormous square seal of Huashan was stamped at the end along with the Grand Master's own seal. Further along the passport were panels for official inscriptions along the way.

The Magistrate grunted noncommitally. The attendant and the guards watched him intently. Every facial expression, every utterance, every gesture meant something. This was the way he communicated. It was beneath him to talk to his minions, let alone those who came to petition him.

The Magistrate stroked his beard as he considered and then seized a brush from the stand. The attendant obsequiously weighted the passport down with bars of white jade and eagerly scrutinized the five dishes of ink on the desk. It didn't matter what the Magistrate wrote. The color of the ink itself would convey his orders.

Black meant no. Green meant yes. Blue signified that the matter would be taken under consideration. White meant that the request had no merit and did not deserve comment. Red meant immediate execution. Saihung anxiously watched the tip of the brush poised above the dishes. Finally, to his relief and the attendant's disappointment, it plunged into the green ink. Saihung could see the little man's disgusted look as he stamped seals on the passports. It had probably been awhile since he'd seen an immediate execution.

The Magistrate beckoned to his attendant and whispered something. The attendant whined a reply to him that so angered the Magistrate that he slammed his palm to the desk. Trembling in fear, the attendant turned to the three of them.

"The Magistrate knows your master," said the attendant.

It was intriguing to hear how his voice conveyed both a cowardly obeyal of his master's orders and yet his complete distaste for them. He continued: "He wishes you the best in your search."

The Magistrate got up without any further comment and left the room. The attendant followed like a dog and the soldiers filed out. Only one remained behind to return the passports.

They went to a teahouse and, by paying a higher price, were able to go to the second story. From that vantage point, they could see the whole city. Out of the haze and the infinite blockhouses of the people's homes, Saihung could see the outlines of the Imperial City with its cinnabar walls and golden tiled roofs. The heat was oppressive, but the sandalwood-lattice windows scented the air whenever a breeze wafted in. The waiter rushed up, inquired what kind of tea they wanted, and took their order for food. As they waited, Saihung squinted against the light and wondered how they might find his elder brother.

They were in the right place to begin. The teahouse was a universal gathering place. Open from dawn until the late hours of the night, people went there to socialize and spend their time. Tea and food were readily available and, in the fancier places, entertainment was provided by lovely women musicians or strolling storytellers. The customers were usually a cross-section of Chinese society: scholars indulging an outrageous fetish for tea, businessmen talking over deals, middlemen arranging marriages, uncomfortably formal relatives entertaining visitors, students exchanging ideas, friends celebrating their cherished ties, or old men relaxing in their unhurried retirement.

By far the most colorful were the martial artists. They were often giants, almost mutant aberrations. They came from all over the North, and one could see by their dress which were warriors from Manchuria, Shandong, or the far West. They sat with their feet wide apart and firmly planted on the ground, always in readiness to spring up. Etiquette dictated that their weapons remained unconcealed. Shorter weapons like swords, fans, daggers, and clubs lay on the table. Maces, spears, and staffs were propped against the table. These knights and warriors were on the verge of becoming an extinct class. But who could tell if the Qing dynasty would return? And even in the current war, the "Big Sword" units had acquitted themselves well against the Japanese. Chivalry and knighthood may have been in its twilight, but powerful and unique exponents of the martial class were still to be seen. Saihung longed to grow old in that very role.

Wuyung saw an old acquaintance and went over to his table. A thin man, dressed all in black, with a broadsword lying within easy reach, he greeted the monk enthusiastically. After some conversation, Saihung saw a brief flash of silver coin. The man smiled even more broadly and saluted as Wuyung returned to the table.

"I dislike bribes," said Saihung in a low voice.

"Consider it tea money for an informer," replied Wuyung simply. "Anyway, it was luck that we ran into him. I got some information."

"What is it?" asked his brother.

"Butterfly lives with his wealthy mistress, a woman in her early thirties named the 'Powerful Tigress.' She herself is a formidable fighter. Her fingers can pierce a body as easily as if they were steel spikes. Her father was an Imperial Shaolin knight who had only two children. The older was the Tigress, the younger now a teenage boy. Since the Tigress was older the father taught her his art unreservedly, but he died before the boy could be fully trained. The sister has probably finished his education and Butterfly has probably added to her technique."

"We'll go to her mansion," said Wuquan quickly.

"Not so fast," interjected Saihung. "We should find out more. There are many women fighters who can be more dangerous than men."

"Exactly," agreed Wuyung. "That's why we'll go to the city coroner's office tomorrow."

The trio spent the night at the famous White Cloud Temple, a holy temple that is to Taoism what the Vatican is to Catholicism. The temple grounds were large and oriented—like all important structures in China—on a perfect north-south axis. A shrine was first built on the site by the Emperor Xuan Zong (A.D 713–756) of the Tang dynasty. After the shrine burned in 1202, the Yuan Emperor Genghis Khan invited the Taoist sage Qiu Changchun to rebuild the temple. More building and imperial patronage followed through the centuries and the White Cloud Temple took on its present dimensions in the Ming and Qing dynasties. Doctrinally devoted wholly to monastic Taoism, the White Cloud Temple was the meeting place for national convocations of abbots, and the name of every Taoist monk and priest in China was inscribed in the Temple's records before any ordination was considered complete.

The temple was fronted by a large polychromed gate, predominantly red and blue with gold accents, that had seven decorative rooftops of grey clay tile. Behind the marble base and iron gates was a large courtyard and another brick gate with three archways and crimson doors. Spirit screens, granite guardian lions, and stone cloud pillars formed a wide barricade to the outside world. The whole compound was surrounded by a high wall and the inner gate was called a "Mountain Gate." Entering it was figuratively to leave the mundane world and enter into a rarified holy place.

The major shrines were situated directly along the centerline with other less important shrines situated on two other parallel axes on each side. On the central axis were the halls to the Lingquan, the Protector of Taoism, the Jade Emperor, the Tomb and Shrine of Qiu Changchun the Four Deities, the Old Disciple, the Pavilion of the Three Pure Ones, and the ordination hall.

On the east axis were the halls to such deities as those of Longevity, the Dipper stars, the North star, Hua Do (a surgeon and doctor), and the Five Patriarchs. In the western compound were shrines to Lu Dongbin, the Eight Immortals, Female deities, and the Ancestral Worship Hall. Other buildings included a sutra hall, drum towers, and bell towers. Placed throughout the grounds were dragon-topped stone steles borne by turtles. These massive memorials, well over twice the height of a man, recorded various words of praise and imperial patronage. At the back of the temple was a large rock garden—a model of Peng-Lai, the Island of Immortality.

It was through the simple metaphors of real objects that the Taoists sought to convey their abstruse philosophical notions to the layperson. A serene atmosphere was conveyed by isolating the temple from the city, providing large expanses of open courtyard and beautiful gardens. The doctrine of Peng-Lai was symbolized by a rock garden. The temporal power of one god was shown by having him hold a *yin-yang* symbol: a graphic statement that he encompassed the entire universe in his hand.

In a way, the temple was an elaborate theater for religion. But the White Cloud Temple also had true spiritual feeling for those who were receptive. Generations of holy men had attained their realization within its grounds and some of their essence inevitably lingered. For someone like Saihung, the atmosphere of the Temple was a welcome solace from the urban world outside the walls. In its cool shrines, he would be alone to renew himself.

Saihung knelt down before the figure of Lu Dongbin. Dressed as he still was in the dusty silk of a layman, he found pause in the juxtaposition between the fighter and the monk. He wondered what to do: Should he pray? Was he eligible to pray? Should he pray for victory? Or to receive forgiveness for the killing he might have to do?

He thought back to the men he had seen in the teahouse and he wished he could be one of them. All his life he had found it difficult to establish an identity for himself. He had never fully wanted to be his mother's scholar, his father's soldier, nor his master's acolyte. All he wanted in life was certainty—the certainty of spiritual truth, the certainty of martial protection, the certainty of a gentlemanly future. But he knew that he was now confronted with uncertainty. Knights were fading before modernity, and it was unlikely that he could ever adopt that role. The complete spiritual truth had not yet revealed itself and so he lacked that assurance. Every challenger might be stronger; he never knew which fight might be his last. He was pursuing his brother in a land of millions and might not catch him. And right there where he knelt, he was a man on a potentially violent quest wondering whether he could even approach the holy.

He cursed his doubt. No fighter could win in battle without confidence. Uncertainty was a weakness, and he knew that he had to seal his vulnerability for the struggle ahead. The answers would not come that day, but he resolved to dig deeper into himself for the strength to face the pursuit ahead.

Saihung, Wuyung, and Wuquan went to the city mortuary the next morning, a grim brick building smeared with coal soot and grime. They showed their papers to the coroner and persuaded him to let them see a body collected two days before. The coroner was an odd man—stranger than one might expect for someone who worked constantly with the dead.

His brow and eyes were vaguely canine, while his lips were always smiling to reveal a terrible overbite. He was cheerful and showed himself every bit to be a man who loved his work. Once he had ascertained their legitimate interest, he led them down a hallway with all the excitement of one about to show off his greatest accomplishment. He had a habit of wringing his leathery hands, not so much from nervousness as from anticipation.

He led the way down into a basement, his white-haired head bobbing like a fish in a dark sea. Saihung might have enjoyed the respite from the Beijing heat were it not for the smell of formaldehyde and the stench of opened bowels. The staircase led into a narrow, vaulted hall with cribs and coffins inadequately lit by oil lamps. An assistant was about to dissect a woman's body, but the coroner dismissed him and almost tenderly covered the body with a greasy sheet. He led the trio into a dark corner where they uncovered a coffin. A foul stench billowed up.

"Fortunately, we have not yet covered him in lime. I thought there might be an investigation, so I waited one more day. But no one cares these days who gets killed."

Saihung examined the body. It was a large and stout Buddhist priest, his shaved head as massive as a cannon ball. The brows were black and thick. The two nostrils seemed like simple holes, and the mouth was parted, a purple-rimmed gape that revealed clotted blood on his broken teeth. Heavy iron rosary beads, each sphere an inch-and-a-half in diameter, hung around his neck. He wore a grey vest and pants that exposed a barrel chest and tree-trunk arms. Wuquan unsheathed his sword and with the tip pushed the vest aside. There was a brown spot beneath the end of the right collarbone, another under the left ear. The most obvious wound was a purple bruise in the shape of a human palm over his heart.

"We don't know who killed him," said the coroner in an academic tone. "But it was fast, and his weapon was broken."

They looked at a shattered weapon that had been carelessly thrown beside the corpse. It was a moon spade, a long, heavy weapon that was the specialty of Buddhist monks. On one end was a large, spade-shaped blade, a derivation of the shovel needed to dig herbs. On the other end was a crescent-shaped blade. Both ends had steel rings hanging from the shaft that made a ringing noise during a fight. The sturdy teakwood shaft had been broken and splintered by a powerful force.

Saihung asked the coroner to leave them in privacy for a few moments and turned to Wuyung.

"What did your informer tell you, and how does this relate to Butterfly?"

Wuyung picked up a hurricane lamp and rested it on the coffin's rim. It threw an acrid yellow light on the corpse.

"This is the story," he began. "Two days ago, this monk came to Beijing with a goal very much like ours. He wanted to stop Butterfly and his mistress from committing more crimes. You know the rule of the martial world: Good and evil men must struggle against one another.

"His strategy was to draw the Tigress out through her brother. He knew from underworld informers that the boy usually left the mansion at a regular time. The monk met him and barred his way. He threw two lead balls into the ground with such force and weight that they sunk deep into the dirt. The monk jumped onto the two spheres and issued a challenge: If the boy could push him off, the monk would teach him his art. Naturally, the boy charged. Confident of his own skill and, like all martial artists, obsessed with the urge to learn more, he attacked carelessly. The monk slapped him over the heart. The boy spit up blood and fled.

"He showed his wound to his sister, who recognized the imprint of an iron palm master. Only one who had trained his hands by a thousand blows to a hard target and soaking in special herbs could have hurt her brother so. She went immediately to avenge him. The monk was waiting. He fought her barehanded at first; but, surprised at her strength and ability, had to resort to his weapon. Even then, the witnesses say, she succeeded in depriving this veteran boxer of his moon spade. In her fury, she snapped the shaft and returned the same blow that had wounded her brother. The monk's years of training were insufficient. She came at him and her deadly fingers broke the slender thread of his life."

Saihung looked at the stiff body. The wounds and bloated areas were as clear as words. They were a distinct warning of a fighter who deserved her name.

"Let's go," he said. "Butterfly may already know we've arrived in Beijing. We'll attack her mansion this afternoon."

The two monks agreed. They gave the coroner some "tea money," and began their walk across town to the northwestern quarter.

"It's such bad luck to visit a mortuary on the day of a duel," muttered Wuyung.

Wuquan cursed his brother's superstition. "Who cares about such ideas? Now the stench—that was real."

"It makes this city smell good by comparison," said Saihung.

Wuyung took a deep breath. The smell of coal smoke— that harsh odor like burning oil and pig grease—was heavy in the air. He coughed.

"Hell," he complained. "It's not that different."

The three companions walked through one of the oldest sections of Beijing. The swaybacked grey buildings and crumbling walls formed twisting narrow lanes—simple, almost accidental corridors left over after building. Although Beijing had at one time been carefully laid out by geomancers on a precise grid, entropy and the chaos of individualism had long ago taken over. It was thus all the more a contrast when they turned a corner to see a long, unbroken expanse of immaculate grey brick. The wall surrounding the Tigress's estate was over thirty feet high and topped by green glazed tile. The gate was flanked by red pillars and the vermillion doors were of timber heavy enough to withstand a tank. Smooth grey, red, and green were all they could see. There was no simple opening, no easy way in. None of the three had Butterfly's jumping skill. They had to use a rope to scale the wall.

Saihung was impressed by the beauty of the gardens within the outwardly grim enclosure. A piece of paradise in the most colorful splendor had been neatly inlaid into the monochromatic dreariness of the aged city. The beauty of the gardens and home had the air of long cultivation. Such refined taste and careful balance of architecture and landscape came only over many years. The Tigress's father must have hidden this jewel from the emperor. Had the ruler known, he would have killed his knight out of jealousy.

A manmade pond fronted the house and a long stream appeared to wind to the west and back of the home. The water was a muddy green, but its opaque surface mirrored the many weeping willows that grew at the banks. The shores were no simple mud; instead, they were lined in an irregular arrangement of the most eccentrically weathered stone available. As if the famous Stone Forest of Yunnan province had been reduced and unwound to form an idiosyncratic bulwark, the rockery portrayed a fairy-tale mountain range rising from the four seas.

It was a garden meant for contemplation, contrived to surround the viewer in nature. The gardeners, with so much space, had not resorted to the foreshortening illusions of smaller literati gardens. They had built a long, covered walkway through the garden. The odd angles of each section had no apparent measure or symmetry. They were placed with a consideration solely for the special vantage points afforded to the stroller. The green roof tile and the red pillars did not seem intrusive to the natural beauty. Rather, they accented the rarified wonder so carefully created. The sunlight through the poplar, pine, and cedar was scattered into a thousand spots of white light; the lotus on the pond flamed into magenta spikes; the chrysanthemum nodded in yellow, purple, and rust accents. More than well-placed trees, more than the chiarascuro of the rockery's shadow play, more than the languid sheen of the still pond, the whole garden shimmered with an ethereal grace and breathed with an other-worldly serenity.

They crept to the brick mansion, a massive two-story arrangement of traditional latticework, sturdy pillars, and upturned tile roof corners. A neat row of glazed pottery planted with cactus stood at the edge of the stone portico. The doors were lacquered red and inlaid with mother-of-pearl that marvelously recalled marine colors.

Saihung withdrew from the splendor of his surroundings and took his outer gown off to reveal a tighter shirt. His body was tied with a rope that had a blade on one end. Saihung looked at his companions, a signal to draw their swords. The naked blades, so straight and sharp in a heaven where smooth and round were the main characteristics, seemed gratingly bright. The Tang scholar Li Quan was right, thought Saihung, "Weapons are tools of ill omen." A sword begged to be used.

He faced the door again. They had to announce their entrance somehow. He kicked it in crudely and it fell with a loud crash. The lacquer chipped and burst from the impact.

Saihung and his companions walked into the room and looked around. They saw a classically symmetrical main reception hall. There were two rows of ornately carved and silk cushioned ebony chairs with tea tables in between, and an extravagantly large silk rug in a pattern of flowers and symbols for longevity. The walls were lined with precious scrolls and ceramics. At the head of the hall was an enormous horizontal scroll of bright red peonies, and a pair of chairs faced the doors. The room light was dim and there was a faint musty trace in the air. The monks heard a frantic running sound and a woman's voice ordering servants away.

Three people soon emerged from two doors on either side of the far end. The first was clearly the Tigress. She was of medium height and walked gracefully. Dressed in gold and blue silk tunic and pants, her shapely figure was lean and athletic. Her feet were strong and unbound. Her skin was smooth and white, like translucent jade. Her eyes were large, dark-lashed, and came to thin trailing points at the outer corners. Her features were delicate and thinly drawn. For a moment, Saihung nearly forgot his reason for being there and his rude entrance. As he savored the gentle perfume, he reflected that he, too, might forsake mountain life had a woman like the Tigress ever tempted him.

Behind her was her brother. A slender teenager with shaven head and inquisitive eyes, he seemed untroubled by his recent wound. Dressed in red silk, he was carefully tucking up the hem of his gown into the black sash to allow for quick footwork and kicks. He carried a spear about his own height, and its red tassel tossed as he leveled the point at them. He smirked, showing teeth that were even and white.

Sister and brother advanced to the center of the room, but

the third person lingered close to the door. It was Butterfly. Instead of the swaggering, self-confident Butterfly Saihung knew, his elder brother seemed reticent, his glance at them almost fatalistic.

"We've come for you, Butterfly!" Saihung shouted across the room.

Butterfly looked up, and then away.

"Master wants you. You've gone beyond what he can tolerate. Come with us now!"

"This is my house," said the Tigress. "You are in no position to give orders."

The Tigress of Beijing.

"Stay out of this, or I won't be polite," replied Saihung hotly. He looked at Butterfly, who took a step back.

"Attack!" shouted Saihung as he charged forward.

The Tigress met his onslaught with ease and Saihung found himself in an unfavorable position. Her skill was greater than his. It wasn't simply a matter of strength. Instinctively, he sensed the overwhelming superiority of his weight and brawn; but she was exasperatingly elusive and quick. She dodged his strikes and did not even bother to block. When she counterattacked, Saihung had to retreat desperately. Striking with her fingertips made her reach longer. She was a lethal opponent.

Saihung leapt to one side and dashed for Butterfly, who retreated calmly. The Tigress leapt at Saihung. He sidestepped and she drove him back, finally connecting with a devastating kick to his chest. There was a flash of metal and both opponents paused momentarily in surprise. She had a blade in the toe of her boot, he was wearing a steel breastplate.

"You cowardly monk," she said in disgust.

Saihung only grinned sheepishly. He wasn't one to take chances. In that brief moment he tugged at the slip knot and whirled around. The rope dart uncoiled and he flung it at her. She was too good a boxer to be picked off, but he at least hoped to keep her off balance.

The rope dart had a whistle on it, and it whined at a high pitch. The rope had to be kept taut and brought back after each strike. As it returned, Saihung could wrap it around different parts of his wrist, elbows, or legs, and then send it flying out at some unpredictable angle. He could also whirl it in all sorts of arcs to cut horizontally. The Tigress was completely unimpressed and pressed her attack. Fifteen feet of rope and a razor-sharp blade were all that kept her at bay. He hoped that Wuyung and Wuquan were doing better.

The two sentry monks were a good two feet taller than their opponent, and each probably outweighed the youth by fifty pounds. But the boy made up for these disadvantages with nimble speed and the long reach of his spear.

Two swordsmen were an easy thing for him, and their devious spinning movements and precise thrusts were countered by a special feature of his weapon. The shaft of his spear was cut from a certain kind of tough vine that retained its flexibility due to lengthy soaking in special oils. If he hit one of the monks along the length of the spear, the shaft would still whip around and embed the blade into the body. At the same time, the spear could still be used to butt, parry, cut, thrust, and smash in all the same ways as a staff. Saihung saw that the teenager was a master of fighting.

The Tigress charged Saihung. He fought back ferociously and hurled the dart straight at her. She sidestepped quickly, but he still cut her shoulder slightly. He stepped forward as the dart came whistling back. The rope flexed powerfully in his palms, he felt the burn of its rapidly shooting fibers on his fingers. He had to keep it moving, yet redirect it. One loop, then another, a rapid spin to gain momentum as he turned his back to her. Just as she came within range, he hit her with a backward tiger tail kick and sent the dart shrieking madly out. It struck the boy so hard that its five-inch blade sunk from sight. Saihung leapt forward and mercilessly threw a loop around his neck. Without hesitation, the two brothers thrust their blades in for the kill.

The Tigress was wild with grief and anger and threw herself at them with her full fury. She had no reservation now, no careful strategy, no graceful moves. A treacherous and magnificent force emerged from her and she struck Saihung with a blow as powerful as any he had felt from a man. He twisted quickly to reduce the force, but was still thrown off balance. He stumbled back as she came with a finger strike aimed at his throat. He caught a glimpse of her glaring eyes, red with hatred and tears. He heard the quiet hiss of her exhalation as the full force of her internal energy was directed with pinpoint accuracy.

But before he could feel her sting, in a blurred flash he saw Wuquan sever her hand. The deadly hiss became a cry of agony as her precious weapon dropped to the floor and her hot blood burst from the stump. She backed out of range with a look so violent that the three monks paused.

She controlled her breathing with great effort and stood up. She saw her dead brother. A look around the room told her that her lover had abandoned her. Even worse, she had lost her hand. She was insulted, dishonored in a way no other form of degradation could have done. Her fingers were famous, her fighting ability was her pride. Now she had lost everything. If nothing else, a martial hero or heroine never compromised pride. The game was played out. She made the only move she could.

The Tigress, who could kill with a straight finger, could harness her full energy and had mastered the ability to direct *qi* and blood instantly to any part of her body. Now she raised it all to her tongue—the junction of the *Du* and *Jen* meridians. As her whole life force rose to this single point, she bit down on her tongue with a ferocious finality. Her throat welled with blood and her spirit burst through her self-inflicted wound. Saihung watched her body swing around and fall like an animal brought down by a hunter. Her last dance spiraled the beautiful Tigress to earth in a fountain of crimson drops.

Saihung unwrapped his rope from the boy. The body was heavy, animated not by life but by gravity. Saihung coiled the stained rope up—he'd have to get it replaced—and carefully cleaned the blade. A raw odor filled the room, a pungent counterpoint to the lingering perfume. Saihung walked to the door and found an oil lamp. In a second the burning fluid soaked into the carpet, and the broken bodies turned orange on a lawn of flame.

In the following days, Saihung, Wuyung, and Wuquan pursued Butterfly by inquiring into the great network of underworld spies. Saihung remembered a passage from the *Art of War*, a treatise on military strategy by Sun Tzu: "The achievements of wise generals surpass ordinary men because of foreknowledge. Foreknowledge cannot be obtained from spirits, gods, analogy with past events, nor from calculations. It must be obtained from men who know the enemy situation." These spies formed what Sun Tzu called a "Divine Skein." If someone knew how to pull the cord, the threads of the net could be activated.

They lost precious time chasing down untrue rumors and false leads. After five days of searching both cities and countryside, they came to a village called Dahong in Hubei province. There, in a seedy wine shop, they found an informer—a small-time racketeer and thief. After a generous payment, he told them what they needed to know.

"Your classmate is in the company of the Hubei Three Tigers. The first is a master of the Eight Trigrams Palm named Li. His teacher was a Zen monk and his lineage is descended from Yin Fu, the master who protected the Empress Dowager when she fled Beijing in 1900. The second is named Wang. He is a disciple of the famous Sun Lutong and is a master of Form and Mind Boxing and the Six Harmonies Sword. The third is called the Flying Cat. A small man, he is nevertheless quite formidable, having been thoroughly taught by one of the last Qing dynasty knights, the Divine Flying Leopard. These men are all in their fifties and thus in the prime of their abilities. You're all too young to beat them."

"Nevertheless," replied Wuquan, "please tell us how we can find them."

The thief considered a moment and then laughed. "Fine, fine. This way, I'll know where to send coffins for you."

They left the still smirking crook and made their plans. This was now solidly an affair of *Wulin*. As such, the only avenue was a personal challenge—and only one person could challenge the three. For all of them to gang up on each of the Three Tigers would be dishonorable. Saihung volunteered, and sent out letters of challenge immediately.

The weather grew hotter. Saihung became temperamental and impatient to catch Butterfly. In two days he met both Li and Wang and had beaten them both. He beat Li's graceful and elusive Eight Trigrams style with the savage grappling and merciless falls of Mongolian wrestling. A fifty-year-old man simply couldn't endure too many throws to the hard ground. Ironically, Saihung used Li's very own style against Wang. The twisting movements and circular strikes were the perfect counter to the straight, crushing advance of Form and Mind Boxing. In neither instance did he kill his opponents. This was a case of martial honor. They had sheltered Butterfly only out of friendship.

Saihung clarified the misunderstanding after Wang conceded. Only then did the two masters realize the trouble Butterfly was in. They told Saihung to hurry southward. The Flying Cat was escorting Butterfly to the Yangzi river.

The three companions hurried to the train station but missed the train, an event that Wuyung immediately took as a bad omen. It was four hours to the next. They could do nothing but wait and catch the next Nanjing-bound train. It was twenty-four hours before they arrived on the north shore of the Yangzi river. There was no bridge across the impossibly wide gulf, and it would take hours to ferry the train across. The three of them rushed to the banks and hired a small boat to take them across.

The Nanjing piers were swarming with people trying to get onto the makeshift wooden junks, steamers, and freighters. Crates were piled everywhere, as were baskets of produce and cages of ducks and geese. The docks stank with gasoline, oil, garbage, and sweat.

Even at that early morning hour the weather was sweltering. Saihung dragged his sleeve across his forehead and the sweat soaked through. As he squinted against the sun, he was startled to see Butterfly, a dazzling figure on the drab docks dressed in a suit of rich sky-blue silk. Beneath his tunic was a pristine white shirt, open to the chest. He was smiling and walking at a leisurely pace. Beside him was a man in black.

Saihung pushed his way rudely through the crowd and the immediate squawking that his rush provoked alerted the Flying Cat. As Saihung pushed the last bystander aside, a shrieking whistle came flying at him. The Flying Cat, master of the rope dart, had made Saihung the target of his weapon.

The screaming crowd backed off immediately, but they did not scatter too far. They paused halfway between fear and curiosity. Saihung and the Flying Cat squared off in this human arena. The Flying Cat circled him warily. He was a thin, short man. His face was shaped like an olive pit, the skin was brown and leathery. His jet-black hair was thickly pomaded and his eyes sharp and narrow.

The rope dart came bitingly, but Saihung produced his weapon, a steel fan. He snapped it open to shield him and launched his counterattack. He quickly closed the distance, but to his astonishment the Flying Cat not only dodged his punches but jumped with terrific gymnastic skill over Saihung's head. He kicked Saihung in midair and then renewed his efforts with the rope dart.

Saihung fell to the wooden planks and felt several searing slivers penetrate his palm. He jumped up angrily in time to deflect the rope. The Flying Cat did nothing to retrieve the dart all the way. He could jump after it, loop it in midair and send it dive-bombing down. The next time he jumped, Saihung cocked the fan back and with a snap brought it open before him. As he did so, he pressed a secret button on the fan's outer rib. Thirteen slender needles propelled by Saihung's rapid wrist movement and a spring-loaded chamber hit the Flying Cat in the leg.

Wuyung and Wuquan joined in. It was too crowded to draw their swords, so they fought barehanded. Though wounded, the Flying Cat fought bravely on, but his opponents soon left him unconscious on the pier.

Saihung pushed through the crowd and ran to the end of the pier. A boat was already pulling away with Butterfly on the deck.

"You know why I'm after you!" shouted Saihung furiously. "Neither heaven nor earth can hide you! I'll get you! I swear I'll get you!"

He was surprised to see Butterfly's impassive look. His elder brother seemed distracted and tentative. Saihung watched the boat drift away and strained to hear any reply. Nothing came. Damn! Why was it that no one in his life talked when it mattered?

The broken-down steamer they took in pursuit was crowded, and Saihung chose to stand at the railing to watch the water. The Yangzi coursed powerfully in its channel. This body of water was too large to be given a ridiculous label like "river." It was an ocean—deep, treacherous, wide, and mighty. All sorts of garbage thrown from boats floated on its opaque, mud-colored surface. As the boat slowly pulled away from shore, the brown expanse became greater and greater. There was a feeling of freedom. Adrift in the smooth expanse of water, great adventure seemed possible.

Saihung watched water curl away from the sides of the boat. The white foam barely frothed. The world took on a very simple composition. Three horizontal bands comprised everything: blue sky, verdant fields, brown water. He watched the green band flow steadily by. Sometimes it was a gentle beach-like bank; at other times it was an eroding wall of loose earth, with little chunks tumbling to the water. Occasionally, a rock formation stood in weathered defiance to the undercutting currents. They passed fields and some mud-brick homes. Towns were mere aberrations to the impassive bands of blue, green, and brown.

Another steamer passed them going upstream. It was crammed with refugees fleeing the occupied zones. Saihung stared at them. They were rough, desperate, and afraid. A surprising number of people were going downstream to look for relatives or to find work. "A job is rare these days," he overheard a man say. "Even if it's in the occupied area, it's better than starving."

There was a flurry of excitement on board as a corpse floated past them. It was surprising how fast it moved. Before long, another one came. The water flowed so quickly, but the figures were still.

"Did you see that?" asked Wuyung excitedly. "A bad omen!"

"Yes," said Saihung. "Was that last one a man or woman?"

"Do you know how to tell?" asked Wuquan. "If it's floating face down it's usually a man. Face up it's usually a woman."

"How did you collect this strange fact?" asked Saihung.

"Somewhere in my travels," said Wuquan casually. "A woman's hips are heavier, so her bottom pulls her down and her face floats up. But a man is more topheavy, with a heavier head. He'll float face down."

Soon another corpse floated by, and they tried to test Wuquan's theory. Unfortunately, this one's head was half-shot away.

Saihung pushed his way through the noisy crowd toward the bow of the boat. There, braving the occasional spray of mist, he continued to stare downstream at the great watery brown triangle of the river. The waves were hypnotic. Somewhere in his lessons his master had told him that water was a special element for him, advising him to gaze at its surface to bring calmness and introspection.

He had killed in Beijing. Who knew how many he had killed in his life? He had been born into a warrior's family, the art of killing was his heritage. He had fought often in his youth to defend his home from bandits, he had duelled in martial challenges, and he had fought as a guerilla soldier. Besides, just as Saihung and all martial artists understood, so the Tigress and her brother would have understood the ultimate price of fighting. But their death nevertheless struck him as tragedy and waste.

He had killed Butterfly's lover. That seemed to make this time different. Now he felt like a destroyer, not a hero. He was a fighter who mowed down those who opposed the fulfillment of his quest. No longer was he an idealistic monk. Instead, he was a man who had been challenged to complete a mission, and he suddenly saw that there was another morality to challenge.

The ethics of challenge were success, and challenge was the heart and soul of the code of chivalry to which he was bound. But hidden within *yiqi* was the sorrow of sacrificing all other principles. Throughout time, men had lived by the quest, but the bards never told the real reason that boys became men: It was by sacrificing nicety and elegant ideals that they finally understood the irony of ethics and reality. As a martial artist, a modern knight, Saihung knew that he liked challenges. There was something about the conflict between principle and circumstance that he craved. But each time he took on a challenge, he had to learn anew the same lesson of sacrifice and compromise. Standing at the boat railing, he accepted again that he had killed, accepted again that his soul would suffer for it, accepted again that he would pay a great price to catch his brother. He felt a feeling of finality as he turned to the boat's side. This was what it was like to be a champion of a chivalrous cause.

He watched the brown water flowing effortlessly by him. He was still too emotional, he thought. Saihung thought back some ten years to a question he had asked the Grand Master as he was trying to understand the concept of *wu wei*.

"What does *wu wei* mean?" he had asked.

"It means," his master had replied, "that everything you do seems spontaneous, natural, and complete. Nothing affects you. Nothing stirs up the emotions to interrupt the precious tranquiliity that you have constantly cultivated."

"Nothing affects you?"

"Nothing."

"What if you were meditating and someone tries to kill you?" asked Saihung.

"If they come to kill me, fine. I shall kill them first."

"And then?"

"And then I sit back down to meditate."

"That's all?"

"Yes."

"Wouldn't you suffer for killing another?"

"Not in this case. They came to kill me. I merely interrupted them."

"Wouldn't you suffer within?"

"No. That's *wu wei*. One event happens, then another. If you are truly *wu wei* then you are always placid."

Saihung had been puzzled. The Grand Master had finally clarified the point in this way: "*Wu* means no. *Wei* can mean for or to. But it also can mean result—or, shall we say, consequences. *Wu wei* means your actions have no consequences either metaphysically, or within yourself."

"Or within yourself . . ." Saihung repeated softly as he leaned pensively on the rocking boat's rail. His meditative tranquility was so distant now. He knew it on the mountain, but here in the midst of his quest it was hidden by a curtain of feeling.

Another corpse floated by. A woman this time. The Yangzi river seemed full with them, and he had a sudden image of being in a procession of the dead. The dead go to hell, he thought. He and the corpses were all going to the same place at the long river's mouth: Shanghai.

SEVEN

Shanghai

Was this hell? Saihung asked himself on the docks of Shanghai. What he saw was so alien, so astonishing, it might as well have been. As he made his way down the swaybacked gangplank, through the shouting, spitting, stinking throng of people, he saw the Shanghai skyline. A veritable mile-long rampart of sky-scraping steel and concrete buildings stood along the famous Bund. They were taller than anything he had seen, except mountains, and with their straight lines, precise rectangular windows, echoes of Greco-Roman architecture, and imposing grey columns and walls, they were stranger than anything he had known. They made the sky jagged with their boasting of the European presence.

It might have been a pretty spot once, he reflected. The sky was a pale blue with high floating clouds, and ocean breezes swept over the flat, open, delta land. Two rivers flowed through Shanghai, the Huangpu and Suzhou creek, with the Yangzi a bit to the north. The richest agricultural lands lay to the west of Shanghai for miles; though they were marred by warfare, they provided fresh produce and bits of green beauty. With the clear light that fell on this city, whose name simply meant "By-the-Sea," Shanghai might indeed have been lovely. But instead, with its clock towers, hotels, and office buildings, Saihung saw it as ugly. With its docks of smelly fish and sweating laborers, it was repulsive. With its noise—motors, honking, screaming—it was no haven. Now he was a part of it, among those rock-like buildings, absorbed in a wash of humanity.

As he stepped onto the dock, he and his two companions
became like small children in a parade. The crush of people
was maddening. Walking was almost as futile as prying
open a hydraulic press. Even by elbowing his way through
the crowd, Saihung could only make slow progress. By the
time he made his way to a street corner, his senses had been
overcome by smell and noise. Where was that fresh air he
had breathed on the river? Now he only smelled an odor like
burning oil. He looked at the streets—a mad race of ped-
icabs, those rickety contraptions pulled by bronzed men
who grew old with their hands on the wooden poles. But
Saihung was almost killed by a few of the other vehicles:
cars. It was they, he discovered, who smelled like burning
oil. Terrifyingly roaring, smoke spitting, gleaming metallic
carriages, ominously black, they sped their well-dressed
occupants carelessly through the crowded boulevards.

Saihung, Wuyung, and Wuquan were bombarded with the
sensory images of the city: massive doorways of colonial
power. Barred windows of the Hong Kong and Shanghai
bank. A Russian woman stepping immodestly from a Rolls
Royce. Prosperous shipping brokers in teahouses. A corpse
stiff in the gutter. Old wizened hawkers selling candy
apples. An Asian banker dressed in top hat and morning
coat. A sniffling heroin addict. Drunken sailors. As Saihung
pushed his way up the urban riot that was Nanjing road,
these impressions multiplied exponentially as he walked
each block.

He could see gangsters on almost every corner—young,
arrogant, and coarse men who would molest anyone they
pleased. Dressed in bright colors, they had their tunics
unbuttoned immodestly to reveal opened undertunics.
Where normal people had their sleeves rolled down, theirs
were rolled up. They affected bits of Western clothing with
their traditional Chinese suits. Pork-pie hats, apple hats,

dark glasses, wide leather belts, and leather shoes were all considered very fashionable. But beneath their clothing were the traditional tools of thuggery: Knives, brass knuckles, blackjacks, and pistols. The population was saturated by mobsters.

Saihung took great interest in these hoodlums. It would only be through the underworld that he could do anything in Shanghai. In fact, nothing was possible without approval from the gangsters. They dominated the city, controlled its banks, government, and police, and preserved themselves between the cracks of the European settlements and the disintegrating wartime society. The millions of dollars that went through the city in a flow mightier than the Yangzi was almost completely tainted by the underworld. Whether it was industry, shipping, opium, heroin, or slavery, the gangsters controlled it.

No one in Shanghai escaped contact with the Red and Blue gangs and the foremost mob of them all, the Green Circle Gang. Famous people like T. A. Soong, H. H. Kung, the Soong Sisters, Sun Yatsen, Mao Zedong, and Zhou Enlai had all been involved in one way or another, and it was said that Chiang Kaishek remained in power precisely because of the money, intrigues, and strong-arm tactics of the godfather of Shanghai, Du Yueshen. It was he who represented the city at its highest sophistication and deepest debauchery.

From the hotels they could hear music, laughter. They could smell savory food: baking bread, roast ham. Once in a while there were sweet traces of opium smoke along with breezes from the sea, and the more pungent odors of the streets. The foreigners even smelled different, Wuyung told Saihung, though they never came close enough to tell. They were supposed to smell of flowers and spice, leather and wood.

In fact, this was one of the few times Saihung had had the

opportunity to see foreigners. It was true he had seen some during large receptions at his family's palatial home, but only a few. Now here was a whole city full of them, and he shivered to recall all the frightening rumors. Did they have tails? Did they have hair all over their bodies? Did they eat their young? Did they really believe they were descended from apes? They were bewildering creatures that no amount of spiritual insight could explain. It was only through Wu-quan's explanations in their flophouse accommodations that Saihung understood more of the foreigners' history in Shanghai, but the people themselves continued to perplex him.

Over the course of many decades, Wuquan told him, the foreigners had carved the city into the famous foreign concessions. The British had occupied the choicest land at the tip of the Bund, while the French took the area between them and the old walled city to the south. Across Suzhou creek in the northern district was the American concession; but, unable to administer their territory with any of the wicked grandeur of the English, they had merged with the British to form the International Settlement.

The settlement had a Municipal Council composed of *tai-pans* and other power brokers, and the French had a parallel governing body. Both had their own police forces, but these were purely tools of colonial mentality. The arrangement actually was a boon to crime. A few miles could put one easily into a different jurisdiction, and gangsters exploited this continually. The police found it more profitable, literally and figuratively, to cooperate with the criminals who dominated Shanghai.

The grandeur of the foreigners had tarnished when the Japanese invaded the city in 1937 and herded the majority of Westerners into the ugly high-rise called the Shanghai Mansions. Once Japanese had settled themselves, they had been compromised by the beguiling corruption and wickedness of the city, and the era of colonialism had begun to molder slightly around the edges. The city now belonged to politicians, assassins, spies, militarists, gangsters, and moneymen.

Japanese soldiers were still a dangerous presence—bullying, carousing, raping, looting—and the monks would have to be careful. But more important still was to avoid the uncanny power of Shanghai to make all who came follow her ways.

Drugs and sex were the foundations of the city's society. Although passion, politics, trade, and at rare times even love played their parts in these two great endeavors, the true medium was money. One could buy any grade of opium, morphine, or heroin to soothe the pains of life and the pangs of a long-acquired addiction. In the opium dens and brothels a man could have "flower and fume," a woman and a smoke. One could buy any sort of woman in Shanghai, from the high-class courtesans or geishas in expensive salons, down the scale to street-walkers who could be cheaply had standing against any alley wall. Nor did the homosexuals feel slighted: Young boys were equally available in number and variety. Anything one wanted could be bought, for all these activities were well organized and run by the gangs.

Over the next few days Saihung and his companions made contact with the streetcorner hoodlums. Bribing and cajoling their way through the criminal hierarchy, chasing down leads in the opera houses, entertaining at teahouses, and fighting to prove their ability, they finally wrangled an audience with the Grey Swan, one of the kingpins of Shanghai's underworld. But Grey Swan was a careful woman fearful of assassination, and she would only see one person. Saihung insisted that he be that one person.

The day of his appointment was sunny but muggy. As he

walked through the French concession Saihung's clothes stuck to his skin, the sweat trickled down the nape of his neck. He clung to the shade afforded by trees planted along the street. The air was hard to breathe. It was almost liquid. The villas were walled and stuccoed with a grey mixture. Behind them he could see wood and brick mansions that were so large they would someday be used for schools and offices. Their style was alien to Saihung. He had not yet been to Paris, London, or Berlin, where these homes would not have appeared so strange.

They came to a heavily guarded walled compound. The men at the steel gates all had holstered pistols. They carefully searched Saihung for weapons and then escorted him down a curved driveway to a squat and ugly brick building. The facade had been built only with a consideration of sturdiness and ostentation. Fake stone columns framed the door of heavy oak. As he stepped into the carpeted front hallway, Saihung noticed a disagreeable odor, like camphor mixed with mold.

Six men accompanied him to the living room, which was decorated in the finest Chinese style. Saihung was surprised. He knew many gangsters affected a show of art and culture after they had established themselves, but their taste usually ran to gaudy and big. Here, however, the porcelain, jade, and scrolls were of museum quality. They were fragile and ephemeral bits of beauty next to the rough men who stood all around the room.

"The Grey Swan!" announced a bodyguard.

There at the head of the cream-colored room full of art and murderers sat a slender woman. Her hair was perfectly coiffed, a fragrant sable-colored cloud pinned with silver, gold, and jade. Her face was a well-formed oval with high cheekbones, arching brow, and thin lips. She wore heavy makeup, giving the impression of a woman slightly past her prime. Her shoulders were a bit wide, but her breasts were well-rounded and full. Her legs, showing at a slit in her tight brocade dress, were long and smooth. She had an affected habit of playing with a dangling earring.

"Ai! What a handsome boy you are!" exclaimed the Grey Swan.

Saihung blushed.

"Just looking at you makes my legs go weak! What a fine body! Ohh! My mouth just waters!"

She turned to a bodyguard with the proportions of a Frankenstein.

"I like him," she smiled. "His skin is so soft, not like you ruffians!"

The bodyguard grinned. Saihung noticed quite a few missing teeth.

"Tell me, have you come to play with me?" she asked insinuatingly.

"I'm sorry, but no," stammered Saihung. "I'm seeking a classmate who is part of the Green Circle Gang."

"What a formal fellow you are!" she pouted. "That's the trouble with men. They always want to get right down to business! Of course I know why you're here. If you want this man so badly, we can tell you where he is. But what will you give me in return?"

"What do you want?"

"A night alone with you would be ecstasy!" said the Grey Swan. "I can just imagine how it would be. Give me one night of pleasure and I'll give you your classmate."

Saihung could feel the veins on both sides of his neck throb in nervousness.

"I'm sorry, but I am a renunciate. I have my vows," he said. "I'm a Taoist."

"So? Why not be a gigolo for the Tao?" she smiled coyly.

"This is out of the question!"

The Grey Swan laughed. "It's so refreshing to see such an upstanding youth. You bullies take a good look. There was never anyone in Shanghai like him."

The bodyguards all laughed sarcastically.

Saihung spoke first. "You don't have my classmate so it wouldn't be an even deal anyway."

"True," she said, her eyes narrowing. "You're shrewd as well as handsome."

"I can see I'm wasting my time. Permit me to take my leave."

"You couldn't leave unless I said so," cooed the Grey Swan. "But actually someone else has an interest in your case. I'm supposed to introduce you."

"Who is it?"

"Mr. Du Yueshen."

Saihung paused. Du was famous. He was the king of the Shanghai underworld. It was not necessarily a good thing for him to be interested, yet Saihung knew that nothing significant happened in Shanghai without his knowledge.

"What do you want from me to see him?"

"You and I are both members of the martial world. I'll chalk it up to chivalry."

"Is that all?"

"Yes. Don't assume that truth lies only in greed."

"That seems to be the rule in Shanghai!"

"Yes, yes," laughed the Grey Swan. "But we'll just say I had too much to smoke today."

Saihung cursed her silently. He knew Du had probably given precise instructions.

"You may go," she said. "You meet Mr. Du tomorrow. They'll take you there."

Saihung agreed and turned to leave.

"Good luck!" called a man's voice.

Saihung spun around. It was inconceivable that a bodyguard would dare to talk. He looked back to see the Grey Swan's laughing face. He was shocked. It was a man's laugh. The Grey Swan was a transvestite.

"I said good luck," he repeated. "Ohhh, what fun it would have been to take you to bed!"

Blindfolded, Saihung, Wuyung, and Wuquan were taken by limousine to a three-storied mansion with balconies. It was built of concrete and stucco and the window frames and balustrades were painted a venetian red. In the narrow front courtyard were parked several more limousines. Saihung glanced around. The walls were about twelve feet high. The gate was bar steel covered with heavy plate. In a corner was a small, wilting garden with an incongruous Chinese gazebo painted red and green. Beyond the walls were more French-styled buildings.

They walked up some steps to the main portico. The front was lined with potted plants, succulents, cacti, and palms. The whole front entryway was a grid of varnished oak and bevelled glass plate. Inside, the interior was dark with walls of stained mahogany, hardwood floors, and a deep carmine carpet. The ubiquitous bodyguards were dressed in dark colors, standing like suits of armor in a haunted house. Unlike the street-corner pimps, thieves, and playboys, these men were grizzled and stoic professionals. The bulges in their clothes signaled both muscle and guns.

A bodyguard opened a sliding set of double oak doors to reveal more men stationed around the perimeter of the big room. It was furnished with large, overstuffed Western sofas and chairs, all with the same shabby brown slipcovers. Photographs and a few murky oil paintings decorated the wall, and a mirror in a rococo gilded frame hung above the cold black fireplace. A few potted palms stretched for light at the windows, but the heavy drapes were all half-drawn. An electric crystal chandelier dangled from the high ceiling. Next to a green lamp at the far end of the room sat Du Yueshen.*

He signaled them to come closer. Saihung examined him. Du Yueshen had a rectangular face. His hair, closely cropped in a crew cut, had receded slightly into a half-circle around his face. The forehead was high but the brows jutted out and the eyebrows were thick, dark and arched in the middle. His eyes glittered with an instinctive ruthlessness. The nose was a straight wedge that flared out into large nostrils, and his mouth was wide, with sensuous lips. His ears stuck out and had earned him the hated nick-name "Big Eared Du." The skin was tight, the flesh hard from years of opium smoking. Most compared his face to that of an ape.

His shoulders had once been heavier, but now they had thinned. There was no young muscle beneath the high-collared gown, only a tough, sinewy, and hardened body. Du Yueshen was forty-five years old then and he was experienced, accomplished, and could still claim to be at the height of his power. Whether it was in Hong Kong, Chongqing, or Shanghai, he controlled everything from the loading of opium in the harbor to the secret society machinations that maintained Chiang Kaishek in power.

In his expressionless face, it was difficult to realize Du's vast history. He had been born in Pudong, across the Huangpu River, and had begun as a small-time drug-runner and pimp in the heyday of Shanghai's lush world of pleasure and corruption. He became the protegé of Huang Jinrong and soon rose in the ranks of the Green Circle Gang. He had

* Most Western sources and scholars believe that Du Yueshen left Shanghai in 1938 with the first invasion of the Japanese. However, Kwan Saihung distinctly remembers having met Du in mid-1941; in addition, two other residents of Shanghai, both daughters of prominent bankers, agree that Du was in Shanghai until he fled to Chongqing around the autumn of 1941.

Du in his mid-forties.

helped to centralize the opium traffic and all criminal activities, making pacts with other gangs or eliminating them outright. By 1927, his power supported Chiang Kaishek's takeover of the Chinese government. Du was a dedicated anti-Communist. It was he who masterminded the infamous 1927 massacre, where his men killed five thousand Communists (some say as many as ten thousand) in the streets of Shanghai. It took hours to kill. It took days to cart away all the bodies.

At the same time, he became a leading figure in the respectable banking circles. This was not necessarily an anomaly in those days, since corruption and the abuse of wealth and power was the standard in Shanghai's money circles. He dressed in fine silks, tuxedos, and top hats, and was chaufeurred in expensive two-tone limousines with bodyguards riding on the runningboards. He was the head of the Shanghai Civic Association, a director of the Bank of China, sat on the Currency Reserve Board, founded a school for boys and established a fraternal organization called the Constancy Society.

Du was an ardent Nationalist and hated the Japanese, although this hardly stopped parts of his sprawling gang from cooperating in the drug trade with the occupying forces. When the Japanese invaded Shanghai in 1937, he offered to sink an entire fleet of his ships to block the harbor. Even now, parts of his gang engaged in an underground resistance against the Japanese.

Some people found it difficult to reconcile Du's many facets. Ruthless killer. Opium smuggler. Respectable banker. Shameless womanizer. Dedicated Nationalist. Drug addict. Opera afficianado. Wealthy socialite. A key to Du's personality could be found in his belief in the martial code. As a martial artist, indeed, elder and godfather of the martial world around the Yangzi River valley, he believed in *Yiqi*, a difficult concept to translate. Its connotations are justice, honor, principle, chivalry, and generosity. Du considered himself almost a knight errant, an upholder of a certain kind of justice. He felt that he treated others fairly and punished those who thwarted his code. A paladin does not question his lord, but merely destroys his challengers. Du's lord was an unholy trinity of power, opium, and money, and he was their champion.

Du's sense of justice was primitive, savage, and unalloyed. But it was this sense of honor, no matter how warped, that made him more than a gangster. Although later accounts would paint him as a cartoon villain, a man of pure evil, Du Yueshen was an infinitely more complex mixture of generosity and gangsterism, idealism and opportunism.

There was no doubt, however, that he was fearsome, and Saihung could feel the man's cruelty as he gazed at him. It was Du who spoke first.

"You are seeking a man," stated Du flatly.

"Yes," said Saihung. "In the name of the martial world, will you help me to find him?"

"Perhaps."

There was a long moment of silence. Saihung could not tell whether Du was contemplating or merely slipping into a stupor.

Everyone stood around respectfully. Du seemed shrunken. Some great men exude glory and charisma, but this was not one's immediate impression of Du Yueshen. He sat for a long time, a cadaverous, unmoving figure. When Saihung looked at his eyes, however, they were alive, shrewd. Aware.

"You are a martial artist?" His voice seemed a little stronger.

Saihung nodded.

"Show me."

Saihung tucked up the hem of his gown. He launched into one of his specialty sets, the famous Willowleaf Palm. As soon as he completed the salute, he saw Du's eyes quicken. He knew he had to impress him.

Saihung felt his muscles flex, the feet firmly forming a steady base for his whirlwind strikes. His waist twisted mightily, his shoulders propelled his quickly arcing arms. He felt a rush of joy, emotion, heat rising in him, and he proudly gave himself over to the pantomime of battle.

"Excellent! Excellent!" shouted Du as Saihung concluded the short set.

Saihung was startled. The cadaver was coming alive.

"What about you two?" Du asked Wuyung and Wuquan.

The two complied by performing a prearranged sparring set of *Xingyi*,—Form and Mind Boxing. An internal system of martial arts, it featured crushing direct strikes. There was little retreating, only sidestepping or turning. Every move was a direct and vicious attack, every reply was counterattack. Du got more excited and motioned for a water pipe. An attendant packed it with what looked like a blob of black tar and gave it to him. Du lit a match and the black opium glowed red. As he inhaled, the pipe made a gurgling sound and blue-white smoke rose up around him. The unique smell of opium—fragrant, sweet, tasty—filled the room.

By the time the brothers finished their set Du was energetic and excited. Saihung could see that he was a martial arts enthusiast, a member of the class of people whose appreciation bordered on the fetishistic and irrational.

"I salute you young heroes," he exclaimed, clasping his hands in salute. He was smiling, almost boyish. "Let me demonstrate too!"

A bodyguard brought forth two sheathed broadswords. Du Yueshen grasped their handles and drew out two gleaming blades. Saihung could hear a rasping sound, which meant that there were sharpening steels in the scabbards. Whenever a broadsword was withdrawn or returned, its blade was honed.

"Eight Trigrams Double Broadsword!" announced Du, and he proceeded to show a unique set.

The set began with the two broadswords held in parallel as they cut to each side, twisted, and cut again. They sliced vertically, horizontally, and in wide arcs. Gradually they began cutting, stabbing, and piercing in different directions, or one would block while the other attacked. At times, both would chop down at once. Du's long arms, like the wings of a big bird, gave him a reach from tip to tip of nearly eleven

Du Yueshen as a young man.
His double broadswords are behind.

feet. This made him a formidable fighter and any opponent would find it difficult to penetrate the blades that swung like propellers. Even if they could, the kicking, jumping, flying kicks, and mid-air cuts would have discouraged all but veteran opponents.

The pace of his set quickened and Saihung could see a thrilled look on Du's face. The smoke had got into him, blood flushed his face, and the pure power of the rapidly slicing blades gave him obvious pleasure. The whirling blades became a blur, cutting so quickly that they made sounds in the air like abruptly ripped bedsheets. Only occasionally did the bright flashes congeal momentarily into an expertly thrust point, a precise block, or a double scissors-like attack in tandem with almost balletic kicks. Grace, speed, and strength were wedded firmly to an absolute homocidal impulse. A faint sheen of moisture appeared on Du's skin, followed by a tight grin of satisfaction.

It was now Saihung's turn to be excited. He himself had learned the Eight Trigrams Broadsword style, but only for a single broadsword. This was a spectacular but cruel set that offered no quarter. He wished that he could learn it.

As Du finished he noticed the gleam familiar to all martial fanatics in Saihung's eyes.

"Did you like it?" he asked.

"Yes, indeed!" responded Saihung.

"Would you like to learn it?"

"Of course!" For a minute, his quest was forgotten. It was Du, ever thorough, who brought the conversation back to reality.

"You want Butterfly. I will let you seek him in my territory. But I want something in return."

"What is it?" asked Saihung.

"Huashan martial arts is famous, as you three have just demonstrated. I know there is a secret manual in five volumes, written by a man who thoroughly mastered the *Seven Bamboo Tablets of the Cloudy Satchel*. It reveals deadly martial arts techniques through the cultivation of internal energy. Get me that manual and I will let you have Butterfly."

"I will have to send for it," said Saihung hesitantly. It was a high price, and he wondered if Huashan would approve its release.

"Good. Have it for me within a week. In the meantime, you can learn this set."

The day that the books arrived in Shanghai via a special courier was grey and overcast. The clouds, dense inkstains on sleek, pale silk, threatened to dissolve not into a heroic storm but a gloomy drizzle. The air was a moist, furry presence outside the dirty windows of Saihung's cheap hotel room. He put the parcel on the square table and opened it. The cloth case was faded purple silk with ivory pins to keep the cover closed. Inside were five volumes. As Saihung opened the book, the wan light fell on yellowed pages with jet black calligraphy.

It intrigued him that Du Yueshen in Shanghai would know of these esoteric manuals in the custody of Huashan's priests. It was a measure not only of Du's position, but the rumors, legends, and information that shot through the communication networks of the martial world. Saihung began reading the manual and immediately saw that Du had not been misinformed. The book laid down profound theoretical principles for internal cultivation and then showed how the superhuman power could be projected into an opponent's body during fighting to rupture internal organs. It was clearly a tremendous risk to allow such murderous techniques to fall into the hands of a killer like Du. Saihung realized that Huashan elders were so desperate to capture Butterfly that they were willing to gamble the books.

Saihung arrived at Du's mansion by pedicab, and found Du Yueshen engaged in his regular habit of opium smoking. He seemed to be having trouble breathing—he was a lifelong asthmatic—and the rims of his eyes were red and teary. Opium was a pleasure and vice with him, but it also helped to mitigate the wheezing and shortness of breath. Without a smoke, Du was unable to call forth his martial abilities. It was for that reason that plenty of armed bodyguards accompanied him everywhere, and that he always sampled from the river of black powder that surged through his territory.

Du looked darkly at Saihung when he opened the case.

"There are only three volumes here." The man who sent a coffin and pallbearers to visit people with whom he was displeased was clearly upset.

"Surely you don't think me naive," replied Saihung boldly. "I give you three volumes in good faith. But where is my classmate? When I capture him you shall have the other two."

"I would not suggest you double-cross me," hissed Du.

"Of course not. But a deal is a deal: the books for Butterfly. I would not think that you would expect payment without the merchandise."

"All right," said Du, after scritinizing Saihung. "I will expect the last two volumes to be delivered to me when you complete your quest. Otherwise, I will forget our friendship; I will find you and burn your temple."

"I understand," said Saihung with a diplomatic smile. "Can you tell me where to find him?"

"Shandong province," revealed Du. "He is at the home of his teacher, the venerable Divine Eagle. This is all the information that these three books will buy."

"It is enough. Thank you."

"I am leaving for Chongqing tonight," continued Du. The Japanese are getting suspicious. I do not know if I will return soon or if we will meet again. But remember that the Green Circle Gang surrounds all of China. I am everywhere. Remember that I want those books."

"A deal is a deal. If I catch Butterfly in Shandong, you will have what you wish."

"Yes. I will have it," said Du in a low voice. "I will always have what I crave."

Saihung made his final goodbyes and rushed back to the hotel where Wuyung and Wuquan were waiting. They gathered their things and set out that afternoon. But Saihung only told them that Butterfly had been sighted in Shandong and nothing else. He suggested that they split up, and that they meet at Taishan, the premier peak of China's Five Sacred Mountains. The mountain was considered to be a sacred place for Taoists, and every Taoist was supposed to make a pilgrimage at least once in a lifetime, much like Moslems visiting Mecca. As initiates, the two brothers had never been to the summit and they readily agreed. They never suspected that Saihung knew all along where Butterfly was hiding.

The home of the Divine Eagle was an isolated and palatial walled villa in the mountains of central Shandong. The peaks did not have the ascetic expanses of rock that Huashan had. Instead they were older, rounded, weathered, and broken. Splintered, battered, crumbled into heaps of rock and dirt, they were covered with a net of dense woods that thrived in the misty atmosphere. The landscape formed an ethereal backdrop to a place that was a virtual fortress. No villages were nearby. The towering walls were a solitary presence in the phantasm mountains.

The Divine Eagle was a friend of Saihung's grandfather, so he welcomed him warmly. A man with the proportions of a legend, he had strong shoulders and hands with fingers that looked like railroad spikes. His white-bearded face was wrinkled, with a bump on his forehead and a hooked nose with a somewhat bulbous tip. There was no space between his thick eyebrows; and his dark, glaring, intense eyes were disquieting and unemotional.

He had received Saihung's letter and, while he did not wish to involve himself in the trouble, had suggested that Butterfly remain to meet with Saihung instead of fleeing again. It was the Divine Eagle's opinion that nothing could be gained by prolonging the chase. Everyone would benefit if the two brothers resolved the difficulties.

The pursuit had lasted two months and had taken Saihung up and down China. Finally, he was about to catch up to his elder brother. He washed himself and changed into a dark burgundy silk gown and went out into the gardens.

Through the round opening of a moon gate in a pristine whitewashed wall, he saw the complete composition of an inlaid rock courtyard, weathered rock, and a massive upthrust pillar of petrified wood surrounded by peonies. He walked through the gate, turned to his right, and came to a hexagonal archway. Above it was an inscription that read, "The Eternal Fragrance of Antiquity."

An inlaid slate pathway led into a lush garden of turquoise pools, grey rockeries, weeping willows, and old pines. Saihung followed the path upward to another wall and then through its oval gate past a pavilion. A large pond, with an artificial island about fifteen feet in diameter, shimmered in the hazy light. There was a zigzag stone bridge over the water and a red and green gazebo to one side of the rock island. Standing with his hands folded behind his back, and immaculately dressed in vibrant cobalt silk, Butterfly stood gazing at the distant peaks.

The bridge was composed of solid slabs of granite a foot thick. It felt hard and unmoving as Saihung walked with quickening steps toward the island. The bright colors of the gazebo and Butterfly's still figure were mirrored on the pond with a background of green willow. In a moment, Saihung merged with the vivid reflections.

"I've finally caught up to you," began Saihung bluntly.

Butterfly turned around slowly, gracefully. Saihung saw that his face was as smooth-skinned and handsome as ever. He did not look troubled at all. Quite the contrary; he was calm, composed, and had an open smile.

"Yes, and you know why. The Grand Master wants you. You've caused a great deal of trouble."

"Have I?" Butterfly motioned to the octagonal marble table that stood between Saihung and himself. There were four stools of fine-textured milky marble carved in the shape of drums. Even details like the nails that held the drumhead and the handles were carved in. A finely painted porcelain tray from the Ming dynasty held a *Yihsing* teapot in the shape of a pine stump and two small cups.

"Will you have some tea, Little Brother?"

Saihung and Butterfly sat down opposite one another. Butterfly placed the teacups delicately down and poured a tea perfumed by narcissus flowers.

"You're ignoring the issue, Elder Brother," said Saihung directly. "You've committed many sins. You've killed many people. It's an abuse of your talent. How outrageous that I never really suspected the scope of your wrongdoing."

"Haven't you also killed? Didn't you kill my lover and her brother?"

"They were martial artists. We all accepted the possibility of dying in a duel when we became members of the martial world."

"Surely, as a Taoist, you understand that taking a life is still just that, regardless of the reason."

"Don't twist things around. You are only trying to divert attention from yourself."

"Myself? I've nothing to hide."

"Nothing? You are shameless! You stand in this garden and ignore the women you've seduced and sold into prostitution, the people you've ruined with narcotics, the innocents who have died simply because they had the misfortune to be in your path. Don't you feel any remorse at all? Don't you feel any guilt?"

Butterfly drained his teacup thoughtfully and put it down. He looked at Saihung with a steady gaze.

"Guilt?" asked Butterfly. "You've become quite a flamboyant orator. Do you really know what guilt is?"

The question stopped Saihung.

"Guilt is a veil that the inferior hide behind. They commit some supposed transgression and then whine that they feel guilty. Is this supposed to purge the consequences of their misdeeds? They say they feel remorse and then they repeat the same acts all over again. Their guilt becomes heavier. Unable to change, unable to accept themselves, they feel inferior because of their continual guilty feelings. Hiding behind their guilt—which is a pious public show— they separate themselves from other people and secretly enjoy their pain. This process becomes a lifelong pattern and cripples them totally."

Saihung was confused. The issue had been so clear to him before. He did not quite understand why it was so complicated now. Butterfly's argument was logical, but the end result did not seem acceptable.

"Guilt comes when a person accepts that his actions were wrong. But guilt is an illness," continued Butterfly. "The only medicine for guilt is to look ahead and persevere. If one climbs a rope, one ignores everything along the way, looking only at the top. Guilt is unnecessary and hinders one's ascent. It is inevitable in life that one will commit some wrongs. The average person hides his embarassment with guilt and then, as I said earlier, hides behind the guilt. But the superior one accepts that actions were wrong and then never does them again. Such a one not only purges a weakness but eliminates the necessity of guilt as well."

"Look, cut the crap," said Saihung awkwardly. "Why don't you admit that you've done wrong?"

"Now you're judging me. Who are you to judge me? Does any person have the right to judge another?"

"There are laws and rules."

"Law is a human conception. It is an artificial and arbitrary standard. I see no reason to accept its yoke. Let the commoner have laws. Let those without imagination accept convention. A herd needs confinement. But I cannot accept such a false thing as morality."

"You've turned into a monster, perverting the very ideas of right living." Saihung was angry.

"All you do is sit there and hurl accusations. If you lived my life you could not say such things. Those who accuse and judge should ask themselves if they have some special right to see themselves as higher than the next person. In truth, all persons are created equal. Don't be so quick to judge another."

Butterfly stood up with a sigh.

"All that matters to me is to experience life deeply and fulfill my destiny," he stated.

Saihung thought a minute. That seemed a perfectly valid goal to him.

"We are all born into this life with a destiny," said Butterfly, as he gazed at the still waters. "All that matters is that we fulfill our destiny. That requires total honesty.

Above all, I've never tried to be dishonest. That's why I despise guilt as a blind for the inferior. They are only hiding from themselves. I don't. I accept myself. I do not trick myself into some artificial conception of myself. I don't take some ideal lifestyle from the sages or some book like the *Seven Bamboo Tablets* and try to bind myself to it. How absurd! The scriptures were written by men, not gods. Why should I accept their word? No, I am determined to live life honestly. I will not violate my nature with the conceptions of others. I will accept my destiny, no matter what it is, and I will live my life only on the basis of my own identity. That standard is my only right and wrong. Let me explore it, contemplate it, coax its meaning out. Let me understand what no other person may give me, but rather what I must decode from the very essence of which I am made. Only then can I feel that I am living my life unadulterated by delusion."

"Brother, what you say is quite worthy. But that hardly justifies killing, robbing, and seducing."

"Am I to shun my destiny because others cannot accept it? Or because it isn't a nice and respectable one? Am I to complain because I was born to this role and not another? An actor mustn't complain about the role he's given. It's only a petty drama. When the opera is over he changes to another role."

"But the killing!"

"I've seldom met a martial artist so fastidious about killing. No, I take that back. The legends are full of stories about sentimental swordsmen. They always die early."

"Elder brother, I can agree with what you say. But it comes too late and as a justification for an evil life."

"You're young. So young. All I can say is that I never seduced a woman against her will. I never killed a man who did not want to kill me. I never robbed anyone who could not afford it and who had not acquired their gold by graft and corruption."

Saihung was quiet.

"Does this satisfy your petty morality?" asked Butterfly sarcastically.

Saihung admitted to himself that it did, in a way. But he said nothing.

Butterfly turned emotionally to Saihung.

"Little Brother. You hold my life in your hands. I appeal to you to let me go. If I am imprisoned on Huashan, I will never rest easily. My spirit will be broken."

A wave of feeling rose up in Saihung. This was his brother, his closest friend since childhood.

"Think, Little Brother. How much in life are we actually free to choose for ourselves? The seasons affect us. The stars direct us. Circumstances hamper us. Destiny guides us. You are the way you are because of what has come your way in life. You made selections, but usually there wasn't much real choice: Out of all the things that came your way, you decided to do what was right for you. Now think about me. A different flow of the Tao came my way. Women fall in love with me. Riches come easily to me. Martial prowess is strong in me. I did not ask for this. They came to me as part of my destiny. I accepted responsibility for it. We are both named Butterfly. We must fly free or die. Give me the chance to fly free. Let me pursue my destiny."

"It will lead to your death."

"That's a farmer's mentality. You and I should try to live like heroes. We will all die. And I know I must come back in future lifetimes. But this is my role now, just as you have yours. Let me continue to play out my role."

Saihung poured himself another cup of tea in a play for time. He agreed with Butterfly, and was impressed all over again with his elder brother's insight. He saw no reason to curtail such a special person's life. Butterfly was a unique and unusual person, Saihung thought. This grey and mundane world needed such spectacular humans.

Saihung stood up and faced his brother. He savored the solitude and the tranquility of the moment. He realized how much he loved him.

Saihung clasped his hands and bowed slightly.

"Will you stop your life of crime?"

"I understand things better now. I assure you I'll stop."

"Elder brother, please take care of yourself. Try to lie low for a while."

"I shall, Little Butterfly."

"I will leave first."

"Please walk slowly."

Saihung crossed the bridge and began down the path. He looked above the waving crowns of venerable trees and saw the celadon colored crest of a distant mountain range silhouetted against a deepening lavender sky. He thought of his master, so far away on a nearly unattainable mountaintop. How distant he was, how like a fairy tale seemed his life on the mountain. He wondered how he would tell his master what he had experienced on the plains. But he resolved that he would. Surely there would be an alternative open to them.

He reached the garden wall at the corner of the pavilion. A bed of roses was just beginning to bud. Lush blobs of red and pink stood at the end of dark green branches. A breeze stirred them slightly and a strong emotion pressed behind his sinuses. He resisted the impulse to look back.

Saihung arrived at the Taishan Railway Station and took a battered bus to the foot of Taishan. Four days had passed since his meeting with Butterfly, and he considered the matter settled. All that remained was to collect the brothers and return to Huashan. He felt satisfied with his quest. He had traveled much, seen much, met unusual people, and had won several difficult duels. This was the life he loved. He truly felt himself to be a martial artist, a man who lived for adventure, a knight who fought for righteousness and justice. In time, he could become a part of that exclusive brethren of unusual men like his master or those he had seen in a Beijing teahouse.

It was cloudy and hazy. The summit of Taishan was obscured by a diaphanous veil. Nevertheless, Saihung could still feel its legendary presence. Taishan, the foremost of China's Five Sacred Mountains, was a series of massive granite peaks with its highest point over five thousand feet above sea level. Its reputation as a mystical place dated from as early as the Qin dynasty, when the Emperor Qin Shi Huang himself came eleven times to pay tribute to the Jade Emperor of Heaven. Throughout history, China's emperors came to offer sacrifices and prayers on behalf of their nation; historical records document seventy-two emperors of past dynasties who came to Taishan.

Numerous shrines and temples dotted the rugged slopes, and both Buddhists and Taoists had places of worship. Much of the symbolism of the landmarks—Immortal's Bridge, Eight Immortal's Bridge, Flying Immortal's Terrace, the Sun Monastery, the Moon Monastery—were exclusively Taoist, and the temples at the very summit were dedicated solely to Taoism. The mountain was reputedly the earthly home of the Jade Emperor, a Taoist deity, and his temple stood at Taishan's crown.

Saihung had agreed to meet Wuyung and Wuquan not at the summit, but on a lesser peak. On the less-traveled eastern route to Taishan was the Triple Yang Temple. It was there that Saihung met his companions and told them about his meeting with Butterfly. They could go back. Huashan was safe and they had only used up a little over two months of the time Qingyi had set.

"Are you mad?" Wuquan burst out rudely after hearing Saihung's account. "You had that bastard in your grasp and let him go!"

"You've made a serious mistake," added Wuyung.

"What are you talking about?" asked Saihung. "It was a misunderstanding. He was accused without complete justification. Besides, he has given me his word to live in obscurity."

"You stupid kid!" cursed the older brother. "He'll never change. You let him bewitch you."

"Bewitch me?" Saihung blurted out. "Impossible. I've been meditating for years. My mind is strong."

"Then open your eyes, you dumb meditating monk," said Wuyung caustically. "You still cannot distinguish between black and white."

"Our orders were to bring him back," continued Wuyung. "You botched it. Now we'll have to begin again."

"No!" shouted Saihung. "Give him a chance. He's promised to stop. I've known him since childhood. He wouldn't lie."

"You've naive!" said Wuyung incredulously. "Even if that were true, he must still be punished for his past transgressions."

"That's past now," said Saihung emphatically.

"That makes no difference to me," Wuyung responded. "I must fulfill my orders."

"I agree," said his brother.

"Let's go back and let the Grand Master decide," said Saihung desperately.

"Show up empty-handed?" asked Wuyung with a sarcastic look. "Then you'll know punishment!"

"And what about Du?" asked Wuquan. "You made that deal with him. Now we'll have him on our trail, too."

"I only gave him three books," shouted Saihung, "and since I didn't bring Butterfly back from the Divine Eagle mansion, it doesn't count."

"But he has the books."

"I've kept the other two. They have the techniques. The first three are purely theoretical. I'll return those to the elders. We haven't lost much."

"Except time and Butterfly, you stupid kid!" burst out Wuyung. "Don't you realize that you've made a terrible mess of things?"

Saihung was quiet and suddenly felt embarrassed. For the first time he wondered if he had been wrong to let Butterfly get away. It had seemed so simple there in the garden. Now he was uncertain.

Wuyung scrutinized him and softened somewhat.

"Look, we'll do it this way: We'll track him through the activities of the Green Circle Gang. If it looks like he has reformed, we'll go back to consult with the Grand Master. If not, then we can still capture him before the time limit."

Wuquan agreed. Saihung also nodded, but said nothing. The more he thought about it, the more depressed he became.

Luck seemed to desert them in the following days, for the railway system was quite off schedule and no trace could be found of Butterfly. They drifted southward towards the Yangzi on the desperate theory that Butterfly might gravitate toward Green Circle Gang activities. This approach brought more information.

China seemed to be a nation of snoops. It was something Saihung had always hated about people, but now he was grateful for it. The countryside was so crowded, and people so nosey, that there was always someone to witness everything that anyone did. In the underworld, such curiosity was an essential method of intelligence. Getting that information only required buying it.

It soon became increasingly evident that Butterfly, far from reforming, was redoubling his efforts. In Yangzhou, where the trio had settled, there came disturbing news. Butterfly had assassinated several politicians in Shanghai, and was escorting a shipment of opium up the Yangzi by way of escape.

Saihung took this news with a heavy heart. There was no romance now. He had to accept that his brother was a simple gangster. He had fooled himself before. Somehow he had looked upon it as a righteous crusade. Now it only seemed like a gritty police job. This was not only mundane, but it brought everything down to a horrible reality. He knew now that he was a rash youth who had allowed his own feelings of adulation and idealism to obscure his duty.

Butterfly was heading towards Chongqing. Once there, he would be impossible to sieze. Both Du Yueshen and Chiang Kaishek were there, and it was certain that the three monks would be killed in that city. They had to get him right away. The spies said that Butterfly would be staying for one night in Nanjing. That was where the three would set their ambush.

Nanjing was a large, spacious city on the southern bank of the Yangzi river. It was an industrial shipping center and a great historical capital as well. One of China's Eight Ancient Capitals, it still had parts of its city walls and the Ming Tombs were adjacent to the city. It had also served for a time as Chiang Kaishek's capital, though the Japanese had driven him out ignominiously in an atrocious and bloody battle in

December 1937. It had been the last time that Nanjing, the "Southern Capital," had sought to compete with Beijing, the "Northern Capital."

In contrast to Beijing, Nanjing had no atmosphere of Imperial rigidity and severity. The weather was finer, the food more plentiful, and the homes and stores were thrown open to the light and clean air. The pace was slow. There were no dust storms and water was abundant. Ponds dotted the countryside and the greenery was thick and lush. The faces of the people were different than those in the North. They were plumper, more sensuous, less sinewy and hard-boned. Their languid air extended even to the architecture. The buildings themselves were smooth, rounded, with undulating walls. Nanjing was a turn-of-the-century river town gently softening in the valley heat.

But a great deal of the city was wrecked in a way Beijing never was. The war had decimated entire city blocks. The rubble and carnage were still clearly in evidence. Burned-out shells of buildings, homes blasted into dirt and sticks, bridges and rails bound in barbed wire, trees shot to splinters, and everywhere cripples with limbs missing, mud on their faces, teeth shattered, eyes filmed over in old yellow tears, crawling ignored through the streets. Freaks. Outcasts. Beggars. No one in Nanjing had survived untouched. They were all in the same city of devastation. This was the war zone, and the Japanese still held the city, patroling the streets and victimizing whomever they pleased. There was no longer a place for martial virtue, for righteousness, nor for heroism. The heroes of China now crawled the streets, pathetic hacked-up derelicts. The righteous lay in mass graves. The virtuous lived in terror and the edema of indifference.

China was changing. The world was changing. The Qing dynasty had collapsed from sheer decadence, beginning a process of decay and rot that stank more and more. The nation had fallen into a terrible state, like a body infested with gangrene, parasites, and cancer. Saihung wondered solemnly how he would neogitate this dying China. It was a monstrous irony now. Here he was, born to nobility, born to be a warrior, trained to be holy. What a joke. The aristocracy was being killed or displaced in prominence by the modern money men. Warriors were dying before gun-toting soldiers who had the mentalities of pig butchers. Holy men could not even control their own disciples.

Saihung waited in an inn's stuffy second-story room for hours. This had started out as a martial crusade. He had been the gentleman-warrior bedecked in jade and silk, petitioning the martial world to bear witness to the great cause he would champion. He should have opened his eyes in Qufu. Half of the elders had been businessmen and even the army was in it. He had battled bravely and heroically when the foes had subscribed to the same ideals. But now he saw that the world belonged to men like Du Yueshen and that warriors were now hacks with guns and artillery.

Saihung shook off these thoughts and recalled himself to the present. He looked out his window and across the balconied courtyard. The walls of the inn had once been white, but now they were streaked with rain stains and soot. He glanced at Wuyung and Wuquan. They were quiet and grim, and their swords were unsheathed. Butterfly was in a room across the way. It was only a matter of time.

At twilight, there was a flurry of activity and several men came out of the room. One was Butterfly. Saihung jerked his head to signal his companions. They crept out and edged around the balcony wall. Saihung emerged from the room holding a four-foot-long blowgun. He looked at his brother and paused. Then he inhaled, a deep, long breath like the one before a sob. He felt his ribs open, his diaphragm strain, his throat tighten. Then all his regrets, all his ideals, all his emotions exploded into the slender tube.

The drugged dart burst silently through the air and struck Butterfly in the neck. The men cried out in confusion. Saihung quickly reloaded and shot two more, as Wuyung and Wuquan sprang forward. Pistols were hurriedly drawn and Saihung threw himself down to escape the fusilade. He took quick glances through a latticework opening. The two swordsmen quickly killed the gangsters. Saihung anxiously checked to see what had happened to his brother. He saw him standing at the edge of the railing. Butterfly pulled the dart out, but it was too late. He reeled unsteadily. As the swordsmen rushed him, he tried to jump down and escape. But his consciousness drained away and Butterfly fell into the garden below.

During the journey back to Huashan, Saihung argued bitterly with Butterfly. It was the voice of one betrayed. Saihung had once idolized him. Now he had shot him off a balcony and was dragging him back for judgment.

"You see what's become of me, Little Brother?" asked Butterfly.

Saihung looked at him in the rocking train. His hands were bound behind his back, his feet bound eighteen inches apart.

"You said many fine words before," replied Saihung. "I believed you. Then you continued on."

"Each of us must make a choice," said Butterfly as he looked out the window. "Sometimes it's wrong. Real life isn't heaven. We can't all act like immortals."

"Real life is always a test," replied Saihung. "Entering heaven requires doing right. It's worth it in the end."

"Perhaps if you lived my life you wouldn't say that. Don't

be like me. Learn from my mistakes. Study hard and discipline yourself. Be good and righteous."

"I can't believe this. You're the one who did wrong and you're trying to correct me?

"It's only because you're my little brother."

"And what do you intend to teach me? More slop like what you fed me at Divine Eagle's home? I'm never going to listen to you again!"

"Don't be stubborn. There may come a day when you'll find that you've made some terrible mistakes. When that time comes, don't feel guilty. Don't hide it from yourself. Just do better in the future."

"Well, you'll have a chance to put your words into action now. When the Grand Master sees you, he won't be affected by your silver tongue."

"I'm not afraid of punishment."

"Wait until you get there."

The train slowed to a stop and Wuquan jerked Butterfly roughly to his feet.

"Here we are at Huayin Station," barked Wuquan. "Let's go, bastard."

They climbed the sheer heights of Huashan in a day and reached the South Peak Temple in the late afternoon. What a contrast monastic life was. The air was clean, the earth itself was unsullied by garbage, feces, or corpses. Ancient pines stood in grand silhouettes above the clouds, roaring cateracts spilled from inaccessible cliffs. Cranes and swallows dotted the skies, songbirds warbled in sweet tones. Although poor and old, the monasteries were clean and still. A feeling of peace enveloped Saihung as he savored the orderliness and tranquility. Something in his heart grew calm.

Inside the temple he could hear the chanting that he had heard since childhood. It was funny to him how something he had sometimes hated now filled him with sentiment. He inhaled the smooth cool air with its undertones of camphor and sandalwood. It was good to be back.

His master and classmates were sitting in the main hall, lined up like judges. He noticed with interest that Phoenix Eyes and Red Pine were missing.

Saihung, Wuyung, and Wuquan fell to their knees. Seeing Butterfly's defiant attitude, Wuquan pulled on the ropes binding his ankles and forced him down.

The room was silent.

The Grand Master motioned them to a small room at the side of the hall and they went in. It was a simple cell with only a window and tiny altar table. Used by the priests to rest between rituals, it was completely bare of any other adornment.

Only the two acolytes followed the Grand Master into the room. The Grand Master stood eye to eye with Butterfly, but said nothing. Butterfly, his hands bound tightly behind him, stood with his head cocked at an arrogant angle.

The silence was excruciatingly tense for Saihung. He looked at Butterfly. The orange half-light of sunset lit his back and threw his face into purple shadows. The sweat from mountain climbing left a sheen on his skin and strands of hair fell over his face. Saihung wondered what Butterfly was thinking as he tested his will against the man who had raised him.

In contrast to their wretched state, the Grand Master was immaculate in his black robes. The creases fell in perfect and orderly folds, the hat was unsullied and adjusted to a studied perfection. His white beard contrasted sharply with his dark clothing and not a hair was out of place. Saihung wondered what he was thinking. Did he feel regret that his adopted son had come to this? Was he sad, angry, or bitter? Would he forgive Butterfly?

The two stood for agonizing moments in complete stoicism. No emotions passed across their faces, nothing moved in their eyes. They were like two statues set face to face by destiny.

Suddenly, the Grand Master's eyes turned red. He took a step forward and smashed his palm over Butterfly's heart. For as long as Saihung had been a fighter, he had never heard the sound of a human heart bursting. Blood gushed out from Butterfly's mouth and nostrils and his eyes rolled to complete whiteness.

"No! No!" screamed Saihung.

Even the swordsmen were stunned as they caught the falling body.

"Why did you do it?" cried Sound of Clear Water.

"Yes, why did you do it?" echoed Saihung as he knelt in grief beside the crumpled body.

The Grand Master only folded his hands and turned brusquely away. He left the temple hall alone.

EIGHT

Ashes

The incense was still smoking. The candles blazed brightly, their melting wax dripping like blood. The flowers were bright, fresh, even cheery, but Saihung knew that they would soon wither, choke, and yellow. He solemnly dipped his hand into the urn he was carrying and felt the gritty ash and pieces of bone. As he wandered over the slopes like some lost ghost, he slowly scattered the last remains of his cremated elder brother.

It was difficult for Saihung to accept Butterfly's death, although everything had reinforced its reality. Saihung himself had washed and clothed the stiff and heavy body. He himself had felt the cold and turgid flesh as he had anointed it with oils and sesame seeds. He had stared at the body for a long time, thinking even during the funeral that he saw it move. But it was only settling, sinking, accepting its final pull to earth.

It had never occurred to him to cry. He felt no sadness, only a shiver of recognition at the absolute nature of destiny's rule. He felt exhausted, empty, tired. He had been striving and struggling a long time, and now it was all over. Although he had groomed himself for the role of a knight, he had never considered the aftermath of a quest. He realized that he had been so involved in the pursuit that he felt drained without it.

Part of the whole struggle had also been the fight with Phoenix Eyes. He had vaguely expected to return to take up that gauntlet. Instead, the elders had quietly moved to expel

Phoenix Eyes, Red Pine, and Intercepting Imprint from
Huashan. Somehow, irrationally, he felt his loyalty had
been rejected. He wanted to fight for his master, to show his
bravery and righteousness. But it had been unnecessary. His
master had triumphed without him and the rebellion had
been quelled.

He heard a commotion down the mountainside and
pulled himself up to see. Any event that would disturb the
sacred solitude of Huashan was significant indeed. Still
clutching Butterfly's funerary urn he saw three travelers
break away from a crowd of monks and begin their long
descent. There were jeers, cries, arguments, urges for return,
as the blue-robed ones stepped away. They were the expelled
challengers, and Saihung saw a hint of defeat in their quivering walks. Phoenix Eyes, Red Pine, and Intercepting Imprint
had flown too high, the brilliance of the Grand Master had
melted their waxen wings. Now they were plunging earth-
ward, leaving the pinnacles that were thought to be heaven's
tripod, losing the lofty glory of that high spiritual community.

Saihung resented them, had wanted to thrash them for
their insubordination. But now he only felt sad. Conflict and
fighting, even the cruel pranks he once played on others,
were normal, even oddly comforting things to him. They
still signified a relationship. He had felt great love for his
two classmates once, and the hatred that came with their
challenge had been bonded to that feeling. Now neither
emotion could exist. Worst was the realization that the
perfect circle of master and disciples was now irreparably
shattered. He never bothered again to find out more about
their challenges to the elders in his absence, nor would he
ever try to locate them again. He only knew that their
departure brought a feeling of crushing loneliness.

The Grand Master had never mentioned Butterfly nor the

expelled priests again, leaving Saihung with many questions he did not dare to ask. His master had never failed to brilliantly answer anything about heaven or earth, but when it came to a personal matter he withdrew to the loftiness of his supreme authority. Although Saihung could say and do anything to his master, no matter how outrageous, he now felt isolated by the older man's silence.

Over the following weeks Saihung tried to fit back into temple life, but his confusion and disappointment hampered him. The contemplation of ascetic austerities discouraged him. He looked at the older priests. Although they had starved, sacrificed, and devoted themselves earnestly to lives of purity, it was still uncertain that they would succeed. They looked bad: wrinkled, stooped, but carrying on year after year with undiminished faith. As far as he could see, they had nothing to show for it. Saihung decided to leave the mountain.

He wanted to travel and search, but he knew that he needed a goal, a guiding star, a role. He considered martial arts, but there were no more knights. He considered returning to his family, but the life of the aristocracy was fading. He finally understood that all he really wanted to be was simply an independent traveler, a connoisseur of art and life. Here was his goal.

He would make of his mind a palace, a rarified place where the utmost goal was beauty. This mind-palace would be a vast place to stroll in tranquility and appreciation. He would have gardens to linger in, rich foods to savor, collections of fantastic art objects, exquisite furniture made by expert craftsmen, and unusual and accomplished people to talk to. Room after room would be dedicated to the pursuit of some special activity, each one a sensitive balance of beautiful furnishings, each one filled with art for contemplation.

For him, beauty transcended the mediocrity of the world. If he feared anything, it was to sink into the morass of banality that normal people called "the good life." He abhorred the possibility of a life without rich beauty. He could not contemplate living without appreciating and absorbing the highest achievements of humanity, art, and knowledge. He wanted to possess both, to collect them, keep them, and arrange them in his palace.

Art could be bought. Fine porcelains, rare antiquities, paintings, old books, handmade furniture—all could be bought and skillfully placed in his orderly interiors. Knowledge was a little different. It had to be studied, learned, and experienced in order to be possessed. It was elusive. It could fade away if not maintained, whereas an object would just gather dust. He needed that stimulation.

All the pieces of his life seemed to fall into place. All the diverse interests could be organized. He could finally see how everything would have a fine proportion in his life. His body would be the landscape, his thoughts the vermillion walls, his eyes the Gate of Heavenly Peace. Within the pavilions and courtyards he could practice his martial arts. In the high towers he could even meditate. In the splendor of his mind there would also be people, those who especially helped him or those whom he simply met in his travels and brought back to live with him. Each one would have his own pavilions, his own gardens. There would be his master and classmates, indeed the whole of Huashan in one part of the palace. His family would be in another. People like Du Yueshen would be there because they had above-average lives. Butterfly, the Tigress, even the Tang poets would come alive again. All that mattered was that each piece of art, each person, would be uniquely beautiful.

Saihung wrote a letter to his master stating his desire to leave monastic life. He then followed his petition with a formal audience.

"I need time to go out," Saihung said humbly. "My spirit is not at peace. I should not be on a holy mountain nor with the gods. I need more experience."

"There are many moments in a man's life when he has a trying time," replied the Grand Master. "Even if he has a strong calling, he may still have misgivings. It is wise to consider such feelings. A man with a calling can go out into the world in an attempt to resolve misgivings, always knowing that he has something to fall back upon. But one should not wander without philosophy: Keep the strong foundation of your youth. Leave your intent fixed in one place. Go out knowing you'll come back."

"Perhaps I was never a committed priest," said Saihung. "I was drawn to it when I was young and without comprehension. Training doesn't have to be lifelong for it to be a part of me that I shall carry all my life."

"Don't be misled by the trappings of priesthood," countered the Grand Master. "Sutra recitation is fine, but one must do good deeds in one's life. It is your life that counts. It is by your life that fate and the gods judge you. You must always strive to live your life for the sake of good. Many people are only good out of fear. Others engage in charity only for the sake of prestige and the identity it affords them. Countless people do 'good' for a variety of reasons, but they all end up being actors playing roles. Don't be attached to the role of a holy man. That makes you no better than the rest. Just do good for true compassion."

"I don't feel that I have anything to prove. I'm not trying to be an example to others."

"That would indeed be unwise," commented the Grand

Master. "Don't try to prove anything. Just act the way you want and don't be a hypocrite. No one is perfect, not even the immortals and gods. Even the Monkey King was naughty. Tung Fengshiu was a thief. The Northern Sea Immortal was once banished from heaven as punishment for misdeeds. What is important is that you have a goal that you strive for. You must try to be good purely as a challenge, an adventure. Then the pursuit of the challenge will become discipline. Just take purity as a goal. If you really want it, you will put all else aside to achieve it."

"I'm unsure, Master. I feel discouraged."

The Grand Master paused. "There's nothing about you that accepts mediocrity."

"True," agreed Saihung.

"Then accept this challenge. Take purity as your goal. This will make you extraordinary. An ordinary person lacks will power, fortitude, and strength. An unusual man is one of supreme determination. Once he puts his mind to it, anything can be done. The sages say a rock can come alive if one worships it with total belief. That is the mind's power. As you wander, turn that power to one goal: purity."

"Purity for what?" asked Saihung glumly. "Good men and bad men seem to end up the same: dead and buried. The priests here on Huashan try to be pure, but have they ever seen the gods? They live for decades in absolute faith and still there's not one shred of evidence that they will be rewarded."

"Don't try to be good for the sake of the gods," said the Grand Master patiently. "Be good for your own sake. Then you will also actually be doing good for the sake of the holy, for the gods are within you. The highest divinity exists within all of us. Don't look outside for it. Look within. But look with the gaze unpolluted by dishonesty, greed, lust, and attachment. Remember that everything we do, we do ourselves. The gods don't intervene, one's friends cannot really help. You can be what you want to be. Be extraordinary not for the sake of holiness, but only as a personal goal."

"Why not let me be anything? Why should I try to be so religious?"

"I said nothing about religion. Religion means other people are on your path too: They'll drag you down. No, you must be your own person and you must resist following others' ideals. Filling yourself with the thinking of other people limits you. You must realize your own nature by yourself. This self-disciplinary realization is the key. You say you want to be free to be anything, but you can't. You must only be free to be yourself. You must know yourself, bring what is within yourself to fruition.

"My only purpose is to see you fulfill your life. You are about to go into the world without the structure of the priesthood. I am trying to show you an inner structure, a method of facing the confusing plethora of influences in the world."

"Yes, Master," said Saihung. He felt more receptive. "Please go on."

"Life is a game, a drama, mere theater. In this epic comedy, the stage is crowded with an amazing number of characters, each with his plots and subplots, each mired in his own petty and pathetic circumstances. How will you make your way through this eternal play? Will you be a clown? A hero? A tragic prince? A dupe? You must have principle and philosophy."

"I will be a man of principle," asserted Saihung quickly.

"But what about philosophy?" asked the Grand Master. "You must have a philosophy that truly perceives the reality of life and understands human feeling. Carefully observe everything before you enter any new phase. Consider before you decide. Use your reason, your powers of discrimination.

Understand the reasons why good and evil exist. Understand how neither is indestructible and how they are even interdependent. Be flexible. Let your philosophy change and evolve. Be aware of how your thoughts progress and take different forms as you age. Think in terms of your whole life, not just the present. Make sure what you do will last a lifetime."

The Grand Master looked at Saihung before he went on. "Little Butterfly, only one thing counts in life: You must look deeply into the structure of your being."

"Thank you for your advice," responded Saihung emotionally. He suddenly realized that he was leaving for an indeterminate length of time. Intellectually, his decision had been so right. But his heart had not had time to catch up. He steeled himself to conclude the conversation.

"May I have permission to descend the mountain?" he asked.

"Yes, but with one condition."

Damn, thought Saihung ruefully. That old fox was never going to stop imposing restrictions on him!

"Everyone must have a task in life. Everyone who leaves Huashan especially has a lifelong task that he must fulfill."

That sounded like a quest to Saihung. Maybe everything would be all right. As he built his mind-palace, he could use it as a fortress from which to sally forth on this quest. It could be quite exciting, he told himself; a last charming souvenir of Huashan.

"What is the task?" asked Saihung.

"I will assign you a task from the *Seven Bamboo Tablets of the Cloudy Satchel*. Will you vow to fulfill it?"

"What is it?"

"I thought you were a knight, an uncompromising champion. What does it matter what it is? Aren't you courageous enough to accept it?"

It's a trick, thought Saihung. Another attempt to control

me. But he was also curious. He decided to accept it—in case it was something really good.

"I accept."

"Good," said the Grand Master with a twinkle. "This is your task: Whenever you meet someone who is suffering and it is within your power to help them, then you must do so at all costs."

Saihung waited. The Grand Master was quiet but smiling gently.

"That's it?" Saihung was almost rude.

"Yes," replied the Grand Master placidly.

Saihung was not at all pleased. This was not a very glamorous task and it was sure to interfere with his goals of becoming a collector, connoisseur, and martial artist. If he stopped to help the suffering, especially in China where literally millions were miserable, then he would never reach his own goals.

"Remember, you accepted this task and you must fulfill it to the end of your days," said the Grand Master as he settled back in his chair. "Whenever you meet the suffering you must help them."

With his descent from the mountain Saihung was plunged into the restless, swirling ugliness of the world. The months that followed his departure from Huashan were convoluted ones filled with drifting and aborted searches for adventure. He put his master's advice far away, determined to pursue his own goals. Returning to his family, he was comfortable in wealth and luxury and spent a fortune collecting art objects and rare books. But he was restless and unsettled. He wanted adventure, to test his skills in the arena of life experiences. So Saihung went to Shanghai.

During Saihung's pursuit of Butterfly, Shanghai had seemed a bizarre place, a maze of danger, diversion, and evil. But now he saw it as the huge city it was: rich, bustling, cosmopolitan. The European buildings now seemed exotic—mountainous edifices of granite and steel, more massive than city walls, almost geometrically regular with their precise windows and their soaring Greek columns. He liked their domes and towers with slender white flagpoles hoisting flags high into the breezes that swept from the Pacific and the Huangpu. The buildings had none of the polychrome and rich detail of their Chinese counterparts, but he was now facinated by the corners, buttresses, archways, and keystones that made sharp and monumental shadowplays across their facades.

From a distance they looked like a hundred fortresses set down against the wide, pale sky. The Chinese buildings—stores, apartments, theaters, opium dens, gambling parlors—filled in the cracks and sprawled away over endless, disorganized streets. They were brown, red, brick, mud, clay, and wood. They were crowded, noisy, busy with cooking, crying, cleaning, and commerce. The European presence was spectacular, flamboyant: It meant to have whole city blocks of the West grafted into the flesh of China. But the Chinese closed back in, bit by bit, until a strange urban symbiosis emerged.

In Shanghai the peculiar meeting of East and West took on mythic proportion. All the stories of rich bankers, puppet politicians, ruthless soldiers, greedy gangsters, opium addicts, sexy women, hapless workers, sincere scholars, corrupt bureaucrats, hardy longshoremen, and ordinary people all existed in one way or another in Shanghai. It was in this fertile mixture of money, power, excitement, pleasure, graft, and drugs that Shanghai thrived. It was exactly in that rich urban environment that Saihung sought to exist.

He lived at a cheap boardinghouse in a room with six other men who came and went at all hours of the day. His possessions were locked in a trunk and it seemed that he locked his past—both as a Taoist and a nobleman—in there as well. He suspended all judgment, forsook introspection. His personality was in a state of seige and was under the control of a dictator. That tyrant was youth.

Like many youngsters, he began a time of experimentation. Attracted to the easy money and challenge, he worked as a mah jong and domino dealer in the casinos. But he soon became disenchanted. He then tried being a guard at gambling and opium dens, thrashing troublemakers and patrons who refused to pay. This was more appealing. He became a cruel and vicious fighter who relied on a variety of weapons, his favorite being brass knuckles. Saihung gradually drifted over to the aesthetic of his martial arts teachers: Choke a man until you see him bleed and his tongue rolls out. Punch a man's ribs and delight in the sound of cracking bone. Torture his muscles with twists and bone locks. Listen for his moans. Wait to hear his organs rupture. Each day he ate in the stalls and restaurants, slept a little by his locked trunk, and went out in eager anticipation of fighting in the dark, smoke-filled hollows of Shanghai.

He felt grim, severe, bad-tempered. But he liked it. He was feared, and to him fear was akin to respect. He did what he wanted, when he wanted. No one could oppose him. No one could restrict him. Those who blocked him were mercilessly brought to the ground. This was his hermitage now. The stone skyscrapers were the mountain ranges. Opium smoke was the poetic mist. Liquor formed the splashing brooks and sacred rivers. Neon and incandescent lights replaced the stars, sun, and moon. Pimps, junkies, gamblers, and whores were the masters, acolytes, and novitiates. His body was the temple, his legs the crimson pillars, his mighty hands the heavy gates.

Day after day he went on, never backing down from a challenge, never failing to do his duty at the places he guarded. He stopped trying to understand life and himself. He would find himself in combat. Although he was aware of different feelings, and though he had reservations about the way he was living his life, he nevertheless refused to back down when the call came to fight. It was a simple matter of survival, a case of injure or be injured.

By winter Shanghai began to turn cold. Saihung tired of the boardinghouse and his shadowy existence. He decided to visit an old martial arts teacher who had moved from Beijing to Shanghai.

The day he went to Wang Ziping's mansion was the first snow of the year. As a servant brought him into the court-yard, Saihung saw the middle-aged teacher stripped to the waist and doing bicep curls with steel and stone barbells. Saihung admired the rippling muscle and determined look, the heaving chest that sent regular bursts of frosty breath into the air. He could see that Wang had not lost any of his hardened 6 foot 4 inch frame, nor had the years brought much humor to his severe, bearded face.

"Ah, Little Two, what brings you here?" said Wang, using Saihung's family designation. Wang was good friends with Saihung's family, and knew him as the second eldest son.

"I've come to join. Will you accept me again?"

"Why aren't you on Huashan?"

"I've descended the mountain for experience."

Wang let out his booming laugh. "Fine, fine. I'll take you in for your grandfather's sake. He'd never forgive me if I didn't look after you. Go fetch your things."

"Thank you, master," said Saihung. He was relieved. There was something in him that needed a master, martial or spiritual. Though he wandered and rebelled and strove for independence, he was surprised at how comfortable he felt with the prospect of a master again directing him.

Saihung thus came to live for a time with Wang, learning with the boxer's live-in disciples, assisting in Wang's osteopathic clinic, and attending the academy with which Wang was associated, the famous Jingwu Athletic Association.

Originally established in 1909 by the prominent boxer Huo Yuanjia, the association would later have Wang Ziping himself as president. In 1918, the association had branches in Wuhan, Nanchona, Guangzhou, Foshan, Shantou, and Xiamen. By the time Saihung joined, Jingwu had forty-two branches and over 400,000 members throughout China and Southeast Asia. The chief virtue and radical innovation of the Jingwu Athletic Association had been its destruction of the rigid stylistic divisions that had hampered the development of martial arts. Whereas traditional teachers were secretive about their styles and forbade their students to learn the techniques of other systems, Jingwu advocated the combination of all the best features of China's martial styles. Dozens of masters taught at the red-brick compound in Shanghai, and students were required to master dozens of styles—like Shaolin, Taoist, and Eagle Claw—and many weapons.

But Jingwu did not stop at Chinese fighting skills, though it was first and foremost a martial arts academy. The open-minded masters soon incorporated Western boxing and wrestling, football, weightlifting, swimming, and chess into the curriculum. This willingness to accept all things of value regardless of their origins was the hallmark of *Mi Zhonqquan* (the Lost Track Style), the centerpiece of Jingwu's martial systems and the specialty of its founder. A synthesis of many other kinds of boxing forms, *Mi Zhongquan* was in itself a universe of techniques: It demanded mastery of fifty sets in order to gain proficiency. Mi Zhongquan's virtue was in the elusiveness of its movements which caused one's opponent to lose track of the practitioner's movements.

As one of Wang's five closest disciples, Saihung simultaneously learned a separate and secret tradition of *Mi Zhong-quan*. This treasured teaching of Wang Ziping demanded the mastery of 108 weapons and the absorption of two sets. The first was called "Chasing the Clouds with One Thousand Steps," a comprehensive set reputedly created by taking the single best technique from one thousand different schools of martial arts. The second set, called "Climbing the Mountain with Ten Thousand Steps," had a peculiar logic to it. The set had been created in such a complicated and lengthy system that it could neither be completely mastered by a single person nor could it ever be humanly possible to complete a total performance. Each disciple selected a section from manuals and specialized in that part for life. The system had had its origins in three Qing dynasty masters and had been codified throughout ten generations of fighters.

Saihung often went into the streets to test the techniques Wang Ziping taught him. He favored an apple hat then, rakishly pulling it over one eye in the universal sign of the troublemaker. But he sometimes lost fights and would go home to complain to Wang that his techniques were impractical. The thought of one of his students losing invariably brought a loud and obscene oath, and Wang would coach Saihung for a return match.

Saihung's only social life was the pleasure of a new novelty, what was called "electric shadows": the movies.

Going to the latest Hollywood films at plush, rococo gilded theaters with red velvet seats was one of the most fashionable pastimes in Shanghai. Unfortunately, it was unacceptable for a young man to go alone to the theater. He had had to find some way to get his master to accompany him. Craftily, Saihung solemnly told Wang Ziping that these were "educational films" showing life in the United States and the ways in which American warriors fought. So master and disciple would go weekly to study the dubbed and subtitled movies of Douglas Fairbanks, Jr., James Cagney, Kirk Douglas, and Humphrey Bogart. Although these were the latest movies, and though there were always newsreels about World War II, the two of them still regarded the United States as an odd place of gangsters, pirates, Robin Hoods, werewolves, air aces, and cowboys.

Cagney was a favorite of Saihung's, and the tough-talking street-wise character he so often portrayed was not much different from the personality that Saihung had developed. Nor did the cinematic world seem odd if he tried to understand it as America. The gangsterism, the money, the style, the masculine bravado, the steets of odd characters, impeccably dressed people, and shiny limousines seemed totally ordinary for Shanghai. Perhaps Chicago and New York were like Shanghai, he speculated. Maybe that was the reason that Hollywood knew the substance of a wickedly sophisticated city and why there was a man like Cagney who understood why a young man had to be so tough.

He took his master to theater after theater. Eventually, it didn't matter whether it was a rerun, a silent film, comedy, newsreel, or romance. Master and student loved to go to the movies, sometimes persuading other elders to sample this astonishing invention from the West. It was at just such an event, a screening of *Frankenstein*, that Saihung saw Liu, a fat Shaolin boxer and a contemporary of his master.

When the lights went down, the man sat peacefully and buddha-like in his seat. He might even have been in total contemplation until the monster came on the screen. At that instant, the frightened man jumped up, smashing his neighbors' faces as he flailed around. Complete pandemonium broke out in the theater, but Saihung was delighted. "Here's my next challenge," he thought.

Liu had a very big reputation in the city, but he was old, fat, and acted like a bumpkin. If Saihung could overcome him, why, just like those gunfighters in the Old West, he'd build a bigger reputation as a fighter. He would be, as they said on the screen, "a mean, ornery cuss."

Saihung challenged Liu the next day in a formal letter. The reply was swift, if a bit terse, and he was still chuckling as he arrived at the master's school the next day.

"Ah, you are Wang's disciple," said Master Liu.

"Yes," replied Saihung solemnly. "Forgive my challenge. I am brash and would appreciate some pointers." Inside, however, Saihung was thinking; "Get ready, fatty, because here I come."

"All right, you may attack as you wish."

"You are a master. I need not hold back?"

"I shall be most disappointed if you do."

Saihung grinned. Here was the pig, and he was the butcher. He revealed two long, sharp daggers.

Master Liu tucked up the hem of his gown and smoothed the few lonely hairs on his scalp. His thick lips pressed together and he stood proudly, hot bothering to find a weapon for himself.

"Pride won't help you," thought Saihung as he attacked.

He was amazed when the old man easily knocked the daggers from his hands in the first skirmish. Master Liu smiled broadly as he brought a ham-sized fist into Saihung's stomach.

But one blow could not penetrate years of training and Saihung retreated. The master came waddling eagerly forward. Saihung hit him several times with full force. He might as well have been massaging a whale.

Unnerved, he ran behind a table to try to gain some time.

He was shocked when the master jumped up and rolled across the table at him like a gigantic cannonball of fat coming full force. Saihung felt that he must use wrestling to win. Sidestepping the master he pinned him from behind. Now he had him where he could overcome him.

He heard a loud sound as the master suddenly farted a mighty blast. Saihung had never smelled a more noxious vapor. Nausea overcame him, and the master turned easily and knocked him unconscious.

When Saihung awoke, he was back at his master's mansion. A scowling Wang Ziping was applying medicine to his wounds. In the background was a concerned but gleeful Master Liu.

"Now Master Wang will be angry for days that one of his students lost," teased Master Liu.

"You dunce," scolded Wang. "Master Liu is quite beyond your skills. You've disgraced me."

"Don't take it so hard, old friend," comforted Liu. "He is good. I was forced to use my secret weapon."

"No . . . not that!" exclaimed Wang.

"Indeed," said Liu proudly. He leaned over Saihung. "My boy, I trained many years to perfect this skill. I eat much meat, eggs, and special herbs. I'll teach you the method, if you like."

"Master is too kind," murmured Saihung weakly. He felt like throwing up.

"Just remember, my box," said Liu with a twinkle. "A master always has a trick up his sleeve."

The two men went to the door, giggling like boys.

"Oh yes," said Liu as he strolled out. "See you at the theater."

NINE

Butterfly Dream

Nearly two years after departing from Huashan, Saihung stood in the wings of a Shanghai opera house. He had felt the need for a career and had longed for travel. Joining the opera provided that chance. More importantly, it was a job during those war years. It was artistic, expressive, literary, and he met many interesting patrons in the troupe's travels. He liked the creativity of being in the arts. Not only was creativity akin to spirituality in its ability to give excitement and new impulse to life, but it also transcended mediocrity, the state Saihung most deplored. In fact, it was not all that different from the temple life or the martial world, just a rearrangement of motifs. He played the role of various gods and generals, and many of the plays had religious themes. He still had to utilize gestures and postures. He participated in plays that alluded to immortals, alchemy, renunciation (especially of historical officials who retired from society in order to escape Imperial service), the gods in heaven, and Lao Tzu himself.

Even his martial impulse was satisfied. He had to train daily for hours to prepare for his roles. He met many masters who coached him in acting, singing, and special theatrical martial arts styles. He immersed himself in the classical literature that was the source of so many operas and explored their military themes from such books as the *Romance of the Three Kindgoms*, *Water Margin*, *Journey to the West*, and *Romance of the Yang Family Generals*. He had even had the opportunity to engage in real fighting, for there were always plenty of rowdy theatergoers interested in seeing whether the actors of warrior-roles could actually fight.

It was the life he wanted. He had adventure and imagination. He was a star. People applauded whenever he performed. Unlike the frustration, restriction, and daily fault-finding inherent in monastic life, he was constantly celebrated. He was realizing his goals of collecting memories, experiences, and skills. His mind-palace was growing into a rich sprawl of pavilions and mansions. Like the three-storied stage in the Forbidden City, his life too had come to revolve around opera, with its pageantry and the sheer fascination of lovely costumes, good music, fine acting, and talented song. This was good enough. Spirituality could wait for retirement. Then, like the scholar-officials, like his own master, he would return to the high mountains. But first he would finally get a lifetime's fill of rich beauty, and here on stage, there was enough to dazzle any eye.

In the center of the stage's dark atmosphere was a solitary figure lit by a blazing spotlight. Blue in the cigarette haze, the beam shot the sparkling embroidered colors of the actor's robe throughout the house. He moved to center stage with a short rapid step. Unseen musicians exploded in a frenzy of stringed sounds, and shouting came from the large and noisy audience.

The actor portrayed the well-known Taoist philosopher Chuang Tzu. He showed all the costume symbols of his character: maroon silk robe with the Eight Trigrams symbols embroidered in gold and silver, immaculately white water-sleeves, long black horse hair beard and stark white make-up startled by rouged cheeks, cinnabar eyeshadow, and arching eyebrows. He held a dragon-head staff in his left hand, and a fly wisk in his right.

"I raise the dragon-head staff," said Chuang Tzu. "My

words shall strike fear into people's hearts. When we are alive we are promised everlasting love; but once dead, we are given only a fan to dry the grave."

He stroked his beard thoughtfully, a classic gesture of importance.

"Men's faces are readily seen, but their hearts are hidden."

He pointed to his heart and suddenly cocked his head toward the audience. A sharp strike of the sticks from the musicians punctuated his gesture.

"I am dead. Truly dead. I am the Taoist of the southern sea. I am Chuang Tzu who feigned death . . . " The orchestra came in with a brief musical statement of support as he flipped the yak-tail whisk through the darkness like a shooting star.

The story was familiar to the audience, as were all scripts in Chinese opera. People did not go to the theater to see original works, but instead went countless times in their lives to see the same themes and dramas. It was therefore the skill of the actor that was most under consideration, and the audience was uninhibited in shouting its approval or disapproval, or even a correction when a line was missppoken.

The Butterfly Dream was no exception in its familiarity to the crowd. In this play, Chuang Tzu, a scholar-magician, received permission from his master to descend the mountains for a reunion with his wife, Tian Xi. On his way, he met a woman fanning a grave. When he asked her why, she told him that she had promised her husband not to remarry until the dirt on his grave was dry. Chuang Tzu dried the grave with his magic powers. In gratitude, the woman inscribed a fan with the words, "Wandering Taoist who pitied me: Tell your wife she would be no more virtuous than I." Upon returning home, Chuang Tzu gave the fan to his wife, Tian Xi, who indignantly swore her lasting fidelity to their marriage. In order to test her, Chuang Tzu, through yogic methods, feigned death and magically created a handsome scholar. Tian Xi fell in love with him, and though still in mourning married him. However, on their wedding night he fell into a coma. His servant, who Chuang Tzu created from one of the paper funeral effigies, announced that only a medicine made from the fresh brain of a relative could save her lover. Since Chuang Tzu had been only dead a week, and though she had great misgivings, she eventually resolved to break open his coffin.

This was the plot known to everyone. As the second scene drew to a close, they saw Tian Xi, resplendent in white, embroidered robes, before a simple altar. On the table was a pair of candles, an incense burner, and a tablet with Chuang Tzu's name inscribed upon it. Behind was the coffin itself.

"But stop!" she said in a high, piercing, nasal voice. "I was married to him. How could I do this? It's impossible! I could never do such a terrible thing."

She brought her palms up to her face and shook her head as she backed away from the coffin.

"What a bitter death is mine!" came the dead lover's voice from offstage.

"Ai! I lost one husband. Must I lose my second? I'll break open this coffin and save my young prince's life!"

As Tian Xi made her exit, the stage darkened again, dark as the scene in which Chuang Tzu had made his monologue. Behind the rear curtain, a stagehand held a bamboo pole. A paper butterfly suspended from it was made to flutter over Chuang Tzu's coffin. The servant boy, the one who was created from a funeral effigy, came on stage with a fan. Using acrobatic and martial movements, while still portraying the puppet-like gestures that suggested his origins, he chased the butterfly. He made a lunge for it, but it was jerked away. He closed his fan with a snap and, squatting low, shuffled across the stage in that position. The boy paused dramatically and then made a second attempt to catch the butterfly in both hands. But when he opened his hands to the audience he showed them his failure. After more acrobatic footwork, he finally lost his patience. Going up on one leg, he snapped the fan open, flinging it wildly left and right as he made a third try. Again, he failed. Finally, he closed his fan in exasperation and marched offstage like a marionette.

The scene symbolized a famous story so well known to the audience that its lines were not included. It was enough to suggest it with the title of the play and the butterfly motif. The story was that Chuang Tzu once dreamed he was a butterfly fluttering here and there in enjoyment. When he awoke he was confused. Had he been Chuang Tzu dreaming that he was a butterfly? Or was he now a butterfly dreaming he was Chuang Tzu?

The scene, in its frustrating attempts to trap the butterfly, mocked human frailties and human attempts at differentiation. Its final irony, however, was that it was a paper effigy, not a person who was pursuing the butterfly.

Saihung went backstage to the dressing room, passing all sorts of costumed actors. Properly arranged in their roles and in their correct dramas, they were quite understandable. But out of context, in the dim corridors of the theater, they became a bizarre and surreal parade of painted-faced generals in armor, lovely women (all of whom were male actors), strange clowns dressed like turtles and shrimp, caricature priests with dangling eyebrows, and a host of acrobats with innumerable stage weapons. Every color was in evidence. The rich hues of dyed silk—cobalt blues, blazing oranges, forest greens, sunset crimsons, along with tiny sparkling silver mirrors, gold thread, and irridescent pearls—made the dazzling carnival a procession of painted images come alive. Here and there he heard disembodied voices, singing, practicing scales, interjecting snatches of poetry from divergent eras of long-past events.

Saihung sat down at his make-up table and looked at himself in the mirror. His large eyes were an asset on the stage, and his wide face with its high cheekbones made the ideal warrior's face. It did, however, ruin him for the more delicate scholar parts.

Peking Opera was divided into four types of roles: the male roles (*sheng*), the female roles (*dan*), the clowns (*chou*) and the painted faces (*jing*). Within each type there were either civil or martial characters. A *wu sheng* , for example would be a military male role.

The *sheng* roles were either old men, young men, civil, or martial. The civil roles demanded perfect diction and a great deal of singing, while the martial roles emphasized acrobatics and fighting movements. The old men, usually scholars, officials, or retired generals, had beards and played their parts with dignity and sang in expert tones. The young men were invariably beardless, refined, and sang falsetto to indicate youth.

The *dan* roles were played by men in Saihung's troupe, as there had been a long-standing convention that women did not belong on the stage. However, that convention was slowly changing and actresses were gradually becoming a part of Peking Opera. The *dan* roles were divided into five categories: the proper woman (matrons, faithful wives, filial daughters), the flower woman (vivacious maidens or women of questionable character (such as Tian Xi in *The Butterfly Dream*), the mischievous woman, the warrior woman, and the old woman.

The *chou* roles, or clowns, could either be male or female, civil or military. They were always in white face with a few black lines to indicate their character. Their main task, of

Saihung as a Peking Opera performer.

Various painted faces for the jing roles.

course, was comedy, and their lines were often dry, pithy, even bawdy.

The fourth type was the painted face (*jing*), and this was the type in which Saihung specialized. He fit perfectly the requirements for a heavily built actor who would have to wear many layers of costume, move in dignified ways, and sing in a rich and robust voice. Though there were both civilian and military painted faces, it was naturally the martial roles Saihung quickly adopted.

Each *jing* actor had his own individual variation for the patterns he applied to his own face. However, the colors had meanings which reinforced the characteristics the actor sought to portray. Red indicated courage and virtuousness. Black symbolized a coarse and fierce nature. Blue signified cruelty and sadism. White was a sign of treachery. Gold and silver were used for the faces of gods—a mimicry of gilded temple figures—and there were also a host of animal spirits and bizarre characters like the legendary Buddhist saints, the Eighteen Luohans.

This was the complicated iconography that Saihung used each time he applied his make-up. That night he was playing the role of Erlang, one of the generals commanding heaven's armies. As he sat staring at his own face he recalled how Erlang was the nephew of the Jade Emperor himself. He was the offspring of a goddess and a mortal, and thus was not qualified to fully enter heaven. He therefore lived on the borders of heaven with his war dog, the Howling Heavenly Hound, and acted as heaven's emissary in dozens of operas. Two details particularly emphasized his importance in theater: The first was the use of four military flags attached to the back of his costume, an allusion to the flags used by generals to issue orders. The second was a third eye prominently painted on the forehead, symbolizing Erlang's divine nature and supernatural perception.

Saihung first tied a tight headband around himself. This led his brows dramatically up and back and made his eyes look even larger. A standard expression of rage or power was the use of glaring eyes.

Saihung next applied a thin white cream all over his face as a foundation for subsequent layers of make-up. He watched as the rubbed-in cream obscured his ruddy skin and dark brows.

He painted a white base at his forehead and above and around his eyes. Then he applied a white powder which evened out the white color and gave it a matte finish. An oily gold film went over his forehead, nose, cheeks, and chin. Carefully avoiding the other areas, he painstakingly completed an even coating. He was beginning to look like a golden idol. He began to apply black around his eyes, slowly painting enormous, sharply pointed brows and shapes like batwings at his eyes. His pointed brush then moved downward to make a stylized beard, covering even the upper lip. The black shapes sprawled across his golden face like razor-cut shadows.

Saihung tilted his head and critically examined his work. He could feel the paint drying tightly over his face like a second skin. He was almost finished. Now he picked up a brush, loaded it with a bright red and began to add two arabesques to his forehead and to paint only the lower lip red. With the upper lip black, it gave a snarling, somewhat canine look to the bottom of his face.

Just as it had taken him a great deal of time to prepare his make-up, he had endured difficult training to prepare for the actor's life. Normally, an apprenticeship required seven years of study, but his background had made the acting coaches and producers notice him. He had risen quickly from being a minor supporting actor to a full star in the course of a year. But it had been arduous. He had spent hours each day improving his singing—demands to sing loudly in alternation with long stage fights taxed even his ability at breath control—and had suffered under the demands of the acrobatic coaches. The troupe would do all kinds of tumbles, flips, jumps, and flip-flops. Balance was trained by walking with stilts—on ice. Dexterity was trained by throwing pins and weapons between partners. He had even learned the precise requirements of make-up from specialists.

Saihung picked up a small dome of metal, applied paste to it, and then placed it upon his forehead as the center of his third eye. He thought of his training in Huashan. If only it had been so easy to open one's psychic perception!

He put on a tight inner cap and then put on his costume, a rich imitation of armor in blue and orange. With four flags in back, the elaborate clothing weighed at least twenty pounds. The headpiece—a crown decorated in blue, orange, gold, and red that bristled with dozens of large imitation pearls and puffy balls of fur that trembled at the slightest movement—weighed at least ten pounds. Not only would Saihung fight, sing, chase, and pose in this cumbersome outfit, he would also have to do full tumbles in the air from a standing start—weapons, flags, and all—and land on narrow platform shoes.

He heard the orchestra working itself to a frenzied climax, and then there was a roar of applause and screaming. The play was over. Tian Xi, having broken open Chuang Tzu's coffin, had been confronted by the black-robed corpse come alive. After hearing his accusation of adultery and being confronted by her phantom lover, Tian Xi had cut her throat with the axe.

The noise of applause was a stimulant to Saihung. He could feel his veins gorge with excitement. He seldom experienced stage fright; there was something liberating about going in front of an audience with his face painted over. Although he, like most monks from Huashan, was shy in many personal encounters, his make-up gave him a mask to conceal his bashfulness. The stage was his freedom.

He stood up as Chuang Tzu rushed in with a sigh, threw his whisk to an attendant, and began removing his beard. Five maidens rushed to take their places offstage. Saihung picked up his spear and walked toward the stage.

The opera was an adaptation of a Hebei opera, "The Magic Lantern." In this story, the beautiful goddess Sheng Mu (Saihung remembered her much differently in her shrine on Huashan) falls in love with a mortal, Liu Yanchang. Erlang is outraged and flies to earth to prevent the union. But Sheng Mu has a magic lantern which wards him off. The two lovers marry and she bears a son. On the one-hundredth-day cele-bration of the son's birth, Erlang sends his Howling Heaven Hound to seize the lantern. Powerless, the goddess cannot defend herself completely. Erlang imprisons her beneath Huashan. Her husband is driven away and eventually dies after giving his son, Chen Xiang, into the care of the Thun-derbolt Taoist. The son learns martial arts and acquires magic powers. Finally, the master reveals his mother's plight and gives him an enchanted axe, and Chen Xiang rescues his mother by cleaving Huashan open.

Saihung stood in the dark wings, waiting. He saw Sheng Mu before the audience, heard the cacophony of the or-chestra, felt the cool air rush up from the bowels of the old theater. He stood alone in the darkness; no audience could see him. Was he Erlang, the Immortal knight who waited for an eternity outside heaven? Was he an actor playing the roles of past generals, heroes, and warrior gods? Was he a fallen monk?

The orchestra wound up to a clatter of drum beats and clappers climaxed by an interlude of warbling melodies. There were several strikes to the gong. It was his cue and, he mused, not too different from temple bells. He rushed onstage to embrace the excitement of performance and applause.

Art imitated life most ironically when Saihung performed in a little-known martial opera called *Purple Cloud Flower.* Its plot was a variation on the famous *White Snake* opera. A beautiful swordswoman, Purple Cloud Flower, finds that her lover has a serious disease. His illness will be fatal unless a medicine can be made with an herb found only on the summit of Huashan. She journeys to retrieve it only to be told by the Taoists who protect the herb that she will not be allowed to take it; the herb is exceedingly rare and precious and, as renunciates, they have no stake in the struggles of the mundane world. She attacks them with her sword. Though the monks are themselves superb swordsmen, she slays a number of them but cannot prevail over them all. The stalemate continues for three days, giving the actors many opportunities to demonstrate their flashy stage technique.

At the play's climax, the head monk finally consents to exchange the herb for her unique sword style. She teaches them her techniques, gets the herb, and returns home in time to save her lover. A number of intriguing themes were contained in the opera. First, it is the woman, not her lover, who is powerful and active. Second, the herb, as a sign of the special place accorded to such herbs as ginseng and the *lingzhi* mushroom, is in itself an echo of the Taoist quests for immortality through alchemy and the search for Peng-Lai. Third, in spite of the value of the herb, it is significant that the Taoists exchange it in order to preserve knowl-edge—a priority with them. Finally, the Taoists, though they are supposed to be completely detached from mortal concerns, nevertheless take action to help their fellow human beings. These themes indicate how many elements of the martial and Taoist worlds were borrowed and even caricatured in popular entertainment. Whatever effect they had on the consciousness of the people was certainly in terms of legend and mythology, not as inducements to seek spiritual salvation. However, Saihung's background was vastly different than that of the average person. While a great deal of the operas had Taoist themes, this one was particularly relevant to his life. His profession had innumerable ways to make him think back over his previous life.

One night he was performing the play in Anhui province. He did not know how many times he had played the role of the head monk, his face powdered white with the arching black eyebrows, heavy mascara, scarlet eyeshadow, and blush. Dressed in his grey cotton robe and brandishing a stage sword, he duelled with Purple Cloud Flower, barely realizing that a former Taoist playing the role of a Taoist on stage was one of the oddest twists of life.

The audience was loud and restless that night. The play was staged in the mid-evening, before the predominantly literary operas full of long arias that the richer patrons who came later favored. The first portion of the night usually featured little dialogue or singing, emphasizing action instead. This meant that a commensurately rowdy and illiterate audience came to see the early shows. They chatted and laughed among themselves, smoked, littered the floor with melon seeds and peanut shells, and shouted obscene remarks to the actors. Saihung ignored them as he came to the center stage.

The orchestra maintained dramatic tension with rapid beats of wooden clappers punctuated with rings of gongs. Saihung stood proudly at center stage and faced Purple Cloud Flower, dressed in lustrous silk that matched her name. She stood for his response with her left leg forward and crossed before her right, her tasselled sword behind her back, her fingers pointing toward him in the sword gesture. They looked like two life-sized dolls with their painted faces and the way they stood glaring at one another.

"We Taoists are renunciates and care not for the petty concerns of mortals," chanted Saihung. As he spoke, he brought his palm down and made a gesture of dismissal. The orchestra followed the lead of his movements—it was his gestures and timing that cued them.

Purple Cloud Flower changed her position, walked in a circle, and pointed once more at him.

"Nevertheless, I must have the herb!" she replied.

Saihung stepped forward, opening his eyes wide to let the footlights catch the whites. The eyes of an opera actor were supposed to glisten like jewels.

"Through three days, we have fought," sang Saihung in a resonant voice. "Neither can prevail over the other."

There was another flurry of orchestral accompaniment.

"Equal value in trade," stated Saihung. "Give us what you most value—your art—and we shall give you the herb."

"Is this true?" asked Purple Cloud Flower.

"Yes. We are renunciates, followers of the Way. The cares of the mundane world hold no significance for us. Yet even hermits may be moved by compassion."

"Hey! Hey!"

Saihung was startled by the loud shout from the audience.

"What would you know about renunciation?" someone demanded.

Saihung turned his painted face rapidly. Purple Cloud Flower was preparing her reply, but he was intent on finding the speaker. Near the front of the audience were two old Taoists.

"Renunciation means to leave the mundane world," cried one of the Taoists, "but enlightenment comes from traveling through the world!"

Saihung was immediately intrigued and, as he continued

with his acting, examined the two. It was unusual to see any holy men at an opera. It was not an acceptable function for them to attend. But there they sat, in their dark blue robes, graying hair in topknots, and long uncut beards. Their status was unmistakable.

At the end of his scene, Saihung rushed offstage and found one of the stagehands. He ordered him to invite the two Taoists for an after-theater meal. He was gratified to receive an affirmative reply.

Saihung was through with his performances a little past midnight. He changed into a dark blue gown and wiped his face one more time. That was the trouble with make-up, he thought. After a while, the white powder seemed to accumulate in the pores and folds. All veteran actors had ghastly complexions, as if their roles were slowly bleaching their personalities into neutral canvases for the colorful parts they played.

He found the two Taoists in the lobby of the theater and politely introduced himself with his family name. The two old men returned his bows with the familiar prayer gesture and bow of their calling. Free of the glare of the footlights and the layered veils of darkness and tobacco haze, Saihung could see them clearly for the first time.

The one who seemed slightly older was a very thin but tall man. This single fact must have seemed his primary rubric, for he introduced himself as the Slender Gourd Immortal. His face was a long oval with a smooth, pale complexion, and his avian eyes were large, serene, but invariably observant. His white beard was long and wispy, and his lips were pressed gently closed.

His companion was heavier, but not quite portly. Unlike the Slender Gourd Immortal, the Crystal Spring Immortal had an expressive, sunny face. He seemed to laugh and smile about everything, and punctuated his actions and remarks

The Slender Gourd Immortal.

The Crystal Spring Immortal.

with sly twinkles of the eyes. His beard was full, his complexion ruddy, and his demeanor was animated and playful.

As Saihung escorted them to a nearby restaurant, he chatted casually. Mentally, though, he was searching his memory. He had heard stories of two Taoists with these names. Reputed to be high-level practitioners, the two had earned the title of "Immortals" as acknowledgment of their great spiritual attainment. What the legends added was that the two had found in each other true soulmates and had been companions for at least two hundred years. It was true that they were already white-haired, and this made them look as if they were only in their mid-seventies. The ages were not unusual for Taoists to claim, but Saihung was a skeptic. He could only observe that the two men gave the air of being old with their manners and white hair, but they seemed young and energetic in all other respects.

After they had been seated in a quiet upstairs room, the Two Taoists examined him in turn.

"You say you have some interest in Taoism?" asked Slender Gourd.

"Yes," replied Saihung modestly. "But I have been away from study for quite some time."

"Ah, well, life itself is study, is it not?" asked Crystal Spring.

"As you say, master," agreed Saihung deferentially. "I am ignorant. However, my two honored guests appear to be of great stature."

"Oh yes!" replied Crystal spring in an outrageously immodest tone. He looked at Saihung with a broad grin. "We've mastered a fair number of things. Wandering here and there, we seek the Mysterious Portal. We've studied invisibility, flying, and we go to heaven all the time. Not bad, eh?"

Saihung looked at Slender Gourd. The man was quiet, with the merest smile. His eyes were fixed on him.

They're testing me, he thought.

"Ever learn to fly without wings, young man?" continued Crystal Spring.

"Yes, I have. Unless one can fly, how could one go to heaven?"

"Quite so. Quite so," giggled Crystal Spring.

Slender Gourd leaned forward.

"What is the technique?" he asked.

"The phrase 'to fly without wings' is, of course a metaphor," said Saihung quietly. He saw Crystal Spring's stage chuckle disappear. "It means to bring one's spiritual essence up the spine."

"What is the secret of invisibility?" demanded Crystal Spring.

"The secret is to sit so still that one is like a lizard on a branch who is unnoticed because it is unmoving."

"Point the way to heaven," ordered Slender Gourd.

Saihung touched his forehead. "The term 'heaven' is a reference to the psychic centers within the skull."

"Is Lao Tzu in your head, then?" demanded Crystal Spring.

"Just so," replied Saihung steadily. "Even the holy one is a symbol of the psychic center associated with the pituitary gland."

"Have you tasted Lao Tzu's Elixer of Immortality?" questioned Slender Gourd.

"Unfortunately not. My progress has slowed."

Slender Gourd sat back and stroked his beard thoughtfully. Crystal Spring looked at him and uttered a sound of satisfaction.

"You truly are what you say you are," concluded Crystal Spring.

"It is always an honor to meet a fellow follower of the way," said Slender Gourd.

"Not at all," smiled Saihung. "It is I who am honored."

The table was quiet for a minute when the food came. Choice morsels of vegetarian cooking whetted their appetites.

"You are much too generous!" protested Crystal Spring.

"Please don't be so formal," said Saihung. "You honor me by accepting my invitation."

They ate quietly.

"May I ask your backgrounds?" said Saihung in a while.

"We have none." said Crystal Spring curtly. Saihung, however, knew that the masters never discussed their personal history.

He knew probes were useless. For masters of their level, questioning was unnecessary. He understood their attainment by the most precise method: pure feeling.

It had been so long since Saihung had been in the presence of spiritual people that the sensations seemed more exaggerated. Being with the two Taoists brought on a feeling of blissful tranquility. He was caught up in some human magnetic field, some intangible wave of reassurance that radiated from both of them. After so many months away from consecrated places, he had forgotten the power of others he had met, people whose mere passing would spontaneously stimulate instant joy, or make one immediately energetic, or bring sudden tears of happiness. Now, in the company of the two Taoists, he rememberd, and felt. He knew that he sat with masters.

Long moments passed as the two Taoists finished eating with great gusto. Saihung felt content, at home. He wondered if it was merely being with Taoists. After all, he had lived with Taoists since the age of nine. It was quite possible it was all mere sentimentality. But he decided it was more than that. Somehow, the occasion was a small reminder that he had wandered a bit too far from his path.

"I would like to study with you," said Saihung. The Two Taoists exchanged solemn glances.

"We do no live in a temple. We are travelers," replied Slender Gourd.

"I am willing."

"Our lives are very poor. Not at all like that of a successful actor," persisted the Taoist.

"I knew the ordination platform before I knew the stage."

"We are leaving tonight," said Crystal Spring.

Saihung was unwavering. "Very well. Please permit me to get my belongings and notify the troupe."

The two stood up.

"We will wait at the East Gate."

"I will be there in an hour's time."

Saihung hurried back to the deserted theater: Most had gone out after the performance since actors favored the nightlife. A few were asleep. But this was a great opportunity for him. After deliberating a moment he wrote a letter, gathered up his things, and prepared to leave.

He stood for a few moments at his make-up table. In the indigo light, he could make out the specter of his own image. The dishes of make-up were huddled to one side. Dry smudges of red, gold, black, purple, and green edged the porcelain rims. He contemplated his letter, the translucent sheet with the black undulations that marked his turning point. To the side of the table was his headdress for the role of a general. The mirrors seemed dull, the fur balls dyed in vivid magentas and oranges did not move. He touched the three-foot pheasant feathers one last time. Pulling them down, he felt the quill flex with its own firm resilience. The memory of applause came faintly to him. He released the feathers and they sprang into the darkness. Before they stopped quivering, he had left the room.

The night was cold. Saihung was glad that the waxing moon was growing full, for he had no lantern. The air made him shiver, but the sparkling spray of stars made his mind shimmer with hopes.

He found the two Taoists without difficulty and they welcomed him. They set off immediately and, before long, came to a long wooden footbridge. As they crossed, Saihung thought that it was an appropriate image. He would not turn back.

Before they had crossed completely, Crystal Spring started laughing hysterically. Slender Gourd, who apparently never laughed, turned to look at Saihung with his sphinx-like gaze and half-smile.

"Listen!" chuckled Crystal Spring.

"I don't hear anything but our footsteps," said a mystified Saihung.

"Ours?" repeated Crystal Spring. "Listen again."

Saihung did. Only then did he realize that his were the only footsteps, and they were grotesquely loud. He paused, listening as the two Taoists walked further. They were soundless.

When Saihung had clunked his way to the end, he found his two new masters still consumed with mirth.

"You have a long way to go," laughed Crystal Spring as he slapped him on the back.

They spent the rest of the night in a ruined temple, a favorite place for the two Taoists. The avaricious did not come because there was no profit, and the rest did not come because of superstition. Abandoned temples were thus ideal shelters.

Saihung was eager to be of service. He awoke at dawn, filled water gourds, and gathered wood for the fire. His delicate actor's hands were now splashed with cold morning water. The fine skin wore against splintered branches. But he was happy. How ironic, he realized, that he should like service so much now, where he had hated it on Huashan. As the two sent him into town for supplies he fell readily into the role of student. It felt good. Only now did he realize the kinship of service and religious devotion.

The road was already crowded with people, though it was barely light. He passed children and adults on their way to early-morning destinations,—farmers with donkey-drawn loads of produce, woodcutters carrying impossible loads of cuttings. Saihung took a deep breath. He was back with masters, and he suddenly felt foolish. He wondered how much time he had wasted by ignoring the wisdom of his elders to strike out on his own. It had been three years since he had left Huashan, three years that he had spent with little spiritual counsel save the whispers of a too-often-shunned conscience. He had been a brawler, recording in bruises and painful breakages the exploits of his challenges. He had been an actor, absorbed in the glory of the art, the satisfaction of acclaim. He had become a young and wealthy gentleman and had built the mind-palace that he had envisioned. But only now did he see how empty it had been.

He cursed himself gently, reproaching himself for his short-sightedness. He reflected that impetuousness and brashness were his greatest faults. Saihung remembered times that his attention had wandered during entire lessons with the priests of Huashan. At the end of the lesson, they had stopped and did not repeat: Knowing that he had missed the knowledge, they would leave him without it. As he thought back, he knew that those precious secrets were gone forever, and the years that had passed since his departure from the mountain had been equal failures to apply himself to his spiritual task.

He was reminded of the task his master had set for him. He had done nothing to ease anyone's suffering except to throw a few coins to beggars. His own whims had been his only concerns. Fame and achievement had become obsessions. In his determination not to fail, to somehow equal in his own way the example of his relatives, classmates, and masters, he had sacrificed that last gift from the Grand Master.

Perhaps a chance still lay open to him. He had the opportunity to study again, to be a disciple again, to redeem himself. He knew that there was no such thing as forgiveness, no such thing as an apology that would negate his blunders: The past was irretrievably gone. The only chance was to look ahead and energetically apply himself to doing good.

Butterfly had been right, thought Saihung. In spite of the disaster that his elder brother had made of his own life, the comments he had made at the Divine Eagle's villa had been correct. The only medicine for guilt was to look ahead and persevere. Pursuing his destiny was all that mattered, and he knew his destiny was to be a spiritual aspirant.

He bought the supplies he had been sent for and started back. It was a two-hour walk to the temple. He could make each step an act of penance, each breath a bead in his human rosary.

In the mid-afternoon, Slender Gourd took him to a shaded corner of the broken-down, weed-invaded courtyard.

"My brother and I will both teach you," he said. "I will first outline the method of cultivating the Way.

"Let me complete what I began last night. You must seek the Mysterious Portal. But it is guarded. You must have an offering to first bribe the guards and then the ability to be invisible so that you may slip through unnoticed. With these preparations you must then learn to fly to heaven, surprise Lao Tzu in his chambers, snatch up the flask of golden elixir, slay the defenders, break down the palace walls, and return to earth an immortal!"

"This is like the opera 'Monkey Makes Havoc in Heaven,'" commented Saihung. "I played that role."

"Yes, but this is no opera," said the master severely. "Sit down and listen to me. The first thing is the bribe for the guards."

"What is that?"

"Gold and jewels do not move the demon generals. It is the human spirit. Your bribe is a vow that should you attain the golden elixir that will liberate you from this earthly plane, you shall not depart into the infinite before teaching others and continuing the lineage."

"I promise. I will do everything I can to walk the holy path," said Saihung. "Master, I will do anything to succeed."

"Not so fast," cautioned Slender Gourd. "You are obviously a man of determination, but you must maintain a certain perspective. For this brings up the question of flying. Flying means weightlessness. Such lightness means shedding weight. Your emotional burden is overeagerness to succeed and anxiety about failing. Gain and loss are not to be taken to heart. You must leave these attitudes behind. Do you understand?"

"Yes, Master."

"Invisibility, as you said last night, signifies stillness in meditation. With it, you can slip through the Mysterious Portal. This gateway is in the region known as the Precious

Square Inch in the center of the head at eyebrow level. It is through this gateway that you will someday glimpse the divine light that is always there. When you can unify semen, breath, and spirit you will soar to heaven—that is to say that you raise this essence to the Mysterious Portal. Snatching the Golden Elixir means that your channels are now open and that your energy breaches the Mysterious Portal. But at that final stage, the guardians will appear and you will have to slay them."

"Who are these guardians?"

"Guardians are the agents of your own involvement with illusion. Your ego will not want you to succeed, for the resulting realization will negate your sense of self. Therefore, it will fight you and attempt to stop you from achieving your goals."

"Is the ego not my very self?" asked Saihung.

"The ego comes and goes, is born and dies. The self is eternal. It neither changes not has substance."

"So when you say to slay the ego, then I suppose you mean that the true self subdues it."

Slender Gourd smiled. "Actually, the ego does not exist."

"If it does not exist, then how can it cause trouble?"

"There is an important inquiry! Ask yourself: To whom is the trouble? The trouble is imagined. The ego is imagined. But we give ego substance and it becomes the means to experience pain and pleasure. We are enslaved. If we inquire into the nature of ego, if we remember that it is our own creation, than ego, pain, and pleasure will disappear."

"Suffering is thus imaginary?"

"Yes. You suffer because you imagine yourself to be something other than who you actually are. In truth, you are the self alone. You are the 'I,' stripped of qualities. You are nameless and formless. Since you cannot grasp that fact you cling to forms, emotions, and thought. Ego arises to give you form. By contrast, the man of wisdom simply *is*. He does not cling to thought. He is still and knows that he is god."

"I still don't understand how to slay the ego."

"Do you think there are two? Wake up! The ego is only imaginary. There is nothing outside yourself. You need only cast off the illusion, forsake your imaginary forms."

"Who casts off the illusion, then?"

"*I* cast off the illusion of myself. Yet I remain *I*."

So the I must cast off the imaginary ego that binds me to illusion."

"Yes we are all mired in the ignorance of illusion. You yourself are an ideal example. We found you on the stage. What could be a more perfect lesson than that? You were an actor, playing a role that people believed, and all the while both actor and audience were themselves victims of the illusion of reality. A play within a play within a cosmic farce: That was your past life. Don't cling to your individuality during meditation. This pathetic little drama we know as life is not reality. We are all just playing roles, put here for a reason, taken off when our roles are finished. But who is behind the painted face? Do not mistake your sense of self for your true nature. Instead, kill the guardians.

"This leaves only one task: to break down the walls of the mind-palace."

Saihung felt a sudden shock, and then an uneasiness.

"The palace walls must be broken down, for they will be the final barrier between you and the Source. Only by smashing the walls can we return to the Source. Once we merge with the Source, temporarily at least for our time of meditation, we surrender all sense of the world and our own individuality."

"Surrender?"

"Surrender is nearly impossible for a fighter like you, but

that is actually what you must do. It means deliberately surrendering all actions, motivations, decisions. Even the form of meditation is transcended. The palace walls are the world of forms."

"How can they be smashed by surrendering? How can illusion be overcome like this?"

"Let me clarify that illusion is not falsehood. Rather, it is the active side of reality. This activity generates forms. From that variety comes illusion. Yet all this variation, all these changes exist only in the mind. You look at me, look at the temple, look at the mountains, and forget your identity with these things. Focus on consciousness, not form, and the illusion of diversity and separateness breaks like a dream. Withdraw from the mind's interplay into stillness. Withdraw from activity to inactivity. Withdraw into the source and all illusion will cease. Then you will know that Lao Tzu, the golden elixir, the guardians, and palace walls existed only in your mind. The only truth lies in realizing yourself as the formless One.

"But talking does nothing. None succeed without effort."

He showed Saihung how to sit and repeated the steps for the meditation, and left Saihung in contemplation.

The poor temple room was a simple cell. Whitewashed walls had been so worn by time, so abraded by dust, and milky layers that they ceased to be dirty or coarse. They had acquired a patina of antiquity. A distant bell sounded and a faint scent of sandalwood lingered far in the background like an ancestral memory. The atmosphere was dense in its stillness. Quietude was a heavy, palpable presence. Serenity had pooled deeply within the confines of the temple and he submerged himself in it. He sunk to its very depths and came to rest in a perfect pyramidal posture.

Perhaps this was what it was like to drown; to feel the

liquid invade your nose, your mouth, every aperture down to your pores and soak to your bones in a few seconds' time. Only here, he breathed in the temple air, heavy enough to feel liquid. He became a rock. A large stone icon at the bottom of a sea of tranquility.

Outside became inside. Inside became indistinguishable from outside. Nothing existed save the world of his meditation. Was time the cycle of the universe, or merely the measured cadence of his energy moving up his spine? He felt it was true when his masters had told him that the body was a microcosm of the universe. Wasn't he now the universe?

In the first darkness, it was his thought that created a thousand suns, a hundred galaxies. It was his breath that set the cosmos whirling. His universe evolved into the five elements, the ten thousand things (only a few named, so many still unnamed and contemplated only in wonder). He could hear his body's functions. He could listen to his nerves firing and even detect the subtle electrical flows. He could smell different smells, some fragrant, some putrid, as they rose from the complex worlds of his organs. He could taste the flows of liquids and gasses. The universe was not a mechanism. It couldn't be compared to the pathetic inventions of puny men. It wasn't an organism. It was eternal. It wasn't a divine being. It embraced both thought and non-thought, being and non-being. All those definitions and metaphors had to be inverted. The universe was of an infinite magnitude. He was a microcosm of the universe.

The masters said the world was illusion. By simple logic, if a human being was a microcosm of the external world, he also was illusion, a phantasm imagining himself to exist in a non-existant reality. He understood that meditation was not merely a state, but a vehicle to understanding. Existing or nonexisting, he commanded the forces inside him, concentrated them, directed them to one point. Illusion nevertheless had substance. He would pierce the veil to find the answer to this question.

The flow of his breath rose in his body, and he felt warm. He concentrated deeply, inhaling deeply. His mind seemed to dive deep into his body, down to its very base, stirring the sexual fluids. Conserved by a lifetime of celibacy, trained since childhood in meditation, it was easy to stir his basic chemistry. He unified semen, breath, and spirit—what the Taoists called "Uniting the Three into One," and directed the resulting essence upwards like a flow of liquid light. The brilliance ascended to his skull.

His meditation was succeeding. He quickly realized that the ascension of energy meant that he was similarly rising towards the spiritual heights. The movement of energy was perfectly precise. He felt his psychic centers opening, whirling. Saihung felt great power.

All the abilities of his masters, which had seemed so unattainable before, now seemed within his grasp. In fact, they seemed absurdly simple. They were as easy to grasp as toys were for a child. He was esctatic. But in that moment he understood that, even then, pride and ego had leapt up. By reveling in the power, he knew that temptation loomed all the more strongly. Balanced at the top of that slender shaft of high-voltage human energy, Saihung finally understood how easy it was to topple off.

The brilliance grew like a sun condensed, contained, but now bursting and burning. Glowing. Here was the golden light streaming through the Mysterious Portal. Here was the blinding stream of infinity. He felt a hesitation. A great inner tension. He knew these feelings were the "guardians." It was his self objecting to its imminent negation. He wanted to go, but something held him back. The light flickered.

Saihung saw the light again, flooding through the portal. It built in power. All he had to do was give in. All he had to do was let the light take his being over. He paused only a moment this time, and then plunged into the rising radiance.

He felt a brief but powerful sensation, like being torn by a great explosion. And then he felt nothing. There was no longer a "he" to feel. There was only golden light and the trace of his surrender.

Hours passed before he came back to awareness. He felt strangely disjointed. It occurred to him that he was dying. The more he thought, the more he felt that he was close to death. All his essence and concentration had been bound into that stream of light. But the rest of his body had been plunged into darkness. He had created a living day within, but this had left a cold and lonely night for the rest of himself. His spirit, confined for so long, had emerged like a beautiful white swan, breathing, awakened, joyous. It had left a trail of brilliant light and breath—a long, heavenly banner. But the rest of his body had begun to wither.

He began to perform dispersing movements that brought him back to reality and restored his own private little universe to proper circulation and functioning. He knew Taoists who had died spiritual deaths by meditating for forty-nine days. After what he had felt, he knew that forty-nine days of experiences such as his would have made him entirely spiritual. His body would have to die: Starved of life force for so long, it would be a wonder if it lasted that amount of time.

The energy drain was the reason for celibacy, diet, rest, physical practice, and sound thinking. He now saw them not as mere monastic affectations, but as desperate measures to prevent a premature death during the struggle for enlightenment. He would have to balance his meditation with herbs, diet, and exercise in order to keep his tie to the earthly plane. The logic of his vow to help others became clear: If everyone passed into the infinite, no one would be left to point the way.

Saihung rested for a while, but still felt weak. He found the two masters sitting casually by the fire. They smiled when he recounted his experiences, commenting that he would soon regain his equilibrium. Meditation would then become smoother and the body would be strengthened to support the critical flows of energy. Slender Gourd seemed uninterested in his feelings of death. Apparently, this was not significant to his quest. However, it did inspire the master to speak further.

"In order to understand the ultimate goal, we must understand death. Dying is life's only certainty. In one way, the Taoist seems intimately concerned with death because his priority is to transcend the mortal plane and escape the cycle of reincarnation. On the other hand, he can be quite unconcerned with death, since he views it as a mere cycle of change.

"There is the parable of the highwayman's victim. The fellow, believing his purse to contain a great store of gold, was horrified to be robbed. If only he had realized that his purse was empty! Then he would have surrendered it with equanimity. This is the true situation: The purse is filled with autumn leaves. The purse is the body. The leaves are the illusion of 'individuality.' There is something real to the human, however. It is a great deal more precious than gold, but it is not our possession. That something did not begin with our birth. It did not grow as we did. It will not cease upon our death. Death, to a Taoist, is nothing."

"I'm afraid that you've lost me," said Saihung.

"Butterfly Taoist! Butterfly Taoist!" laughed Crystal Spring. "Don't you know the parable of the butterfly? It was even an opera that your troupe performed!"

"Yes, I know it," responded Saihung. "But I do not see the connection."

"Let me quote," said Crystal Spring. "'I, Chuang Tzu, dreamed I was a butterfly. Now, when I am awake, I do not know if I was Chuang Tzu dreaming that I was a butterfly, or whether I am now a butterfly dreaming that I am a man.'"

"Yes, I am familiar with this tale."

"Then let me ask you this," said Crystal Spring with a sly twinkle. "What would an onlooker have seen?"

Saihung was bewildered. He had been thinking only of the paradox of Chuang Tzu and the butterfly.

"I don't know," he stammered.

"An onlooker would have seen no difference," announced the master triumphantly.

Saihung was thoroughly confused.

"Change is constant in nature," explained Slender Gourd. "But there is an unchanging principle underlying all change. Take water, for example. Water evaporates and becomes clouds. Clouds become rain, sleet, or snow. Lakes become ice. But throughout all these changes, water does not lose its essential nature. Some might say that when water becomes ice, it has 'died.' Or when it evaporates, it has 'died.' But this is absurd. In the same way, death is a mere transformation, not an end. We need not be terrified of it. In fact, our sentimental emotions are totally irrelevant."

"So you see," added Crystal Spring, "that Chuang Tzu is either befuddled or throwing us a diversion. He is neither Chuang Tzu nor the butterfly. He is both at once. What is important is not to be deceived by the dualistic question of whether he was one or the other, but to realize that there is some underlying essence beneath it all."

"Do not fear the sensations you feel during meditation," concluded Slender Gourd. "Let all phenomena come and go. Even death is a part of such illusion. Don't identify with phenomena, but instead look deeply into the Tao and its source. Forget the illusion of a separate existence. Cast off this imaginary limitation that separates you from the Way. Let your finiteness merge with the infinte. Far from becoming diminished, you will become infinite yourself. When you have this perception, you will then know the true secret of the sages: The mind of one who returns to the Source becomes the Source."

T E N

The Golden Embryo

Saihung stayed with the two Taoists for months of relentless travel. Their nomadic lifestyle took them over the length and breadth of China. They found inspiration in any event and any place they happened upon. Whether it was the mist-shrouded peaks of China's ethereal mountains, the parched plains of the northern deserts, or even the crowded and bustling urban centers, the two Taoists taught Saihung that everything was a part of the Way. They taught him that when one identified oneself with the universe, then the universe was real. If one perceived the universe as outside of oneself, then it was unreal. Illusion and reality were yin and yang and thus one and the same. Thus, swimming in the current of the universe was as important as still contemplation. Experiencing life, testing their learning and philosophy among people who cared nothing for such things, and confirming speculations that arose from their contemplations were crucial priorities. Life experience, they said, would always be superior both to mere book learning and the artificiality of the cloistered world.

Their unconventional approach and their great insight gave their teaching an unusual character. While they would give their lessons the support of Taoist proverbs that Saihung had been familiar with for many years, they frequently interpreted them in startlingly new ways. They found precedent for their life of travel in the phrase, "Without going out of my door, I can know all things on heaven and earth." Surely, Saihung thought, this was an argument for austere contemplation. But no, the two had countered with great delight. They interpreted the phrase from a greater point of view. "Without going out of my door" meant without dying too soon. "Knowing all things on heaven and earth" meant the completion of one's life task and the purging of all consequences of past lives. Therefore, the meaning they saw was that one should complete one's earthly destiny in a single lifetime. Such a goal could not be achieved by mere monastic living, for "know all things on heaven and earth" would require personal investigation.

They spurned traditional book knowledge and laughed at the efforts of scholars, though they were both educated, intelligent, and well-read. Theories were merely the idle speculations of others. Stories could never substitute for real adventure, manuscripts and scriptures were inferior to direct transmissions from masters. The division and partisanship of schools and styles was useless. The intellectual was only valid when tested and proved upon one's own body and self.

Book-learning was a violation of the basic human nature. Etiquette was a tiring yoke on the spontaneous will. Social duty only dulled happy spirits. Morality was repression. As they trekked through China, they sometimes came upon backwoods villages, or some of the even more socially primitive minority tribes. In the example of uneducated people free from the rigid socialization of mainstream Confucianist China, they found their ideal of a more pure and innocent human. Honesty, contentment, lack of striving, and simple lives close to the earth and seasons were the beautiful qualities of such people. The two Taoists pointed out that their unspoiled state was not derived from book-learning, but the simple people still had wisdom.

Wisdom was a necessary pursuit for humans, not only because humanity had the inborn capacities for reasoning and higher learning, but because proper understanding could lead to spiritual liberation. Mastering a sufficient body of knowledge was a great challenge, because the Taoists demanded high degrees of excellence. Yet, while they encouraged the pursuit of skill and understanding, they used the ideal of the uncarved block as a balancing element. In the often frustrating search for perfection, it was useful to remember that the ideal state was not to be pursued, but uncovered. It was not to be searched for far and near, but to be found by realizing its presence within.

The two Taoists thus embodied a paradox of learning. They spurned education, yet they insisted that Saihung continue with his own.

They eschewed monastic living, yet they sequestered themselves daily for meditation. They advocated innocence, yet practiced complex arts. They lived wandering lives among all levels of society, yet they clung to very disciplined standards for their diet, thought, conduct, and actions.

"It is only on the extreme limits of knowledge that one encounters paradox," Crystal Spring told Saihung. "Yet if one would seek all knowledge, one must accept paradox.

"The conventional say that things must always be one way or the other. They would say that one must either be a monk or a layperson. An untutored innocent, or a cynical erudite. This kind of dualistic thinking is why the Confucianists and Buddhists remain locked into dogmatic schools.

"That's why they hate Taoists. They dislike our nonconformity. But in fact, it is only due to their inflexible viewpoint that they fail to see the true substance and creative potential of our methods."

"So in essence," added Slender Gourd, "the paradox of learning is that you must be both artful and artless."

"That's it," said Crystal Spring. "You have to be both. Yin and yang together. Yin and yang oppose one another, define one another, complete one another, destroy one another. If you are to be learned, you must do the same. Embrace paradox, my boy. For unless you do, you will be doomed to contradiction."

"Pardon me?" asked Saihung.

"Contradiction!" snapped Crystal Spring. "Don't confuse that with paradox or we'll never be done with this blabbering."

"I'm sorry," said Saihung. "Couldn't you just explain a little?"

"All I mean," said Crystal Spring, "is that those who don't embrace paradox in their knowledge will forever stumble upon the contradictions that will inevitably arise from their rational and logical calculations. Since they cannot account for these contradictions within the rigid framework of their doctrines, it renders their thinking completely sterile."

Knowledge and its history formed tradition, and tradition was also useful, even to the iconoclastic Taoists. They explained that traditional knowledge was an aid in shaping the early crude efforts of the beginner. It was a rich and varied source of all the tried processes, the improved methods, and even the dead-ends of investigation. It stood as the delineation of the boundaries of the human imagination. Inviting spontaneous excursions inside its borders, or allowing reasonable attempts to expand its frontiers, tradition was the crucial matrix for an individual's efforts.

Since it was larger than any single human, traditional knowledge offered the seeker the choice of many precedents. Surely, the two Taoists told Saihung, tradition was superior to the efforts of novices, and certainly of the disdainful, or the ignorant. It was reasonable to learn as much as was necessary in order to reach the frontiers of reality; and then, from having saved one's creative efforts by profiting from learning, using one's creative efforts to make the leap into the unknown.

It was human nature to pursue learning, yet it was important to note that even the genius did not have truly encyclopedic knowledge. Human knowledge could not be mastered by a single person. There were twelve thousand documented herbs, but not even the most brilliant doctor used them all. There were more than ten thousand words in the Chinese dictionary, but not even the greatest scholar could explain them all. The pursuit of knowledge was the exploration of an infinite universe that curved back upon itself, that frayed into paradoxes and contradictions at its extremes. All that was important was that Saihung continue to learn and gather experiences, to stave off the mental rigor mortis of the content individual and cling to the Way.

The two Taoists' attitude towards learning and skill was best summarized in their maxim, "Know magic, shun magic." Magic truly existed, they taught Saihung. One should learn it—not to use it, but to avoid it. Ignorance made one a victim. Knowledge provided a defense. Only through understanding could one be free of its influence.

They then took the example further, substituting all sorts of words for magic: knowledge, tradition, martial arts, politics. The equation applied to all those things and more.

Saihung had the chance to observe this philosophy when he realized that he was never in any danger in the time he was with the two Taoists. Bandits never attacked them. Animals did not threaten them. Soldiers never stopped them. Without any structure or conflict, Saihung realized that there had never been any need to fight while he was with them. His masters had gone beyond art and artfulness. Just as they could cross a bridge silently, they could follow the Way without disturbance from themselves or others.

They wandered here and there fearlessly. They had indeed embraced paradox by being highly learned yet completely spontaneous and natural. It came, no doubt, because they knew magic yet shunned magic.

Saihung noted this observation, and the two Taoists merely gestured toward a faraway temple.

"Magic is for simpletons. Idols are for the unthinking," said Crystal Spring. "Truth is evasive and subtle. What you notice is not the product of knowledge, but a sign of something much greater. Yes, knowledge is essential, but it is not the ultimate thing."

"What is truth?" asked Slender Gourd rhetorically. "What can we put our trust in? Certainly not the world. Ultimately, the world is an illusion. It is a stage play of elaborate costumes, bedazzling sets, intoxicating music, and fascinating characters. It is full of pathos, tragedy, happiness, and aspiration. But it is no more real than the operas of which you once were a part. All that you experience, all that you see, is but a play of unseen elements. We see the five colors, taste the five flavors, hear the five tones; we take this as reality, but it isn't so. 'Know magic, shun magic,' we tell you. 'Experience the world.' 'Travel to follow the Tao.' In the end, even these phrases are merely provisional. These just help you play your part on this ludicrous opera stage. I tell you, the world is a farce, a kaleidescopic play of shadows, colors, and reflections.

"All knowledge is infinite," said Crystal Spring. "Yet compared with the ultimate truth, it is an inexact approximation. Know knowledge to shun knowledge: You can put your faith in nothing but inner perception. Shall we base our truth upon the gods? Yet we know little about them. They are nothing of what they appear to be. The temples and scriptures are just religious theaters for the ordinary person.

The gods are nothing like that. No, truth is to be based not on any ideal, no matter how purportedly divine, but on something else."

"But the scriptures are holy," protested Saihung. "Aren't they truth?"

"The scriptures were written by human beings," explained Slender Gourd patiently. "They are useful as rough guides. The degree of truth they contain, when compared to the befuddled state of the average person, is extraordinary. But to the enlightened, the scriptures are mere funeral money and the gods but straw dogs."

"When I was on Huashan, they told me that mastering the *Seven Bamboo Tablets* was essential. I have never read it, I've never determined how far I have to go. Now you teach me that my efforts were illusory?"

"The *Seven Bamboo Tablets* were, according to legend, brought to earth by the God of Longevity," said Crystal Spring. "Even in antiquity, the earth was not spiritually cleansed and the gods would send emissaries to earth to help people. Sometimes they would bring scriptures and leave them as instructions for the worthy. *The Seven Bamboo Tablets* were such a gift.

"But the god left the tablets in a cave on a high peak in the Kunlun mountains. Humanity had to prove itself worthy by sending a hero to retrieve the tablets. The sages selected a baby and raised him from childhood with his sole goal the seeking of the divine gift. This baby was quite unusual. According to legend, he was born from an egg that a farmer found while gathering wood. Since he and his wife were childless, he took it home. It hatched and a handsome boy emerged. It was this boy who was groomed to take up the quest.

"He brought those tablets back many centuries ago. The original tablets still exist, but they were hidden away at

Maoshan during the Opium Wars with Britain. Now all we have are copies with many commentaries attached by generations of masters. Additionally, there are different versions according to lineages and sects.

"In essence, *The Seven Bamboo Tablets* detail 360 methods of attaining enlightenment. The number 360 corresponds to the number of degrees in a circle. Thus, the entire range of methodologies is accounted for in this work. The methods range from the purely ascetic and meditative, to controversial sexual techniques of dual cultivation. Philosophy, breathing, alchemy, drugs, ritual, ceremony, devotion—every possible means of achieving higher states is discussed, analyzed, and recorded for the sake of future generations. Even martial arts are a part of this sacred work, not as a fighting art, but as a complete way of study, discipline, and practice.

"*The Seven Bamboo Tablets* represent all that you must master, it's true. But don't mistake mastering the book for mastering the knowledge. What is important is that you fully complete your spiritual task."

"Look beyond this mere book," said Slender Gourd. "As it has 360 ways, so must you become a complete and well-rounded man. Do not cleave to narrow doctrines. Take it as a framework, a scaffolding. But once we circle constantly back to tradition, we shall soar forth again."

"It matters not," Crystal Spring concluded, "whether you read the *Seven Bamboo Tablets* or not. You could read it and it might be as dull as a dictionary. In fact, that would be its exact appearance. But take its components, benefit from its tradition, use them as alloys to be blended in the crucible of life, and forge them into your own unique personality. Don't follow any book dogmatically, not even the most sacred scripture. It's stupidity to think any book is the word of the gods."

"Truth ultimately lies not in learning, for one inevitably reaches the limits of one's art," said Slender Gourd. "Therefore, one can attain truth only by transcending the self. The petty self is but a part of this grand comedy. The spiritual is the force that animates the play, and through meditation, one can merge with the spiritual. At the highest stages, the self is absorbed in a larger consciousness. Individuality is lost, accomplishments from skill become irrelevant. The pursuit of knowledge is vital to the continuing growth and health of the practitioner and is useful for helping others and cultivating attitudes of perfectionism. However, one's ultimate endeavor lies in the artless art of meditation, where all skill is finally transcended."

The truth. Something in Saihung awakened. All this time he had searched to accumulate knowledge, struggled to complete methodologies, collected ancient manuscripts, studied with many great teachers. Despite years of experience and accumulated understandings bound by the monastic structure, he had been left with nothing. He thought again of the parable of the highwayman and the purse, and thought of the *Seven Bamboo Tablets of the Cloudy Satchel*. His masters had truly shown his purse to contain autumn leaves. And the Cloudy Satchel—what a monstrous joke, what a piece of compassion. All the knowledge of the sages was a tender way of leading the student to the realization that there was something beyond knowledge and facility, something on the other side of high learning. All of civilization was a mere shadow play, a crude projection from the light of truth that had need of neither conceptualization nor structure.

He stood up. What a thing to absorb. What a dunce he had been! But, he reminded himself, it was better to suffer a moment of embarassment than a lifetime of shame. He strolled to the edge of the mountain and looked out, and thought of his master on Huashan with gratitude. The old man had begun the process, had worked for years with patience to prepare Saihung for this very point.

Being in the mountains always seemed to calm Saihung. Their loftiness gave him an entirely different perspective on life than when he was down on the plains. The pure grandeur dwarfed whole cities with their thousands of inhabitants engaged in their myriad pursuits. The exquisite splendor made his own emotions and anxieties seem superfluous. There on a high peak of pristine granite, he felt as if he were on the world's rim, only a breath away from heaven's borders. Whenever he looked to the wide horizon, he lost his frustrations and abandoned his mental troubles. His soul yearned to fly, to float, to become absorbed in that narrow band of mountains and sky. The day was warm and sunny. He sat back down in the shadow of a venerable pine to again listen to Slender Gourd's lecture.

"Our bodies, imagination, and breath are the only immediately available tools to we who begin spiritual practice. Deeper states and powers cannot immediately be tapped. We must first utilize those parts of ourselves that can most readily be brought under conscious control. These can then be gradually directed towards the attainment of more specialized abilities.

"The paradox is that these facets of ourselves can be our hindrances if left unchecked. Our bodies may deteriorate to the point that poor health makes practice impossible. Our imaginations can run wild, obscuring our true souls in wild and lurid fantasy. Our breathing, left only under the automatic control of our subconscious, can never become anything more than a way to provide oxygen to this physical shell.

"But the first stage of spiritual practice begins with the

tangible. The body is disciplined by stretching, postures, herbs, martial arts, and meditation; its raw material and good health become the basis for further progress.

"The imagination is used to suggest goals and direct the movement of energy not normally under conscious control; its powerful message can overwhelm both mind and body. The breath represents not only the first organ that we can bring under our conscious control, but it is the physical link to the mind; its rhythms, ratios, proportions, and timing can cause the mind to respond with correspondingly altered states.

"Discipline makes achievement possible. Reins direct the wild horse; constraint directs the spirit. When a bow is pulled back, the arrow is aimed while the bow is at its highest constraint. Its release sends the arrow mightily to its target. Today, I want to teach you a very special technique vital to your development: the creation of the Golden Embryo."

"The Golden Embryo is our expression for creating a powerful force field in the abdomen. It fortifies the body and bolsters the organs. Loss of hair, wrinkling of the skin, stiffening of the joints, dulling of the eyes, diminishing of hearing, loss of memory, weakening of muscles, faltering of will, and decline of vitality all represent the progressive deterioration of the glands and organs. The Golden Embryo, if practiced faithfully, becomes a storehouse of energy distributing life force to rejuvenate the body."

"Does this make one immortal?" asked Saihung.

"Yes, but not in the sense of living forever in this mortal form," replied his master. "It does mean that your breath and lifetime will be extended and maintained long enough for you to gain realization. But it also is related to a very critical point: spiritual death."

"The spiritual death is not exclusive to Taoists," said

Crystal Spring seriously. "The Buddhists call it *nirvana*, the Hindus call it *mahasamadhi*, and the Taoists call it 'merging with the void.' Isn't that odd? At the moment we introduce the idea of an embryo, we must also discuss death."

They told Saihung that every human being had three selves: animal, astral, and spiritual. The animal self was the instincts, drives, lusts. Created at birth, it was trapped in the body upon death and decayed with the body. The astral self was the hereditary self. It carried with it the imprint of the parents, embodied their genetics not merely physically, but mentally and emotionally as well. This inherited personality determined a great deal of a person's destiny, for it established the basic parameters of potential progress and contained the metaphysical qualities of the parents. Education, parental upbringing, and the person's own actions would complete the elements of his destiny. Aside from that, the function of the astral self was to judge, reason and learn.

The spiritual self was that element of a human that was on a journey, the immortal spirit that no physical force could destroy. Its sole aim was to return to the cosmic Source. In order to do that, it had to learn, be purified, purge itself of all negativity in order to merge with the great One.

All three selves were active in everyday life. Whenever action was required, the three selves acted as a tribunal. However, one or the other self could predominate in the decision making, giving the person's actions a particular emphasis.

The two Taoists reminded Saihung that the critical thing in life was to die a spiritual death, to merge with the Void. In order to do so, one had to be free of the cycle of reincarnation. This meant absolutely no earthly ties. The important point was that having children automatically tied one to the circle of reincarnation. How could it be otherwise? By passing on one's metaphysical and physical genetics, one perpetuated one's earthly karma. This was why the sages had no biological children.

Assuming that a practitioner fulfilled all the requirements, he could, through his austerities, merge his three selves into one super-dynamic new self. This composite spirit would emerge from the body at the right moment and would transcend the cycle of earthly reincarnation. It would then rise as high as it could to another plane of existence. There were few, even among the sages, who could return immediately to the Source. More than likely, the new Spirit would go on to an astral realm where there no longer was birth or death, but where everything was accomplished by thought alone. Then the spirit would go through more transformation in order to finally merge with the Void.

Superhuman achievement as it was to combine the selves and transcend the earthly plane, the two Taoists reminded Saihung that it was not enough in itself: They believed that one must pass through thirty-nine levels of existence in order to return to nothingness. Earthly life was the very lowest level.

All this was relevant to the creation of the Golden Embryo, because this was the goal of practice. Otherwise, the technique was nothing more than a sophisticated health exercise. It was the Golden Embryo that supported the energy to maintain the adept and power his final ascension.

There was one curious footnote to the whole doctrine: A master could, just before death, project his Golden Embryo into the body of his student. This in effect made the student his child. The disciple then received incredible power, but with a catch: He also received his master's destiny, both good and bad. This meant that he then had to work off more destiny along with his greater power, and that his own master would return to earth again. Such a technique was rarely employed.

The Golden Embryo technique required that Saihung first master a complex system of *qigong* or breath control. A variety of options were open to him, such as the microcosmic orbit, meditation on the Twelve Meridians, or Using *Qi* to Open the Eight Psychic Meridians. Saihung had already learned these techniques on Huashan. They all opened the twelve regular meridians and the eight psychic meridians.

Once this had been accomplished, Saihung was to perceive—not simply imagine—the light of the Mysterious Portal. This light was pure life force. Then he had to direct it, to bring it down to the *dan tian*—the Field of Cultivation. He would then repeatedly raise and lower this light from his *dan tian* to the Red Palace just at the base of his heart. This current of energy created the Golden Embryo.

It was a dark, quiet night when Saihung first sat to practice this new meditation. He found an empty cell in the ruined monastery they had temporarily inhabited. How, he wondered, had this consecrated place been destroyed and its community dispersed? What danger or superstition kept it barren? Yet it was because of its wrecked status that his place made a perfect shelter for them. In the shattered shell of the aspirations generations before him had left, he sat down for his own attempt.

He sat cross-legged on a grass mat, without the luxury of prayer rugs and deer skin he had had on Huashan. He arranged his limbs exactly, clasped his hands in a particular way. He placed his body into an idealized alignment. His body and mind, so used to their everyday whirling about— mind racing and clicking into innumerable overlapping patterns, his limbs flailing and gesticulating—were contracted into a stable structure. His personality withdrew to an exact set of concordances. He breathed down to the root of life. The energy released could go nowhere but up into the channel he had left for it.

His meditation progressed according to a geometry of its own. The psychic centers of his body lay on a straight line. They each had their own colors and inner patterns. His energy flowed in lines, coursing through the meridians. Lines connected points. The network moved, glowed with high energy. Sequentiality came into the structure. Unfolding began.

He followed his masters' instructions exactly in order to direct the flow of energy. In daily life, energy and the distances between points in the body and mind varied and revolved. But now, by setting the structure of his personality into a particular form, concentration occurred. Energy was stepped up or down. Taoism knew no separation between materialism and spirituality. By beginning with the physical and tangible, he would pass into the metaphysical and ethereal.

He felt power. What a thrill it was! A confidence, an assurance, a danger. He knew that without meditation he would never gain spiritual maturity. Only by endeavoring to raise the energy high in his body could he gain the power to fulfill his quest. But the geometry into which he had set himself knew no morality. Patterns of lines and points embodied no ethics. He gained power through meditation, but, he realized, the choice of good and evil still was his to make. Nothing about meditation made an evil person good; it only put a formidable weapon into his hand, and good people found themselves tempted. This was meditation's safety device, its trap to catch the unworthy.

He built his energy higher, mindful of the danger, the temptation to linger in spheres that yielded great power and ability. He urged himself higher, into the realms above the heart, where he would feel indifference to the outside world and the realm of the senses.

All was still. The slightest external movement would

alter the fragile route, snap the glowing strand. He breached the gate to the skull, the Jade Pivot, entered Lao Tzu's grotto, and his soul was bathed in a golden light. He took that light, like the life-giving glow of the sun, like the divine fire of a thousand stars, and embraced it, merged with it, loved it. Here was bliss, here was happiness. Here was god, or good, or whatever label there was for this force so divine and holy. Here was utter serenity and immortality.

How simple it all was, and how much like doting old aunties all his masters had been! He had thought them obtuse, secretive, and enigmatic people stingy with their realization. Now he knew them for the babblers they were, the caring, sentimental old fools who spent every day pointing out to their students what was absurdly obvious. Divinity and immortality were within us all. That could truly be known "without going out of the door."

His masters must have worn themselves out pointing out what to them must have been as obvious as the nose on his face. Now he saw. Now he realized that nothing in the external world could compare to this. Not martial arts. Not fine porcelains. Not great literature. Not a career or fame and fortune. Nothing could compare with this blazing glow of life force.

This pure energy, the pure essence of virility, was alive, and could give life and create life. It was inspiration, it was the movement that first set the universe into motion. It was that ray that first sliced through the dark chaos and brought reality into being. Now that ray flashed down through his body to the Field of Cultivation, to that place of fertility. It flashed like the warm rays of the sun, it stirred the rich soil of his soul watered by the fluids of his body. It warmed the valley and he knew in time that creation would take place, and the Golden Embryo would emerge.

Words fail. They cannot describe the beauty of spiritual

fulfillment. Emotions fail. They cannot encompass the profundity of birth. Men and women are filled with awe and wonder when they come together to create a child. How much more difficult it is to understand spiritual birth, where the mystery of life is ours to at once create and perceive. In the end, the intellect fails. Inevitably, this mortal shell, too will fail.

For our lifetime, we live dependent on this physical cocoon. We love this vessel of flesh and blood, this vehicle of complexity. It is adorned, pampered, damaged by illness and violence, fed by consuming other bodies, joined in intercourse sometimes pure, other times unholy. In youth, we revel in its power. In old age we curse its betrayal. Eventually we see that over our lifetime, we have been imprisoned in a gradually rotting pillar of flesh.

The Taoists found the potential of the human. They found its potency, its fertility. They discovered ways to transform and direct that vitality so that what was immortal—the sliver of the spirit that was hurtling through millennia of the universe's existence—could be liberated from the physical shell. That was the purpose of the Golden Embryo meditation: to maintain the physical body until the immortal soul could emerge intact.

He had been reborn, knew birth, knew creation. But life is nothing without death; and it was in the moment when Saihung truly began to know life that he also had to know death.

It was late in the year, just past the autumn equinox, that the three of them wandered towards Maoshan in Jiangsu province. They went into the mountains and found a quiet and secluded cave. In the morning and at dusk, twice a day like some atmospheric tide, mists would roll through the passes and chasms. Like the ocean rushing between rocks, they obscured what lay below. On the solitary peak there were no other people. Birds sang, the small stream nearby splashed a subtle rhythm, and the wind rustled the drying bones of trees. Saihung looked at his mentors. They were at peace.

"In a short time," said Slender Gourd, "we will leave this world."

"Who knows how long we've wandered this dusty vale," added Crystal Spring. "Alas, its charms are so ephemeral."

"Go into town, and buy some supplies" continued Slender Gourd. "Then you must build us a pyre."

Saihung bowed and turned toward town obediently, but inwardly he was disturbed. He had seen other masters on Huashan leave their bodies and had been a part of the witnessing students gathered to honor one of the greatest accomplishments possible for a Taoist. But it had never been one of his own masters, and he had always remained unemotional about it. Confronted with the imminent departure of Slender Gourd and Crystal Spring, he panicked.

They were going to die. Though a lifetime of study had taught him that a normal death was a mere transformation, and that spiritual death meant an ascension to a higher dimension of consciousness, he nevertheless felt a sudden loneliness. They were abandoning him, leaving him to his own efforts, depriving him of the guidance that gave him utter confidence that any sanctioned action was absolutely correct. He had become used to having masters again, indeed, he had never been free of that structure—even his rebellion was still tied to the authority it professed to reject. He wondered what he would do without them. Should he return to Huashan, the opera, or Wang Ziping? He found no appeal in any alternative except for the one he instinctively knew: that he would always be committed in some way to spirituality. Everything else was temporary and unsteady.

Even as he split wood and spent days building a pyre, he understood that everything manmade inevitably comes to an end.

The dawn of the appointed day was cold and misty. Inside the cave, the two Taoists sat in meditation. At its conclusion, Saihung looked at them by the red light of the fire. Slender Gourd, thin but upright as a pillar, seemed older, a little more wrinkled. By the firelight his fine white hair seemed like flaming lightning. But his eyes were still those limpid, enigmatic jewels. Crystal Spring seemed to sit with more presence. As he gazed dispassionately out through the mouth of the cave, his gentle visage was calm and heroic. Saihung found it amazing that these two men would be dead within a few hours. He wondered if they felt emotion or longing as they contemplated their voyage into the unknown.

"A sage knows how to send his soul into the great beyond," whispered Slender Gourd. "He has already seen higher planes of existence. Thus, at death, he firmly fixes his mind upon the place he wants to travel to. At death, his soul goes there."

"An ordinary person, however has his three selves scattered," said Crystal Spring, "enmeshed again into the turnings of the wheel of life, they return again in a new form—but, sadly, to the same earthly hell. Remember to keep practicing, so that you may deliver yourself from this mortal plane."

"You are still young," said Slender Gourd compassionately. "It is a shame we did not meet earlier. But our time has come. Keep on with your spiritual path. Return to your master on Huashan. He will guide your progress with care and kindness."

"Do not feel grief upon our passing," said Crystal Spring as he noticed Saihung's reddening eyes. "This is only our physical shell. It is like a set of clothes that we discard. Our true selves shall emerge radiant and pure. Don't feel sad. Instead, rejoice at our victory."

"Goodbye," said Slender Gourd as his eyes gently closed.

"See you on the other side, my boy!" said Crystal Spring. He smiled reassuringly, until his eyes closed too.

Saihung watched the two motionless bodies. But inside their stillness, he knew a dynamic movement was taking place. Within each master, a flow of energy mightier than any other each had ever manifested was rushing upwards into the skull. Slowly, their bodies were passing into night. The arteries were pooling. The organs were stopping, drying up. The nerves were dulling. Every trace of life force was drawn upward. There, it was closed off. The body was in eclipse. The sun was contained in the head. The three selves became one, until in a powerful fusion, their souls launched themselves away.

Watching, Saihung saw none of this. He knew the process took about twenty minutes, but he waited for twice that long, anxiously peering at his two masters. Were they gone? Or just still? All along he kept rehearsing in his mind what he should do next, as if that would give him some reassurance.

Finally, he rose to check them. He found neither breathing nor pulse. They were dead. They had transcended life, died a superhuman death, perhaps they had cheated the cosmic cycle itself. He was left behind on earth with only the memory of their extraordinary lives. He was left open to injuries, accidents, illnesses, tricks of fate, and weaknesses of character. He felt like a lost boy, stuck in a house with objects whose meaning he had never completely decoded, alone after the adults had left. He realized that part of Taoism, indeed part of the human psyche, idolized a myth of invulnerability.

Everyone wanted to believe that heroes were unbeatable, that hermits could become physically immortal. They all wanted proof that death could be cheated. Legends, religions, even childhood fairy tales all reflected the immature fear of dying and the equally childish admiration for those who could break the final law. That was why there were heroes, so that those who did not reach their stature could at least take solace in the vicarious victory over the last enemy. Throughout history, they had enshrouded the fallen ones in myth, conveniently glossing over actual death. Guan Gong, though in actuality beheaded by his enemies, was deified as an immortal. Thousands of Taoists were supposed to have ridden up into heaven on the backs of dragons. Generations of alchemists—perhaps even the Emperor Qin himself—had died eating substances that they had speculated to be the elixir of immortality. Stupid humanity twisted its heroes. It wanted *bodhisattvas*, Christs, Immortals. It wanted desperately to have people willing to accept upon their bodies the overwhelming sins of all humanity. It wanted someone else to spare them the punishment of dying.

But here he was. Alone. His masters had gone, leaving him with all his own physical and spiritual vulnerabilities to cope with. They had wordlessly left him with the responsibility not only for his own existence, but for his own transcendence. They had shown him a way to transcend death not for the sake of the burlesque that was religion, but for his own private moment. He knew he had to work out all his own problems, bear all his own injuries and illnesses, endure each brush with his own gadfly mortality until he too could leave the earth in a solitary and pure way.

He sat down. In respect for the moment he tried to absorb it, to bear witness to it. A sense of his own mortality made him shiver involuntarily. He looked at the two Taoists again. Already they seemed a little smaller, a little less human. With the candles and incense, he could even have been in a little mountain shrine. They were like statues, unmoving, unyielding. After the two years he had been with them, he knew no more about their history or background than the night he met them. They were still enigmas. With their passing they had revealed nothing more and had left him with hundreds of unanswered questions.

The veil that had dropped between them could not be moved. It was opaque. He wished that they could talk to him from behind death's curtain. He wanted them to tell him what it was like there. What was on the other side? He sighed. Death was meant to be a mystery to the living.

The light in the cave was slowly brightening. He realized that he still had his duty to do. It was a lucky thing for the living to have duty, he reflected. It kept them from being totally paralyzed whenever death made its appearance and took people irreversibly into its depths. Saihung carried each man tenderly out of the cave and laid him upon the bier.

He sprinkled sesame seeds all over their bodies to make them burn better. It occurred to him to wait. Maybe they would come back. After all, they looked like they were only sleeping. But no. He realized that he was only being sentimental. The two Taoists were gone forever.

He walked into the cave, picked up a torch, and set the mountain of wood aflame.

The fire was gentle and small at first. But it soon began to climb up the criss-crossed timbers and the fountain of flame began to caress the two corpses. Panic rose up in him with the rising flames. It was shocking to see human beings burn. He had to stop himself from rushing to put out the fire. The taboo against watching helpless people being destroyed was strong.

Soon the bodies began to glow. The cloth was stripped away and consumed in the brightening inferno. The fire leapt higher, the wood cracking, splintering, sparks exploding as the blaze consumed it. Smoke rose up and Saihung had to back away from the intense heat. The mists were still thick, the sun a pale disk. He sat down to watch. The blaze dominated the quiet birdless morning.

Two days later, Saihung gathered the ashes, crushed the bone fragments and scattered them in the forest. He returned to the cave and carefully obscured all signs of his presence. The scorched earth was swept over and the rock was washed clean.

The way seemed traceless. Two men were gone as if they had never existed. He stood on the craggy cliff looking out over the silvery mists. It seemed as if his whole life had been a dream. He wondered if his master, the two acolytes, Butterfly, or he as the warrior, actor, or renunciate had ever existed. But then, who was asking the question?

It was he—he who had straggled off the Way but who, at least for the moment, had found it again. Following the Tao meant integration with it, all the time warding off confusion, emotionalism, and all other things that would oppose such unity. Through his life, he had had to cope with the difficulties forced upon him by his clan, his own mischievousness and wavering nature, his desire for fighting, his attraction to beauty, his dislike of discipline. Each time he had given in, he had lost his touch with the Tao; and when he had left Huashan for the streets of Shanghai, he had been no different than Butterfly in his fall from grace.

Slendor Gourd and Crystal Spring had helped him to see beyond emotions. Their instructions had helped him understand his swings between enthusiasm and wild rebellion. They had helped him to leave behind his feelings so that it might truly be possible for him to fly without wings.

The two Taoists had taught him to look beyond mere

technical knowledge, intellectualism, and even the substance of sacred literature. His body was the temple, and the divine was in him. Once that simple reality was grasped, all learning was a superfluous burden. Had the sages given some hint of that irony when they had identified the *Seven Bamboo Tablets* as being "of the Cloudy Satchel"?

All his slipping from the path, all his returns to try once more, all his perceptions of the elements both good and bad that shielded his perceptions were unavoidable events in his progress. He had striven, fallen, ascended. He had found the way again, and having plunged so far from it, was better prepared to stay with it. He truly could feel something growing within him—not just the physical field of energy promised by practice, but a new shining nature.

It was his original true self, finally bursting forth with clear brilliance. He glimpsed what it was to be "the uncarved block": pure, unmarred by emotional turbulence, misconception, or socialization. Through the grace of the Tao, there would grow in him a Golden Embryo of light and innocence, eternally in touch with the truth.

As the day began to brighten, he started down the mountain path. The trees were a vibrant green, made all the brighter by their white trunks. Some leaves were turning red and yellow, and the forest floor was carpeted by tiny maple leaves with slender stems pointing straight into the air. He took a deep breath, noticed the smell of the rich moist earth, caught the scent of botanical respiration. The sun broke through the clouds and he smiled. He wanted to travel.

Epilogue

Today, the Grand Master and the two acolytes, Mist Through a Grove and Sound of Clear Water, live in obscurity, the only inhabitants of an island temple in northwestern China. Only five of the original thirteen disciples are still alive. Red Pine and Intercepting Imprint disappeared after their expulsion from Huashan and are now presumed dead. Phoenix Eyes is still active in the Taoist hierarchy.

Du Yueshen returned to Shanghai in 1945 and, until the Communist takeover in 1949, revived the old Shanghai world. He fled to Hong Kong, where he died on August 16, 1951. His body was eventually interred in a tomb on Taiwan.

Saihung traveled for some time, visiting Europe, India, and other countries in Asia. He returned to China, studied at Peking University, and eventually returned to his master. During the Cultural Revolution, all of Taoism was tragically interrupted.

Huashan was overrun by the Red Guard. Monks were killed, temples burned, holy ground desecrated. Scriptures and relics were destroyed, among them, one of the oldest surviving copies of the *Seven Bamboo Tablets of the Cloudy Satchel.* The original may still be on Maoshan, but that place is fearsome and shunned, and its priests are powerful sorcerers unlikely to bother with the world. Other versions are considered to be fragments overly laden with later commentaries.

In 1963, the Grand Master sent Saihung out of China, still in pursuit of his quest. Saihung wandered through Hong Kong, Japan, Europe, and the United States, finally settling in California. He currently lives in seclusion in the San Francisco Bay Area.